Handbook of Procedures
for the Design of Instruction

Second Edition

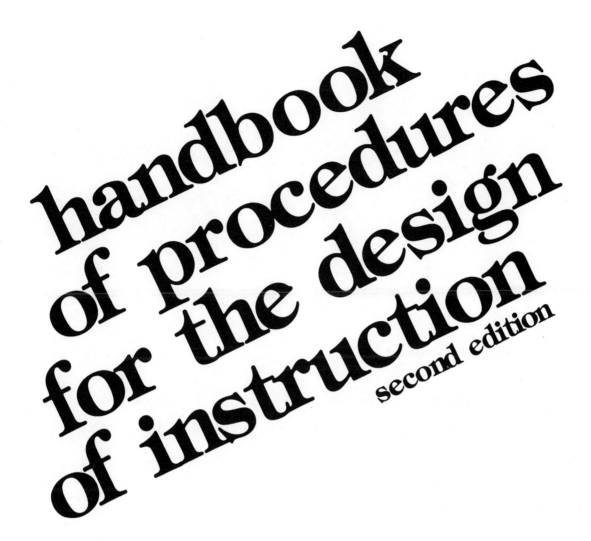

Leslie J. Briggs and Walter W. Wager

Florida State University

Educational Technology Publications
Englewood Cliffs, New Jersey 07632

Library of Congress Cataloging in Publication Data

Briggs, Leslie J
    Handbook of procedures for the design of instruction.

    Bibliography: p.
    Includes indexes.
    1. Instructional systems--Design and construction.
I. Wager, Walter W., 1944-   joint author. II. Title.
LB1028.35.B74 1981   371.3   80-20920
ISBN 0-87778-177-X

Printed in the United States of America.

Library of Congress Catalog Card Number:
80-20920.

International Standard Book Number:
0-87778-177-X.

First Printing: January, 1981.

Second Printing: January, 1989.

Preface

In this Second Edition of this book, we have retained the title of the First Edition, not only to serve as identification for those readers familiar with the earlier edition but also to emphasize that this book is a *handbook* rather than a *textbook*. This distinction is made to call attention to the instructional design *procedures* that are a prominent part of this book. Therefore, the instructor and other readers will find information tests and performance objectives for chapters, and how-to-do-it explanations, examples, exercises, and answer keys. These are features not found in many textbooks.

Consistent with the above distinction between handbooks and textbooks, readers are urged to use one or more of the three textbooks which are cited at the beginning of each chapter. Those textbooks give theoretical background, explanations, and further examples of the procedures presented in this book. While this book alone could be used by readers who wish only an overview of instructional design, for those wishing to achieve deeper understanding or actual skill in design, reading of the other books is strongly recommended. An instructor may wish to choose which of the three textbooks most clearly fits into the purpose of a particular course. In choosing the three textbooks, we have unabashedly selected the ones that are most consistent with the particular "systems model" presented in this book. It has not been our purpose to review the literature concerning other systems-oriented textbooks which are available.

The present edition retains the overall purpose of the earlier edition: to give instructors, students, and on-the-job designers a resource for establishing or sharpening their skills in instructional design.

The "model" of design espoused here has features of other "systems" models, as described in Chapter 1.

The central focus of this book is upon the design of instructional materials, whether print or nonprint. The book is most useful, then, for learning to develop *predesigned*, materials-centered instruction, as distinct from *teacher-centered* instruction. This is not to minimize the role of the teacher or instructor, but rather to suggest that the teacher's role can shift from information presentation to the management of learning. In short, our approach is to design into the materials those instructional events which are best accomplished by carefully designed materials, and to leave to the teacher those events which are best handled by the teacher. However, we do attend to the planning that teachers need to do when they design lessons that utilize selected materials. Thus we intend this book to be helpful to teachers in their *planning* activity as distinct from their classroom management activity. This book, therefore, does not deal with the platform performance of teachers, but with the planning of their own activities and also those of the learner.

This book is intended for teachers, curriculum specialists, trainers, administrators, and those who wish to become professional designers of instructional materials and programs.

Both editions of this book were developed initially for use in a graduate course in the design of instruction at Florida State University. The senior author began teaching those classes in 1968, resulting in publication of the First Edition in 1970. The co-author began teaching those classes in 1974, at first in a team teaching arrangement, after which the two authors alternated in teaching the classes. This Second Edition reflects changes which both authors initiated in the course over a period of time.

This edition is almost completely rewritten, even though the central concepts of the original edition are retained. Major changes in this edition include:

1. Expansion of coverage from learning of intellectual skills only to the inclusion of learning of information, attitudes, cognitive strategies, and motor skills.

2. Changes in vocabulary to bring it more into conformity with the three recommended text-books.

3. Introduction of the use of instructional maps to complement the use of learning hierarchies in planning sequences of objectives for courses, course units, and individual lessons.

4. Coordinating media selection and utilization more closely with planning of utilization of class time.

5. Attention to how learning in the different outcome domains becomes mutually supportive (attention to domain interactions).

6. Expansion of examples, exercises, and chapter objectives to cover all five domains of outcomes.

7. Updating of references to other sources.

8. Adoption of a tear-out format which enables instructors to use information tests and exercises either for evaluating students' work or as learning aids. This choice can be implemented by removing answer keys (placed at the end of the book) for the instructor to retain until the course is over, when the first of the two choices is adopted.

9. More emphasis upon sequencing of lessons.

10. More emphasis on attitude and motor skill learning.

11. Organizing the performance objectives for the reader by chapter rather than in larger units of study and design practice. This is to enable an instructor to ask students to turn in their design work either after each chapter is studied, or to turn in larger segments of work at a time, as suggested in Chapter 1.

The authors and the publisher wish to thank the American Institutes for Research for publishing the First Edition and for relinquishing copyright of that edition so that selected parts of it could be used in this Second Edition.

This edition may be considered a companion text to the book, *Instructional Design: Principles and Applications*, edited by the senior author and published by Educational Technology Publications in 1977. We also acknowledge the pioneering work of Robert M. Gagné, our colleague, whose concepts are heavily utilized in this book.

We wish to thank the several persons, some of them our past or present students, who gave permission for including some of their work in this book. Their contributions are acknowledged, by name, at appropriate places in this book.

Finally, we acknowledge our debt to all our students whose errors and successes helped us to write this book, and to our respective wives who were patient with us during the writing process.

LJB
WWW

Tallahassee, Florida
July, 1980

Cross-References to Recommended Readings

As noted in the Preface, since this book is a *handbook* rather than a *textbook*, we have used much of our space for examples, exercises, information tests, and performance objectives. For this reason, we have not included as much textual materials on the theory base for our model of instructional design as is found in many textbooks.

Consequently, we open each Chapter with cross-references to textbooks containing additional discussion of the theory base upon which our model rests. For the convenience of the reader, these cross-references opening each Chapter in this book emphasize the corresponding Chapters in the three textbooks, but they also list references for the Chapter preceding and following the Chapter being dealt with. A summary of these cross-references for the entire book is found on the following page.

Cross-References to Recommended Readings

Chapter in This Book	Chapter Title	Recommended Readings		
		Briggs, L.J. (Ed.) *Instructional Design: Principles and Applications*. Englewood Cliffs, N.J.: Educational Technology Publications, 1977.	Gagné, R.M., and Briggs, L.J. *Principles of Instructional Design*, 2nd ed. New York: Holt, Rinehart, and Winston, 1979.	Gagné, R.M. *The Conditions of Learning*, 3rd ed. New York: Holt, Rinehart, and Winston, 1977.
1	Introduction	Chapter 1	Chapters 1, 2	Chapter 1
2	Determining Needs, Goals, Priorities	Chapters 2, 12, 13	Chapter 2	
3	Determining Resources, Constraints; Delivery Sys.	Pages 262-265 Pages 278-307 Chapters 12, 13	Pages 25-28 Pages 175-178	
4	Writing Objectives & Test Items	Chapter 3 Pages 158-170	Chapters 2, 3, 7	Chapter 2
5	Organizing the Course	Chapter 4	Chapter 8	
6	Organizing the Unit	Chapters 4, 5	Chapters 6, 8	Chapter 11
7	Organizing the Lesson	Chapters 5, 7 Pages 179-193	Chapters 6, 8	Chapter 11
8	Factors in Media Selection	Chapters 8, 9	Chapter 10	Chapter 12
9	Designing Lessons, Mats.	Chapters 7, 8, 9	Chapters 4, 5, 9, 10, 11, 13, 14	Chapters 3-10 Chapter 12
10	Student Assessment	Chapters 6, 10, 11	Chapter 12	
11	Formative Evaluation	Chapter 10	Chapter 15	
12	Teacher Training; Summative Evaluation; Diffusion	Chapter 15	Chapter 15	
Total Book	Examples of design products by students of instructional design	Chapters 16, 17		

Table of Contents

Handbook of Procedures for the Design of Instruction

Second Edition

Chapter 1
Introduction

Chapter in This Book	Recommended Readings		
	Briggs, L.J. (Ed.) *Instructional Design: Principles and Applications.* Englewood Cliffs, N.J.: Educational Technology Publications, 1977.	Gagné, R.M., and Briggs, L.J. *Principles of Instructional Design*, 2nd ed. New York: Holt, Rinehart, and Winston, 1979.	Gagné, R.M. *The Conditions of Learning*, 3rd ed. New York: Holt, Rinehart, and Winston, 1977.
①	**Chapter 1**	**Chapters 1, 2**	**Chapter 1**
2	Chapters 2, 12, 13	Chapter 2	

Background

As indicated in the Preface, the "model" of instructional design presented in this book may be called a "systems-oriented model." The word "model" refers to a particular organized set of procedures for actually carrying out a problem-solving process for a particular purpose. In the present context, the "problem" to be solved is how to provide either more effective instruction for an *existing* course, or effective *new* instruction for a needed new course. The instruction to be designed may be for an entire curriculum, for a course, or for a single lesson objective.

If the real-world problem (lack of desired performance on the part of a group of people) should be solved by new laws, administrative changes, new directives, or more money, then the "solution" is not to design instruction. But if the problem (need) can be best met by arranging for people to learn something they have not yet learned, then *instruction* is one solution to a learning need (Chapter 2).

The planning of instruction is not always carried out systematically, with the result that it is not always effective or efficient, and hence does not meet the need. Of course, there are a number of proposals for how effective instruction should be planned, designed, and carried out. Many of these "Models of Teaching" have been summarized by Joyce and Weil (1972). Some of these models are for a single purpose such as "science education." Others, like the model presented in this book, are intended for application in any subject area.

A conventional way to design instruction is to select the "content" to be presented to the student by teachers or by instructional materials. This may work well for a teacher, working alone, but it has the defect that the objectives of such instruction are not described in terms of what the learners are to do as a result of the instruction that they could not do before, except to recall the new "content." Our proposal is that needs, goals, and objectives for a lesson, course, or curriculum should be specified first, because these *do* describe the new performances expected of the learners as a result of the new instruction. Then content can be selected or developed for the purpose of promoting the achievement of the intended new capabilities by the learners.

Features of a Systems Model

The "systems approach" to the design of instruction results in a model to be followed to be sure that all components are designed to fit with each other. In part, this is accomplished by planning that the objectives, the teaching, and the testing of learner achievement are all congruent with each other. The systems model presented in this book (and in the three textbooks recommended for reading along with this book) has the following features:

1. All components of the instruction are planned to work together to achieve the goals and objectives of the instruction.

2. Components are analyzed and developed in a planned sequence, although each is reviewed again as new components are planned.

3. The entire design process is orderly but flexible. There is both "feedback" and "feedforward" in iterative cycles of work.

4. The procedures are based on research and theory when possible, supplemented by logic, common sense, and frequent review.

5. Empirical data are gathered to test assumptions underlying the work, and to test the effectiveness of the designed instruction. These data are gathered while the instruction is being planned and first tried out, and also after the instruction has been field tested. These efforts are called, respectively, formative evaluation and summative evaluation.

6. There is a characteristic order of stages in which the work is accomplished (see the next section, *Stages in Design of Instructional Systems*, in this Chapter).

7. The specific functions to be performed by teachers, learners, materials, exercises, media, and tests are planned jointly.

8. A delivery system is developed to include all components needed to make it operate as planned, including: the physical environment, the characteristics of learners and teachers, and the instructional procedures.

9. The overall model of procedures is based on an intellectually consistent set of key concepts. This helps assure compatibility or congruence among the resulting designed components.

10. The model is planned to assure an honest and open relationship among the designer, the teacher, and the learner. The resulting instruction is thus humane.

11. The model is consistent with the concept of accountability for the value of goals adopted and for the effectiveness of instruction.

12. The model provides for setting criteria for evaluating the success of the instruction.

Stages in Design of Instructional Systems

Each author describing a systems model for design of instruction may use somewhat different terminology and may list varying numbers of stages in the work. Also, any one author may present a somewhat different list of stages to different audiences upon various occasions over a period of time. The list presented in Figure 1 is our latest list, arranged in the general order in which work on the different stages is performed. Recall that, in practice, one works "back and forth" in this list as new insights are gained which lead to corrections to earlier work and changes in thinking about work yet to be done. Opposite each stage in our list is the chapter in this book relating to each stage. Note that the stages reflect the sequence of tasks as performed by the *experienced designer*, while the chapter sequence was arranged to help you, the reader, to *learn how to do* each stage. An instructor may, of course, wish you to adopt a chapter sequence different from that shown in Figure 1.

Often, writers show the stages in design of an instructional system in the form of a flow diagram rather than as a list of stages like the list in Figure 1. The advantage of a flow diagram is that it permits identification of some of the "feedback loops" which represent the "iterative nature" of the design task in actual practice. Such a diagram may serve to remind the designer to look for additional opportunities to reappraise prior work and to modify plans for work to be accomplished in remaining design stages. We present such a flow diagram in Figure 2. It is more condensed than the design stages shown in Figure 1.

Organization of This Handbook

The chapters in this handbook may be classified by their correspondence to five different purposes. These purposes, in turn, guided our decision about chapter sequence. We have already shown, in Figure 1, how the chapter sequence differs from

Stage of Design	Chapter in This Book
1. Assessment of Needs, Goals, and Priorities	2
2. Assessment of Resources and Constraints, and Selection of a Delivery System	3
3. Identification of Curriculum and Course Scope and Sequence	2
4. Determination of Gross Structure of Courses	5
5. Determination of Sequence of Unit and Specific Objectives	6
6. Definition of Performance Objectives	4
7. Analysis of Objectives for Sequencing of Enablers	7
8. Preparation of Assessments of Learner Performance	4, 10
9. Designing Lessons and Materials: a. Instructional Events; b. Media; c. Prescriptions (utilizing appropriate conditions of learning)	8, 9
10. Development of Media, Materials, Activities	8, 9
11. Formative Evaluation	11
12. Field Tests and Revisions 13. Instructor Training 14. Summative Evaluation 15. Diffusion and Operational Installation	12

Figure 1. Stages of design as performed by the expert, and chapter sequence for readers just learning to perform design.

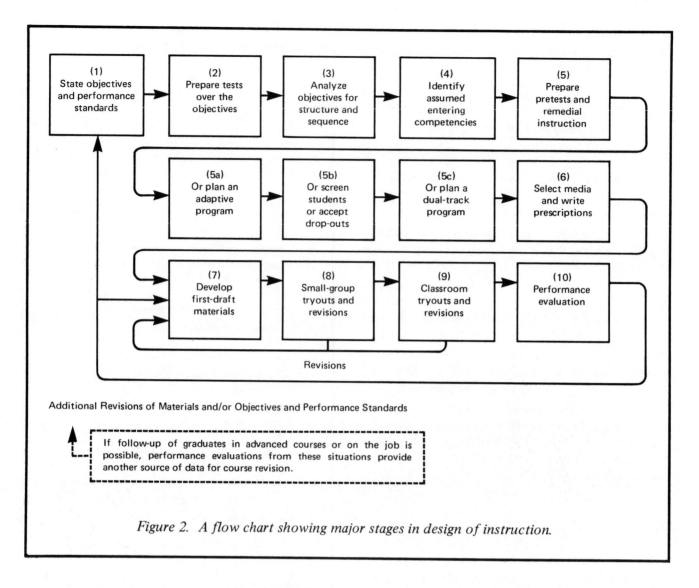

| (1) State objectives and performance standards | (2) Prepare tests over the objectives | (3) Analyze objectives for structure and sequence | (4) Identify assumed entering competencies | (5) Prepare pretests and remedial instruction |

| (5a) Or plan an adaptive program | (5b) Or screen students or accept drop-outs | (5c) Or plan a dual-track program | (6) Select media and write prescriptions |

| (7) Develop first-draft materials | (8) Small-group tryouts and revisions | (9) Classroom tryouts and revisions | (10) Performance evaluation |

Revisions

Additional Revisions of Materials and/or Objectives and Performance Standards

If follow-up of graduates in advanced courses or on the job is possible, performance evaluations from these situations provide another source of data for course revision.

Figure 2. A flow chart showing major stages in design of instruction.

the sequence of the stages of design as performed by the expert. The chapters may be classified as follows:

Chapter 1. This Chapter introduces the concept of a systems approach to an instructional design model, and shows the stages of work to be accomplished according to this model. It also suggests how to use this book for courses having different purposes.

Chapter 4. This Chapter presents the "basic skill" of how to write instructional objectives for various types of desired outcomes of instruction. It also deals with writing performance test items which are valid for measuring the accomplishment of the objectives by the learners. We thus wanted *you* to learn *how to write* objectives and test items before you learn how to organize a course by writing the desired objectives.

Chapter 8. This Chapter is intended to stimulate your thinking about various media of instruction before you are asked to select and develop media presentations for use in the lessons which comprise the course.

Chapter 12. This Chapter is a brief description of work often done with an instructional system after the designer's task is finished. This Chapter is merely an information chapter, not a skill-development chapter.

All other chapters. These chapters are arranged in the order of the stages of design, and are intended to enable you to learn *information* about design, or actual *skill* in design, or both—whichever you and an instructor take as the purpose of a course utilizing this handbook.

Components of Chapters in This Book

Each chapter in this book has specific components to enable you to achieve *information objec-*

tives, skill objectives, or *both*. The information objectives are reflected in the *information tests*, usually placed at the beginning of each chapter. The *skill objectives* are labelled *performance objectives*, and they are placed near the opening of each chapter which is intended to develop skills for a specific stage in design. These performance objectives are the *terminal objectives* for the chapter—objectives which describe the design stage you are to prepare and submit to your instructor for evaluation, if the purpose of the course is skill development (see the next section for courses having other purposes).

Supporting the attainment of the chapter terminal performance objectives are these kinds of chapter components:

(1) background about the design stage;
(2) references for further reading;
(3) descriptions of how to do the design stage;
(4) figures containing more information;
(5) exercises to help you develop the part skills which make up the chapter terminal performance objectives; and
(6) examples of completed design stages to serve as models for your design efforts.

No summary has been written for each chapter; it was deemed of more importance to close each chapter with exercises closely related to the performance objectives.

Also, there is one set of references at the end of the book rather than after each chapter, to avoid redundancy.

Answer keys at the end of the book are labelled to correspond with the titles and numbers of information tests and exercises.

How to Use This Handbook

If you are studying alone, after reading each chapter we encourage you to first take the information test in the chapter and then to do each stage of design as reflected in the performance objectives stated near the beginning of most chapters. Read the information test and the performance objectives, and study the chapters and the recommended readings for the purpose of accomplishing those objectives. If you have a colleague or supervisor who is already familiar with this model of design, ask for a critique of your work on the objectives.

If you are in a formal course or training group,

the instructor may wish to use this book for any of several distinct purposes. Such purposes may include the following:

1. *To gain only an overall introductory understanding* of design procedures and the theory on which they are based. This might be called an orientation or information course. In that case, the instructor may not wish you to actually produce your own course design, as reflected in the chapter performance objectives. Instead, the instructor may wish you only to take the information tests or to describe the purposes and procedures reflected in the performance objectives.

2. *To gain actual design skills.* In this event, the course takes on a "workshop" flavor, in which mastery of both information objectives and design skills may be demonstrated by the generation of actual design plans, analyses, and script writing. For this purpose, the exercises may be considered as "enabling objectives," the practice of which leads you to be able to perform the chapter performance objectives.

3. *To look for research which needs to be done.* As you read the book for this purpose, you could ask yourself: "Which parts of the design model lack a research basis? What alternative techniques might be developed and evaluated by comparison with the recommended techniques? What knowledge about how learning takes place is still lacking? What hypotheses could I develop and test which might lead to improved instructional design practices?"

4. *To convert principles stated in the context of design of instructional materials to practices which teachers can employ.* One source of ideas for this purpose may be found by comparing two chapters in another book (Briggs, 1977, Chapters 8 and 9). Those chapters show how basic strategies for instruction (Briggs, 1977, Chapter 7) can be employed by teachers as designers and by teams as designers.

5. *To identify classroom organizations and administrative changes* which would be compatible with instructional systems designed by a systems model. Examples of applications in group instruction and in individualized instruction, respectively, are found elsewhere (Gagné and Briggs, 1979, Chapters 13 and 14).

Remember that this book contains only brief condensations of theory which is presented in greater detail in the recommended readings. After reading those sources, you should be able to more effectively practice the techniques emphasized in this book.

If the purpose of using this book is other than purpose No. 2 above (to gain actual design skills), the instructor may wish to prepare chapter objectives different from those listed in each chapter in this book. Doing this would represent application of the principle that the same information source (such as a book) can be adapted to a variety of purposes by writing objectives appropriate for the purpose, and teaching and testing the learners accordingly.

1. Some instances of lack of desired human performance do not require instruction as the solution. List some other kinds of solutions to such problems.

    a. ....

    b. ....

    c. ....

    d. ....

2. What is the disadvantage in organizing a course by first selecting the course content? ....
....

3. List features of a systems model for the design of instruction.

    a. ....

    b. ....

    c. ....

    d. ....

    e. ....

    f. ....

4. Why is the chapter sequence of this book somewhat different from the sequence in which the expert does course design? ....
....

5. Arrows in a flow chart representing design stages show both a linear progression of work stages as well as ....
....

6. State the purpose of these chapter information tests for two kinds of courses:

    a. orientation courses ....
....

    b. skill courses ....
....

7. What is the function of examples and exercises in this book when used for a skill course? ....
....

8. A single information source, like this book, can be used for courses having different purposes by
....

9. List different purposes for which this book can be used.

    a. ....

    b. ....

    c. ....

    d. ....

    e. ....

    f. ....

10. A systems approach brings congruence (agreement) among what three important aspects of instruction?

    a. ....

    b. ....

    c. ....

Chapter 2
Determining Needs, Goals, Priorities

Chapter in This Book	Recommended Readings		
	Briggs, L.J. (Ed.) *Instructional Design: Principles and Applications.* Englewood Cliffs, N.J.: Educational Technology Publications, 1977.	Gagné, R.M., and Briggs, L.J. *Principles of Instructional Design,* 2nd ed. New York: Holt, Rinehart, and Winston, 1979.	Gagné, R.M. *The Conditions of Learning,* 3rd ed. New York: Holt, Rinehart, and Winston, 1977.
1	Chapter 1	Chapters 1, 2	Chapter 1
②	**Chapters 2, 12, 13**	**Chapter 2**	
3	Pages 262-265 Pages 278-307 Chapters 12, 13	Pages 25-28 Pages 175-178	

	Special Reading		
②	**Kaufman, R., and English, F.W. *Needs Assessment: Concept and Application.* Englewood Cliffs, N.J.: Educational Technology Publications, 1979.**		

Note to Students and Instructors

This systems model of instructional design may be used to plan entire curricula, such as for grades 1-12, or for a single "course" of any duration, or for a single lesson or "module."

Therefore, the concepts of needs analysis, goal setting, determination of priorities among goals, consideration of resources and constraints, and selection of a delivery system can all be done either for an entire curriculum or for a single course.

Some of the material in Chapters 2 and 3 deals with how to go from general goals (attainable only over long periods of instruction) to increasingly specific objectives for courses, course units, and single lessons. Because of this, you may wish to skip Chapters 2 and 3 if you are designing a single course, or you may wish to interpret the performance objectives for these two chapters in terms of a single course instead of an entire curriculum. A third alternative would be to take the information tests for these two chapters, but not do actual design as called for in the chapter performance objectives. It would be possible to begin the course with Chapter 4 in the case of designing for a single course.

In any event, the chapter information tests and the performance objectives may be submitted to the instructor for evaluation either after each chapter, or after groups of chapters. For example, an instructor may consider Chapters 1-4 to constitute a unit of the course; then the students might submit their work for performance objectives 1 through 12 as the "first assignment." It is a matter of how often the instructor wishes to review students' work and provide evaluation and feedback to the students. The second unit could then include Chapters 5-7, organizing courses, units, and lessons. The third unit, lesson design, would then include Chapters 8-9. Chapters 10-11 would comprise the evaluation unit. Chapter 12 would be the closing information unit. Other arrangements of units are also possible, of course, depending on the purpose and emphasis of the course.

Both the information test and the chapter performance objectives are placed near the beginning of each chapter. The information test items can be *read* as if they were information objectives to provide a "set" for reading the chapter in order to answer those questions; then the test can be actually written out after studying the chapter. Similarly, the performance objectives can be read at the outset to enable the reader to foresee the design work to be accomplished after studying the chapter.

Introduction

An *instructional system* is designed as a solution to a *problem*. It is first necessary, then, to define the problem so that one is able to decide with confidence that the solution to the problem is best arrived at by offering *instruction* rather than by some other means, such as legislative action, policy changes, institutional changes, budget changes, or administrative action. The appropriate sequence, thus, is to define the problem and then to seek a solution. The inappropriate sequence, often encountered, is to select a favored solution and then seek a problem to which to apply the solution. When some person (or group of persons) *perceives* that an unsatisfactory state of affairs exists, it is then relevant to *verify* that the unsatisfactory state of affairs does, indeed, exist. That action identifies a problem, or need for a solution, so that it is then relevant to seek a solution. If further analysis suggests that a certain group of people are not performing as desired because there is something they should learn to do which they do not know how to do, then an *instructional need* may have been identified, provided that those people can learn the required knowledge, skills, or attitudes better through *instruction* than from learning entirely upon their own resources.

A *need* has been defined as a gap or discrepancy between the present state of affairs and a desired state of affairs (Burton and Merrill, 1977; Kaufman and English, 1979). For example, suppose that many high school graduates cannot maintain a checking account because of faulty mathematics skills. Suppose it is established that to survive in society as an independent adult it is necessary to maintain a checking account. Then a gap, or need, has been identified, since such skills can be shown necessary for survival (which itself is held in high value), and since the facts show that many graduates do not have the relevant skills. A *goal* would be set, therefore, so that "within five years 95% (for example) of all high school graduates will have the skills to maintain a checking account at a bank."

Once such a goal is established by the responsible group, means for achieving the goal would be considered. If *instruction* is adopted as the best means to the goal, priorities and resources would be allocated to this goal, so that an appropriate *instructional delivery system* could be designed, within available resources and constraints, in order to achieve the goal.

One aspect of the instructional delivery system might involve the development of a new or revised *curriculum scope and sequence* plan, which would spell out the *performance objectives* to be achieved each year by students at appropriate grade levels in school.

This Chapter (and following chapters) outlines procedures for beginning with identifying needs, goals, and performance objectives which are used to guide the development of the solution to the problem defined in the needs statement.

The reader is advised to pause at this point to consult the references cited at the beginning of this Chapter. The purpose of reading those references is summarized by the following information test and the chapter *performance objectives,* which may be used by an instructor to help define the requirements of a formal course of instruction or workshop, or which may be used by a reader working alone to guide his or her application of the information read here and in the references. These objectives may serve the reader as a study guide, a set of skills to be exercised, and an outline for self-evaluation of the design work produced. These objectives may also be used as a guideline for an instructor to evaluate a student's work. In a non-formal study or training setting, the reader may work with peers to provide interactive study and evaluation.

For readers wishing a more detailed overview of the entire process of instructional systems design, including the identification of needs, goals, and alternative solutions, see Gagné and Briggs (1979, Chapter 2).

<u>*1*</u>. *A needs analysis can be done at several levels in education. What are these levels?*

    a. ....

    b. ....

    c. ....

    d. ....

<u>*2*</u>. *Needs analysis, goal identification, arrangement of priorities, consideration of resources and constraints, and choice of a delivery system may all be made at either of two levels, or both. What are these levels?*

    a. ....

    b. ....

<u>*3*</u>. *Which sequence is advisable?*

    a. solution; problem ....

    b. problem; solution ....

<u>*4*</u>. *What is a need?* ....

....

<u>*5*</u>. *In education, a step between a needs analysis and setting of course objectives is development of a*

....

....

<u>*6*</u>. *Goals often refer to desired performance of students at the end of the twelfth grade. What would goals become at the level of courses, units, or lessons?* ....

....

<u>*7*</u>. *Name and give an example of five kinds of needs.*

    a. ....

    b. ....

    c. ....

    d. ....

    e. ....

<u>*8*</u>. *Which schools have developed an entire network of layers of goals and objectives to show exact connections in curricula from broad needs to single lesson objectives?* ....

....

<u>*9*</u>. *What influences have normally determined the goals of education?*

    a. ....

    b. ....

    c. ....

    d. ....

<u>*10*</u>. *What is a common industrial equivalent of a needs analysis in education?* ....

<u>*11*</u>. *Name five broad steps in doing a needs analysis.*

    a. ....

    b. ....

    c. ....

    d. ....

    e. ....

Background

From Needs to Lessons

Burton and Merrill (1977), drawing upon the work of Bradshaw (1972), have identified five kinds of needs. Each of these, along with examples, is listed next.

1. *Normative need*: an individual has a deficient diet, compared to established minimum daily requirements (norms); students in a school score below the national average.

2. *Felt need*: a teacher advocates the "need" for a particular course because he or she "wants" to teach it, or someone else "feels" it should be taught.

3. *Expressed need or demand*: if more students sign up for a course than there are chairs in the room, a "need" is seen for another section of the course.

4. *Comparative need*: if Central High School has no chemistry laboratory, and East Side High School does, Central "needs" a laboratory.

5. *Anticipated or future need*: it is predicted that workers will have more leisure in the future, hence there is a "need" for teaching leisure time activities.

It is apparent that some of the above examples appear more like "wants" than "needs." Kaufman and English (1979) have tried to avoid this problem by recommending that needs be related to preparation of people to at least *survive* in the society as it is expected to be when they legally leave school. They further differentiate among survival as a dependent in a protected environment, survival as an independently functioning adult, and survival plus contributing to the change of society for the better. In their distinction between the "Alpha" and the "Beta" levels of needs analysis and assessment, they differentiate between an open and a restricted setting or set of assumptions as the context of the analysis. In the "Alpha" analysis, there is willingness to aim for the best possible solutions to problems by being willing to ignore present conventions relating to the nature of schools and their established curricula. In the "Beta" level of analysis, one accepts certain restrictions and constraints which limit the range of solutions which will be considered.

An example of an "Alpha" situation in industrial training would be the willingness of management to make possible *any* mode of learning, when performance deficits of employees are viewed as lack of relevant skills rather than due to company policies or other causes of poor performance. Thus *any* reasonable way to learn *any* required goals would be open for approval as a solution to the problem. In a "Beta" situation, the existing training department and modes of training operations would be retained; only the content and objectives of training would be open to some degree of change. Kaufman and English (1979) go on to define other kinds of restrictions in viewing problems and solutions, labelled as "Gamma," "Delta," "Epsilon," and "Zeta." Each of these refers to the degree to which consideration is restricted in going from needs, to solutions, to evaluation, and redesign of the resulting training (when "training" is adopted as the "solution" to the problem).

Somewhat related to the above forms of needs analysis are the levels at which needs are determined. While needs and goals are often stated at the National and State levels, in the United States the curriculum is most subject to reconsideration and change at the level of the community, the school, or the individual classroom. This may be labelled as a decentralized system of education. On the other hand, in military and industrial training, needs and solutions are more likely to be decided in a centralized fashion, by Commanding Officers, training directors, or boards of directors.

A major problem in education is the existence of "gaps" between goals and specific performance objectives. Goals have traditionally been stated in very broad terms, such as "basic skills," "citizenship," "health," or "vocational competency." Verbs used in describing these broad goals include such words as "understand," "appreciate," and "comprehend." While these broad goals may be sufficient to gain citizen approval, they are difficult to measure, so discrepancies between what "is" and what "ought to be" are difficult to detect and interpret in such a way as to provide clues for how the curriculum should be improved.

Perhaps no group has ever satisfactorily bridged the large gap between such goal statements and the performance objectives which may be found for individual courses or for a curriculum scope and sequence statement. It is, therefore, not known how many "layers" of increasingly specific goals, sub-goals, and objectives would be needed to assure a direct linkage or network of sub-goals connecting broad goals to lesson objectives. A further difficulty is that some goals are not fully measurable at the time students graduate from high school or college, since the goals refer, in part, to adult activity after schooling is over.

While much more concentrated effort is needed to form a more complete network of connecting sub-goals and objectives, making possible a direct link among lessons, units of instruction, courses, competency at the time of graduation, and adult life, the techniques of needs analysis and assessment offered by Kaufman and English (1979) and Burton and Merrill (1977) are a start in the right direction. Once a more effective means can be found to connect end-of-schooling goals to curriculum scope and sequence, and on to specific courses, it is *less* difficult to make the remaining connections. For those latter connections, Briggs (1977, Chapter 4) has demonstrated how end-of-course objectives can be broken down into unit objectives, which in turn can be broken down into performance objectives for single lessons. This is accomplished by the important technique of task analysis, which can further reveal the subordinate

enabling objectives, whether classified as essential prerequisites or supporting prerequisites (Gagné, 1977a; Gagné and Briggs, 1979). Further, a method for showing the relationship among objectives representing different domains of learning in a taxonomy of learning outcomes has been demonstrated in the form of "instructional maps" (Wager, 1977). Later in this book, three "levels" of instructional maps are illustrated: the course level, the unit level, and the lesson level. These maps range in scope and degree of specificity analogous to maps of a Nation, a State, and a City.

Ways of Identifying Goals

Traditionally there have been several means by which the curricula of schools have been formed.

Some subjects or skills appear in present curricula because there has been such common agreement as to their necessity that they have never been seriously questioned. The familiar "reading, writing, and arithmetic" fall into this category, although emphasis upon them has waxed and waned from time to time. There appear to be cycles of shifts in emphasis, depending on the moods of educators and the public.

Academic disciplines have also had their influences in science, mathematics, social studies, and language arts in the curricula.

Some elements of curricula are mandated by legislation for elementary and secondary schools, and by requirements for certification of educational personnel.

In industrial training, the nature of the products and services offered by a company becomes translated into job requirements for personnel to produce and market products and services. In the military, the nature of weapons and missions is the source of job performance requirements.

Some elements of the curriculum represent the interests of teachers, but overall the public must have control. Various ways of arriving at consensus are discussed next.

The most traditional means for defining the broad goals of education at the National and State levels have included formation of groups of educators and others to prepare written goal statements. Such formulations often contain goals such as "health," "vocational competency," and "communication skills." These statements, of course, refer to the desired outcomes of the *entire education* of young people; they do not specify the year-by-year objectives, which, over a period of many years, result in achievement of these goals.

While educators try to keep these broad goals in mind when determining the curriculum for an entire school system, from kindergarten to the twelfth grade, much gets lost along the way. It seems logically possible that planning groups could design many "layers" of sub-goals and objectives, thus making possible a complete "audit trail" from the goals at high school graduation to the individual lessons, taught day by day, in each subject area during each year of schooling. But the fact is that such a complete network has never been undertaken. It would clearly be an enormous task, worthwhile perhaps only if we had a clear definition of the skills "really needed" to be a successful adult in the society as it will exist when students finish school. Thus the study of the future would be a good starting point. Many attempts to predict what the future society could or should be like are presented in issues of the magazine *The Futurist* (1979), and in other sources. While predicting the future is itself an uncertain activity, because it is not known whether society will make the decisions necessary to result in a desired future, outlining the skills needed in some predicted future would appear to be a worthy undertaking. Coupled with this could be studies of skills possessed by present successful survivors and contributors to society.

The study of the future and the analysis of skills apparently needed now and in the future are ideas which might expand upon the needs and goals assessment techniques presently used. Armed with the predicted skills for both the present and the future, the general procedures outlined in the references given at the opening of this Chapter could be modified and employed. This, itself, is a hope for the future, not a present practice.

Nevertheless, the procedures now available can yield goals more specific than such broad (and vague) goals as have resulted from earlier efforts. Kaufman and English (1979) provide many examples of goals, resulting from needs assessments, which are more readily converted to performance objectives for school curricula than were the earlier forms of goal statements. Such efforts can retain the idea that in a democratic society, the citizens (including the school children) should have a voice in the process. Thus the better informed are the members of the consensus groups which set goals and priorities, the greater the likelihood that the goals will be appropriate for the pupils to be served.

How to Do It

Burton and Merrill (1977) have presented a brief account of a method for identifying needs, goals, and priorities. A brief synopsis of their recommendations follows.

1. Identify the persons who are to serve as members of the consensus group.
2. Identify a broad range of possible goals.
3. Rank order goals in order of importance.
4. Identify discrepancies between expected and actual performance.
5. Set priorities for action.

The specifics for achieving each of the above steps are also outlined by Burton and Merrill, broken down into lists of inputs, operators, and operations. The role of the instructional designer in such functions is also described, and simple data processing procedures are discussed.

Kaufman and English (1979) also list a series of general steps for needs assessment. A synopsis of their recommendations follows.

1. Decide to plan systematically.
2. Obtain agreement by participants to range beyond existing goals and objectives.
3. Achieve representativeness in the participant group.
4. Obtain a commitment to refer to external criteria for what "should be," not merely to criteria internal to schools.
5. Obtain data on current survival/contribution levels of graduates.
6. Identify requirements for current and future survival.
7. Translate gaps between present and future survival/contribution levels into post-schooling outcome statements, not just school processes and outputs.
8. Place the gaps in priority order, considering the cost of the present status (the cost of ignoring the gap) and the cost of closing the gap.
9. Identify disagreements among sub-groups.
10. Reconcile the disagreements.
11. Re-rank needs, considering former and present decisions.
12. If required by continuing disagreements, cycle through steps 9-11 again.
13. List needs in priority order.
14. Select the needs in priority order.
15. Plan a continuing effort to review and revise.

16. Be ready to consider new needs that might arise during problem solution.

17. Thank the participants personally and publicly.

An interesting feature of the output of such a needs identifying group, as recommended by Kaufman and English (1979, p. 193), is a needs statement matrix, which is composed of six cells formed by three rows (learners, implementors, and society/community) and two columns (what is, and what should be). The cell entries describe what is being done now, and what would be done when the new goals are met successfully. The goals for learners are identified, as well as goals for actions to be accomplished by educators and by the community.

Levels of Analysis

As noted earlier, goals may be selected for the Nation, for a State, for a community, for a school, or for a single course or classroom.

Within these levels, the probability of being able to do an "Alpha" type analysis, rather than one of the other types listed earlier, rests largely upon freedom to build anew the entire institution, facilities, and curricula to be associated with the delivery system selected as the solution for the problem. For example, if a new community were just being established, an "Alpha" analysis would be possible, because no prior established goals, curricula, or school system would restrict the range of needs and goals that might be adopted. Under normal circumstances, however, there are often "givens" to be accepted at the outset; these givens might set limits on goals that can be selected as well as upon the range of means which could be developed within the existing system. Existing school buildings and administrative conventions, and the investment in money and power they represent, as well as laws and customs, may demand that education be achieved in schools rather than in homes, churches, business establishments, libraries, etc. These "givens" may set restrictions on both the goals and the delivery systems that realistically may be adopted.

One reason for the slow pace of educational change is these "givens," mentioned above. Nevertheless, changes in the content and methods of instruction do take place over a period of time. While there is a tendency to perpetuate traditional content and methods, new ones do gradually appear in response to perceived needs. These may appear as new "subjects" in a curriculum or as new "degree programs," as in higher education. In recent years, long-established university "majors" have expanded from the traditional liberal arts and professional degree programs to include new ones, such as the study of futurism, instructional systems design, adult education, medical technology, and many others. Often such new programs arise, not because of formal, systematic needs assessments as discussed in the previous section of this Chapter, but rather by an informal consensus among educational planners.

Examples of Need Identification

Example One: An Instructional Design Course

Teachers and other educational and training personnel for years have devised curricula and courses of instruction. Sometimes rather large groups were formed, and well funded, to develop new curricula, as in the new science and mathematics curriculum development projects of the past 20 years.

Beginning during the two World Wars, psychologists were employed in the selection and training of personnel in military specialties. At the same time, industrial psychologists were performing similar functions in industry. There, especially during the 1950's, these psychologists became increasingly aware that techniques were needed which were not provided by current learning theories, prediction tests, and measurement procedures. Techniques of task analysis were developed, supplemented by new instructional media techniques, teaching machines, simulators, job aids, and performance measures. Gradually all these and others were merged with the idea of systems analysis, to result in a technology of instructional systems design.

Before 1965 no universities were granting degrees in the new instructional systems technology, although education and training organizations were creating a demand for such people. Due to this "demand" type need identification, various universities began to hire faculty to develop such a degree program.

In 1968, at Florida State University, a doctoral degree program in instructional design and development was begun within an existing Department of Educational Research and Testing. Faculty already located there had previously been conducting graduate training in research methods and statistics, and in evaluation and measurement. Other faculty members were operating a computer-assisted instruction facility. Building upon existing courses taught by those faculty members, new courses were designed by both those faculty members and new ones arriving in 1968 and thereafter. This group of faculty members began holding regular meetings to continuously define and redefine the new degree program. These meetings continue to the present, and are expected to continue in the future.

These faculty members, beginning with their own experiences in instructional design, continued to revise courses and degree requirements on the basis of increasingly systematic data—knowledge of duties required in existing jobs, data from newly advertised job openings, and feedback from students before and after graduation from the program. The "need" for the new program is continuously redefined, and the program revised accordingly.

One of the "core courses" (as distinct from "background" and "specialty" courses) identified early for the program was a course entitled "The Design of Instruction." This course offers procedures for the design of both teacher-conducted instruction and for courses heavily dependent upon self-instructional materials. The "need" for this course was thus informally identified by consensus of the faculty. The first textbook written for this course was the First Edition (Briggs, 1970) of the present book. That text first listed publicly the performance objectives for the course. A revised statement of those course objectives appeared in a later text (Briggs, 1977, pp. 464-468). The performance objectives listed near the beginning of each chapter in the present book represent a second up-dating of those objectives. The experience of teaching this course began for Briggs in 1968 and for Wager in 1974. No doubt a somewhat similar process has taken place in other universities now offering a similar program.

This account began with how the "demand" type need for trained personnel developed, and followed by showing how a degree program and a course within it emerged. Other courses in the program include those in the history and theory of instructional technology, learning theory, research methods, media, evaluation, modular design, alternate teaching models, and others. This represents a type of curriculum scope and sequence for a single degree program.

The course in "Design of Instruction," in turn, is broken down into "units," not unlike the chapters in this book. Then performance objectives are stated for each unit. The instruction itself further attends to the "enabling objectives" for each performance objective, and each "lesson," in turn, attends to the "conditions of learning" and "instructional events" needed to master the enabling objectives of each performance objective (discussed in later chapters of this book).

Perhaps the above example of how the "need" arose for a new degree program, and for specific courses within the program, is fairly typical of how most "needs" are identified. This is not to say that the more systematic, formal methods recommended in the sources cited in this Chapter are not feasible.

Just as the "need" was identified primarily based on the practical demand reflected in the job market, the design of the course mentioned was accomplished *while the course was being taught.* The instructor did not have the luxury of a design and development period of time (or a budget for it) before the course began. Again, this is more typical than not, so again, the total "pre-design" (e.g., before delivery of the instruction) activities recommended in this book often take place concurrent with instruction. So, ideally, we recommend orderly periods of design, development, production, installation, evaluation, and revision of instruction, knowing that often in practice these gradually emerge at the same time the instruction is being carried on.

Example Two: A College Teaching Course

Another example of a course that has been developed following a systems approach was one taught by Wager beginning in 1972. Assigned by Florida State University to teach certification courses for prospective junior college teachers, Wager had to determine what needs existed. The fact that the course had existed for eight years before Wager's coming to the university was evidence that someone had perceived a need for some kind of teacher training for prospective junior college teachers.

In an attempt to define a curriculum for the course, Wager searched for documentation of the need. There was much literature that described what has been called earlier "an anticipated or future need"; the authors of articles and books advocated training for this group of people because of the demand for new professionals in the field. Furthermore, there was a "felt need" that related to the heavy emphasis on teaching at the junior colleges. It was felt that students exiting most disciplines with a masters degree would be capable of providing better instruction after having some further training in instructional practices.

From this information one could also detect a "normative need"; experienced teachers and administrators expressed the deficiencies observed in "new" junior college teachers, e.g., lack of organization, poor teaching methodology, poor resource utilization, unrealistic attitudes and expectations, etc. Wager went to the local junior college and observed and interviewed teachers about their role as junior college faculty, and what they felt it was important to know before starting a job as a new faculty member.

It is interesting that many of the faculty interviewed said they had never given the situation any thought before this, but reflecting upon their experience, they produced a list of teaching skills, such as:

    (1) constructing classroom tests;
    (2) administering tests;
    (3) lecturing skills;
    (4) discussion skills;
    (5) writing instructional materials;
    (6) writing a syllabus;
    (7) grading students, etc.

Many of these skills corresponded to those described in the literature; however, most were more specific and could be related directly to competency statements. Wager did not attempt to verify the level with which these skills were being performed by existing teachers in the field; instead, he attempted to specify a level that might be considered suitable for an entry level teacher.

The list of skills was divided into two basic groups: those related to teaching methodology and classroom management, and those related to curriculum or course development. It was decided to teach these skills in two sequential courses. On the first day of class the students were given the list of skills that the first course would attend to, and they were asked to indicate the extent to which they felt they needed the skills and the extent to which they felt they already possessed them. They were also told to add skills they expected to attain by taking the course (e.g., skills that were not already on the list).

This procedure of determining a curriculum shows how many different types of needs analysis procedures can be combined to determine the discrepancies between what is desired and what exists. It was also interesting to the author, that when the course was offered off-campus to practicing junior college faculty, all felt that they had learned much that would be of value to them in future teaching. This suggests that although they knew what skills were needed (in the initial interviews), they did not themselves possess them to the degree they desired. Needs analysis is an enlightening process, and to omit it from the design process is to take the risk that instruction will be designed for unneeded skills or for skills already possessed by the learners.

Chapter 3
Determining Resources and Constraints;
Selection of a Delivery System

Chapter in This Book	Recommended Readings		
	Briggs, L.J. (Ed.) *Instructional Design: Principles and Applications.* Englewood Cliffs, N.J.: Educational Technology Publications, 1977.	Gagné, R.M., and Briggs, L.J. *Principles of Instructional Design*, 2nd ed. New York: Holt, Rinehart, and Winston, 1979.	Gagné, R.M. *The Conditions of Learning*, 3rd ed. New York: Holt, Rinehart, and Winston, 1977.
2	Chapters 2, 12, 13	Chapter 2	
(3)	**Pages 262-265** **Pages 278-307** **Chapters 12, 13**	**Pages 25-28** **Pages 175-178**	
4	Chapter 3 Pages 158-170	Chapters 2, 3, 7,	Chapter 2

Introduction

Once a needs analysis has been conducted, as discussed in Chapter 2, and the goals have been ranked in order of priority, the next step is to begin planning the means for achieving the goals. It is assumed that *instruction* has been determined to be an appropriate approach to reaching the selected goals.

Depending upon the time estimated to be required for the learners to achieve the goals, a decision is reached either to design a single "course," or an entire curriculum consisting of several courses.

In the latter case, a curriculum "scope and sequence" is to be designed, or a "degree major," or a series of courses.

Regardless of whether "education" or "training" is the name given to the *instruction* to be designed as the solution to the problem, three matters need to be considered:

1. The overall goal or goals selected for solution must be viewed in terms of the magnitude of the learning task represented by goals. Thus the learning to be accomplished over a long or a short time period must be expressed as a progression of courses, possibly in the form of a curriculum scope and sequence, or merely as a course or a series of courses. In the case of a single course, the major units must be identified. (The organization of a single course is discussed in Chapter 5.) For a larger learning task, consisting of several courses, or years of instruction, the *relationship among courses* must be outlined.

2. Once the overall learning task has been organized to show relationships among courses or units, the *resources and constraints* must be appraised, so that alternate instructional solution strategies may be considered.

3. Based on step 2, above, *a delivery system is selected*—one that can be designed within the resources and constraints.

These three activities are discussed, in turn, following the presentation of the information test and the performance objectives for this Chapter.

Chapter 3 Information Test

_1_. After terminal goals for an entire curriculum (or degree program) are prepared, the next step is to prepare a curriculum ....

....

_2_. Name three reasons for analyzing resources and constraints.

    _a._ ....

    _b._ ....

    _c._ ....

_3_. List several types of resources and constraints to be considered.

    _a._ ....

    _b._ ....

    _c._ ....

    _d._ ....

    _e._ ....

_4_. What are some possible results of a review of resources and constraints?

    _a._ ....

    _b._ ....

    _c._ ....

_5_. List several reasons for designing from general goals to increasingly specific objectives.

    _a._ ....

    _b._ ....

    _c._ ....

_6_. Distinguish between a delivery system and media of instruction. ....

....

....

....

_7_. List five delivery systems.

    _a._ ....

    _b._ ....

    _c._ ....

    _d._ ....

    _e._ ....

_8_. List three features which may be found among systems of individualized instruction.

    _a._ ....

    _b._ ....

    _c._ ....

_9_. Show some differences between a non-mastery model and a mastery model. In a mastery model:

    _a._ ....

    _b._ ....

    _c._ ....

_10_. List problems in implementing individualized, mastery instruction in higher education.

    _a._ ....

    _b._ ....

    _c._ ....

    _d._ ....

Chapter 3 Performance Objectives

(Beginning with this Chapter, objectives will be numbered sequentially for this entire book, for ready identification and reference. Thus the numbering here takes up from Chapter 2 objectives.)

5. Write a description of the entire series of courses, or years of study, needed to reach the goals. Express this as either a curriculum scope and sequence statement, or as a description of how various courses relate to each other in sequence.

6. List the resources and constraints which influence choices among possible delivery systems. Name the systems most desired for adoption, and show how the final choice was made in view of the resources and constraints. Arrange lists of resources and constraints pertaining to the assumed development environment and the assumed learning environment.

7. Outline the major media, materials, teacher (or instructor) roles, learner roles, and learning activities to be designed. (Note that the final choices of media for each lesson or small unit of instruction are deferred until Chapter 9.)

8. Identify a course to be designed; write a one-paragraph description of it so that a student could decide whether or not he or she wishes to take the course.

Background

After needs and goals have been determined, questions like these are asked: How could the learners develop the ability to do the things described in the goals? What kind of learning environment and resources would be needed? Would the learning take place in schools, in a learning center, in the community, or at home? Are there reasons why the preferred location of learning is impossible because of policy, legal, or financial restrictions? How much money do we have for design of a delivery system and for conducting the instruction? What is our time schedule for developing a delivery system? When must the instruction begin?

A delivery system is everything required to operate an instructional system in a defined environment; the choice of a delivery system is made with questions like those above in mind, as well as other questions.

What kind of personnel are available to *design* the delivery system, to *develop* all of its component parts, and to *conduct* the instruction? Are some delivery systems, media, or methods prohibited by cost, personnel available, or user attitudes? Does a single delivery system fit the entire curriculum, or must different systems be selected for portions of the curriculum? Do we build new physical facilities and organizations, or conduct instruction in existing facilities? Are expensive mechanical/electrical simulators to be used, such as for pilot training or driver education, or is "real" equipment to be used? Are part-task trainers and devices more advisable (Branson, 1977)? What institutional traditions must be observed (Wager, 1977)? Are large *development* costs tolerated at the outset in return for lower *operating* costs, all amortized over a period of time (Wager, 1977)? How can team processes in design and development of the delivery system be organized; what design model can be followed by the design personnel; how can the work be managed (Carey and Briggs, 1977)?

In the process of answering such questions as the above, many compromises may be made either in the solution planned, or in the goals and priorities themselves. Some goals may be abandoned as unreachable with available resources and constraints. Others may be redefined, with levels of expectation reduced. Priorities among goals may be changed. Decisions will be made whether to attempt to modify existing resources and constraints, to pare down expectations, or to design a second-choice delivery system. Conflicts in the area of human relationships must be resolved. The composition of the planning team may change. Some citizens who served in the original consensus group for the needs analysis may now retire from the project, and a new planning team may be formed consisting of fewer citizen members and more educational personnel—administrators, teachers, subject-matter experts, instructional designers, and evaluation specialists.

At some point in designing the curriculum scope, in the analysis of resources and constraints, and in selecting delivery systems, publishers and contractors may enter the discussions to help estimate requirements for developing alternate delivery systems under consideration.

In the total set of operations from needs analysis to completion of a delivery system, the progression from one work stage to another will not be as clear-cut as we describe it in this book. In practice there is as much "looking ahead" and "backtracking" as there is progression in a linear, systematic fashion, described here for convenience and clarity as a constant forward progression. With this caution, however, we present the entire process as a systematic progression from stage to stage, knowing that in practice there is much "recycling," some of this in fact deliberately intended, as in the use of "formative evaluation" to correct prior decisions.

How to Do It

Establishing Relationships Among Courses

If the goals established refer to learner capabilities at the time of graduation from high school, then a decision must be made as to whether the entire curriculum, from kindergarten to the twelfth grade must be revised, or whether only the high school curriculum requires changing. After a review of the existing curriculum, a new scope and sequence would be drawn up. This is a familiar task for educators, and ways of accomplishing it will not be presented here. Suffice it to say again, though, that efforts need to be made to improve the "connectedness" of each successive year of study, so that a more complete relationship may be established between broad end goals and the curriculum of each school year.

Also familiar is the process of establishing relationships among courses in a degree program. These relationships may be looser in a liberal arts program than in a professional or vocational program.

In industrial and military training, experience in the past has also resulted in series of courses for career progression, as for officers and enlisted personnel. Some such career programs, consisting of both formal courses and on-the-job training and experience, may be broad in nature, as for the eventual goal for senior officers; other career progressions may represent specialties.

We simply recognize here, then, that ways of establishing sequences of courses and other learning experiences are by no means new; what is needed is improved precision in drawing up such relationships among courses to achieve more effective instruction, in terms of defined goals. Thus a single course or an entire series of courses must be reviewed as to the actual contribution in a long sequence of learning experiences which are goal directed.

We emphasize again a need for more explicitness in showing how each course contributes to a series of sub-goals which end up in achieving the broader, long-range goals. Just as lesson objectives need to be justified by showing their contributions to a unit objective, and units in turn must be shown to contribute to course goals, so course goals must be shown to contribute to the end-of-program goals. As said earlier, this has seldom, if ever, been done in any complete fashion, but improvement in that direction is desirable.

Relating Resources and Constraints to Delivery Systems

For each course in an entire instructional program, resources and constraints must be analyzed in terms of alternate delivery systems which might be employed to reach the goals adopted.

Alternate delivery systems. Gagné and Briggs (1979, pp. 176-177) have presented a table listing six delivery systems, along with possible media, learner activities, and methods and teacher roles associated with each delivery system. The six delivery systems listed there are:

(1) group instruction;
(2) individualized instruction;
(3) small-group instruction;
(4) independent study;
(5) work-study programs; and
(6) home study.

The above delivery systems are seen as total instructional contexts within each of which a variety of media may be used. These delivery systems were chosen for examination because they are suitable for consideration in public education. At any given grade level, more than one delivery system may be used, and in an entire school, all may be employed at times. Also, the delivery systems listed are not necessarily mutually exclusive. For example, an overall individualized instruction program, while employing extensively those media which permit individual self-pacing by learners, also includes both small-group and large-group instruction. In fact, most widely used individualized programs do employ such a range of media and methods (Gagné and Briggs, 1979; Talmage, 1975). The selection of a delivery system is thus a macro decision, while selection of media within the system involves micro decisions. In both cases, resources and constraints must be considered, as well, of course, as the appropriateness for the goals, the learners, and the teachers.

While the six delivery systems listed above are some of those in common use, there exists no widely recognized list of delivery systems. Appropriate terms for industrial and military training often include classroom training; field training; on-the-job training; correspondence courses; and peer teaching. Some industries develop other descriptive phrases reflecting features of the industry—e.g., "tail-gate training" in telephone companies—training conducted at the equipment installer's truck.

One central focus when selecting a delivery system is, of course, its appropriateness for the goals. Another focus is the characteristics of the learners. A third focus is the assumed learning environment and the capabilities of teachers, all within constraints of costs, time available, and the personnel who are to develop the delivery system.

Resources and constraints. The first-choice delivery system for the goals adopted may, of course, prove to be outside the reach of available funds, personnel, or time schedules. In such a case, it may be well to attempt to change the constraints before abandoning the preferred delivery system. So *constraint removal* efforts may be indicated—efforts to increase a budget, to change a policy, or to modify a law. In short, political effort may be expended to modify resources and constraints before a good plan is given up as infeasible. If this fails, the next step is either to choose another delivery system or to find a different set of media and methods for implementing the preferred delivery system. For example, a computer may have been preferred to afford drill and practice for a broad segment of the curriculum, but if it is infeasible to obtain the required resources, a less expensive drill and practice mode may be developed. In seeking compromise solutions, it is well to examine all components of the system—space utilization, equipment alternatives, forms of materials, media, methods, teacher roles, and learning activities. A cost may be cut in one component to increase resources available for another, provided that some support and operating procedure can thus be achieved. At this point, the planning team may review priorities among goals, thus again illustrating the "iterative" (recycling) nature of the total planning process.

The end of this stage of planning is reached when a delivery system (or systems) has been chosen which would (a) be effective in goal attainment and (b) could be developed within the resources and constraints. The actual *development* of the delivery system, however, is not begun until many more steps are taken. The *design* steps outlined in Chapters 4-7 come next, and then the actual delivery system development (Chapters 8-12).

Examples of Application

Example One: An Instructional Design Course

Here we continue the discussion, begun in Chapter 2, of the graduate course in "Design of Instruction." Recall that the need identified was a "demand" type need for instructional designers trained at the doctoral level. This implies that the total curriculum for this doctoral degree program would include courses in theory, research, and practice. The faculty decided to classify course in this program as "background" courses, "core courses," and "specialty" courses. Examples of background courses included general and educational psychology. An example of a "core" course is the course described here: "Design of Instruction." Examples of "specialty" courses include management of research and development projects, design of print materials, design of audio-visual materials, evaluation and measurement, alternate models for the design of instruction, and computerized instruction.

Within the "core" area, some further examples of courses are those listed below.

Theory courses. Theories of learning relevant to education; history and theory of instructional technology; theory of instructional design; and theory of evaluation.

Research courses. Methods of research; design of experiments; research in special topics in instruction; non-parametric methods; methods of multivariate analysis and factor analysis.

Practicum courses. The design of instruction; design of instructional modules; formative evaluation; delivery systems; adaptations for school practice.

Within the above types of courses, the program for an individual student is arranged to accommodate individual goals and future plans. The sequence of courses is arranged to fit the prior education and experience of the student and prerequisite relationships among courses in the program.

The resources and constraints within which the course "Design of Instruction" was developed were typical of university teaching situations in which there is no budget or time for *developing* the course as distinct from *teaching* it. Therefore, a delivery system such as individualized instruction by use of self-instructional modules was ruled out. The actual resources and constraints, and their influence upon selection of the delivery systems are described below.

- *Resources.*
    1. An instructor.
    2. A classroom with a chalkboard.
    3. One month for preparation time.
    4. About ¼ of a secretary's time.
- *Constraints.*
    1. No design and development budget.
    2. No direct funds except for the above resources.
    3. A fixed schedule for learning; that is, students were expected to complete the course within an academic quarter; "incompletes" were to be used only for emergencies, not to allow students to take more than a quarter to complete the course.
    4. No suitable textbook was available; a few texts covered portions of information desired for the course.

Choice of delivery system. Due to the above resources and constraints, a "mastery model" in its pure form was not feasible as the delivery system. It therefore became necessary to combine features of the conventional (non-mastery) model and a mastery model. Features of the two models were analyzed as shown in Figure 3.

A comparison of Figure 3 with the resources and constraints listed above for the course being described will make it evident that the best that could be done under the circumstances was to choose a delivery system of a "mixed" nature. Some features of both mastery and non-mastery models were combined, resulting in a delivery system having the features noted below.

The resulting delivery system. The features of the course, as first taught, were as follows:

1. Objectives were given to the student.
2. Due to the nature of the objectives, a design product accomplished by the student replaced conventional written tests.

Conventional instruction: A Non-Mastery Model	Individualized instruction: A Mastery Model
1. No objectives given to students.	1. Objectives given to students.
2. Tests usually made by sampling the instructional content of materials.	2. Objective-referenced tests designed for determining when mastery is achieved.
3. Fixed times for all students to complete each lesson and the entire course.	3. Each student works on each objective until mastery is achieved.
4. Instruction is group paced.	4. Instruction is self-paced by the student.
5. Since time is fixed, a "normal distribution" of scores results.	5. Since time is variable and second attempts on tests permitted, achievement scores often range only from 80 to 100 percent.
6. Usual procedure is lecture, discussion, and study of a textbook, if available.	6. Usual procedure is self-instructional, self-paced modules.
7. Teacher salary is the major budget item.	7. Cost of developing the modules is the major budget item.
8. A teacher is the only person for delivering the instruction.	8. Teaching assistants often used to monitor the system, in addition to an instructor.

Figure 3. Typical features of two models of instructional design: non-mastery and mastery models.

3. The design products were evaluated by criterion-referenced methods. That is, a standard of 90%, based on specific scoring criteria given to the students, was set for an "A," and 80% for a "B," etc.

4. Due dates were set for completion of each of four design stages which constituted the student product. If a student did not receive an "A" for the first or second assignment, he or she was allowed to revise it for a second evaluation *provided that* all four assignments could be completed by the end of the quarter.

5. Lectures and demonstrations were, of course, group paced, but students studied the few readings available at their own pace.

6. The scored evaluations of student products were neither a normal distribution nor confined to a range of 80-100%. Since second attempts were allowed, within the quarter time limit, the majority of students earned A or B grades; the percentage of such grades increased year by year as new materials were available.

Due to the circumstances described for the first offering of the course, the instructor immediately began preparing mimeographed materials, a few pages at a time, for use by students. In 1970, these collected materials were published as the First Edition of this *Handbook*. Later on, a *Student's Guide* and an *Instructor's Guide* were published. When all those materials became obsolete in some respects, the faculty of the program worked together to prepare the more recent text (Briggs, 1977) referred to at the opening of these chapters.

Example Two: A College Teaching Course

Scope and sequence. The aim of the "College Teaching Program" is to prepare prospective Community College teachers for their first jobs. To this end, three courses and a supervised teaching experience have been designed. The courses are (a) "College Teaching Methods," which concentrates on instructional activities, (b) "Course Design," which concentrates on curriculum design, and (c) "History and Philosophy of the Community College in America," which lays the foundation for the development and growth of this institution.

The two courses, "College Teaching Methods" and "Course Design," are sequential in nature (it is assumed that one should know how to teach before one designs the structure and resources of a particular course). Therefore, "College Teaching Methods" is a prerequisite for "Course Design."

It is assumed that all students in the "College Teaching Program" are subject-matter experts at the Master's level. This means that no instruction will be directed toward teaching mathematics to potential mathematics teachers—and no English to potential English teachers. However, there are other objectives to the program that are to be attained from other courses, namely, a "Supervised Teaching Internship," and "History and Philosophy of the Community College in America." In addition to "Course Design," "College Teaching Methods" is a prerequisite to the "Supervised Teaching Internship"; however, the "History and Philosophy" course may be taken concurrently.

Resources and constraints. The University has a wide variety of instructional delivery systems that can be used, provided that the software is available. It is desirable for the "College Teaching Methods" course to employ those types of delivery systems that a student might find in a typical community college in Florida. It is also desirable to design classroom presentations that employ different lecture and discussion techniques so that they may serve as models for the student's future behavior. Since most college courses rely heavily upon printed text, it will also be desirable to use this medium in an effective way. The college will provide videotape, slide-film, and audiotape for materials development, and the audio-visual center will supply needed equipment. Mediated materials may be placed in a learning resource room with computer terminals, sound-slide systems, videotape playback units, and reading carrels. Since this equipment is also available in most Florida community colleges, there are few constraints, and there are adequate resources to allow for the designer's choice of media.

The chosen delivery system. Listed next are the chosen activities and media:

1. use of the computer as an instructional delivery system;
2. use of sound-slide;
3. use of 16mm instructional film;
4. use of lecture discussion techniques;
5. use of student role playing—simulation;
6. use of videotape—instructional television; and
7. use of live model (teacher role).

Basically, a wide variety of media is appropriate for the content being conveyed, when linked to appropriate text and lectures.

Chapter 4
Writing and Classifying Objectives; Writing Test Items

Chapter in This Book	Recommended Readings		
	Briggs, L.J. (Ed.) *Instructional Design: Principles and Applications.* Englewood Cliffs, N.J.: Educational Technology Publications, 1977.	Gagné, R.M., and Briggs, L.J. *Principles of Instructional Design*, 2nd ed. New York: Holt, Rinehart, and Winston, 1979.	Gagné, R.M. *The Conditions of Learning*, 3rd ed. New York: Holt, Rinehart, and Winston, 1977.
3	Pages 262-265; 278-307 Chapters 12, 13	Pages 25-28; 175-178	
④	**Chapter 3 Pages 158-170**	**Chapters 2, 3, 7**	**Chapter 2**
5	Chapter 4	Chapter 8	

Explanatory Note

At this point in the book, the authors had to choose between two alternatives of chapter sequencing. The first alternative is the sequence in which an *experienced designer* actually designs a course. This is called the *job sequence*. The second alternative was to arrange the chapters in the order in which *you, the reader,* could best learn to design the course.

We have chosen the second sequence, the *learning* sequence. However, for convenience, we list the two sequences next, so that the significance of the above may be grasped (see Figure 4).

The Job Sequence	The Learning Sequence
Step 1—Needs, goals, priorities	Chapter 2—Needs, goals, priorities
Step 2—Resources, constraints, delivery systems	Chapter 3—Resources, constraints, delivery systems
Step 3—Organizing the course	Chapter 4—Writing and classifying objectives; test items
Step 4—Writing and classifying objectives; test items	Chapter 5—Organizing the course

Figure 4. Two sequences: The job sequence and the learning sequence.

The significance of Figure 4 may be summarized as follows:

1. A course of instruction is organized by writing objectives and arranging them into major course units. The relationships among the units are shown in a "course map." Next, the structure of each unit and the objectives which comprise it are shown by "unit maps." Then, lessons within each unit are planned and exhibited in the form of "lesson maps." These three "levels" of maps are comparable to a map of a *Nation*, then maps of *States*, and then maps of *Cities* within states. So, the three "levels" of maps go from general to specific, with increasing detail shown at each level, from course, to unit, to lessons. This process is described in Chapters 5-7.

2. But before you can show the organization of a course by constructing these three levels of maps (Chapters 5, 6, and 7, respectively), you must first learn to write objectives, which is one purpose of this Chapter. Hence, the placement of Chapter 4 before Chapters 5, 6, and 7.

In this Chapter, we show the relationships among: (a) categories of learning outcomes; (b) the writing of performance objectives for those categories of outcomes; and (c) the preparation of test items which are congruent with the objectives.

There are two different possible sequences for accomplishing the above three design steps:

• *Sequence One*

1. Decide upon the categories of outcomes desired from the instruction in the course.

2. Write objectives and classify them by type of outcome.

3. Prepare tests over the objectives.

or

• *Sequence Two*

1. Write the objectives.

2. Classify the objectives by types of outcome.

3. Prepare tests over the objectives.

In other words, one can first write the objectives for the course and then classify them, or one can first determine the types of outcomes sought and then write the objectives. An advantage of using the "standard verbs" presented in this Chapter is that you can write objectives so as to show their classification. Thus both steps are done at the same time.

In either event, the purpose in classifying objectives into categories of outcome (or domains) in a taxonomy of learning outcomes is to bring about economy in planning teaching strategies. Since there are different conditions of learning for each type of outcome in a taxonomy (Gagné, 1977b), grouping objectives according to outcome categories can reduce the number of strategy decisions to be made. Thus only one general strategy for teaching a cluster of *information* objectives and only one strategy for teaching *defined concepts* may need to be designed.

The purpose of writing performance objectives is, of course, to serve as guidelines for lesson planning or design of instructional materials, and to serve as a basis for developing tests to evaluate the achievement of the learners.

Each of the above three design stages will be discussed, in turn, following the presentation of the information test and the performance objectives for this Chapter.

In summary, the purpose of this Chapter is for you to learn a specific method of writing objectives which has several advantages over other methods. We will show sample objectives written for all 11 types of learning outcomes to be described in this Chapter. After learning to write objectives for these 11 types of outcomes, and to write valid test items for each objective, you can use this skill to organize instructional courses, units, and lessons (Chapters 5-7).

In this Chapter, then, we identify the 11 types of learning outcomes as domains and sub-domains in a taxonomy of outcomes, and we show you how our method of writing objectives automatically signals the type of outcome intended by each objective. The matter of classifying objectives is thus simplified.

Chapter 4 Information Test

_1._ Explain why the classification of objectives into their appropriate domains and sub-domains of outcomes assists in designing teaching strategies. ....
....
....
....

_2._ List the five major domains of learning outcomes.
   _a._ ....
   _b._ ....
   _c._ ....
   _d._ ....
   _e._ ....

_3._ List three different procedures for using outcome domains to classify objectives.
   _a._ ....
   _b._ ....
   _c._ ....

_4._ List the sub-domains for information learning.
   _a._ ....
   _b._ ....
   _c._ ....

_5._ List the sub-domains of intellectual skills.
   _a._ ....
   _b._ ....
   _c._ ....
   _d._ ....
   _e._ ....

_6._ Name the 11 types of outcomes (domains and sub-domains), and list the standard verb for each; then give an acceptable example of an action verb for each.

Type of Outcome	Standard Capability Verb	Action Verb
_a._		
_b._		
_c._		
_d._		
_e._		
_f._		
_g._		
_h._		
_i._		
_j._		
_k._		

_7._ In the context of objective-referenced teaching and testing, how is the validity of a test item determined? ....
....
....

<u>8.</u> *What does reliability of a test mean?* ....
....
....

<u>9.</u> *Name the five components of an objective.*
  a. ....
  b. ....
  c. ....
  d. ....
  e. ....

<u>10.</u> *From the point of view of open, ethical relationships between teachers and students, why should tests be valid?* ....
....
....
....

<u>11.</u> *List some synonyms for validity.*
  a. ....
  b. ....
  c. ....

<u>12.</u> *Define validity.* ....
....

<u>13.</u> *Define reliability.* ....
....

The Domains of Learning Outcomes

The taxonomy of educational objectives developed by Bloom (1956) is well known in educational circles. It was designed to assist in writing and classifying objectives and in preparing tests over the objectives.

We have chosen here to utilize the learning outcome taxonomy developed by Gagné (1977b) because it, also, serves the above two purposes; and, in addition, it is related directly and specifically to the learning and teaching of each type of outcome.

Classroom Experiences and
Learning Outcomes

Suppose that the students in a classroom watch a ten-minute film on the solar system. Is this a performance objective? It could be, depending upon the intent of the instruction, but more than likely it is not. The student watches the film in order to be able to do something else—watching the film is an instructional experience. It is important to be able to differentiate between the ends or objectives of the instruction and the means for accomplishing the ends. Why does the student watch the film? It may be that the teacher expects him or her to be able to name the planets in order from the sun, or to state which planet has rings caused by the reflection of light off solar dust. Whatever the reason, the film becomes the learning environment from which the student is to gain a new behavioral repertoire. After watching the film, the student will be expected to do things (exhibit behaviors that he or she couldn't exhibit before watching the film).

Is the film mentioned above a "good" instructional experience? This can only be determined if it is known ahead of time what watching the film was supposed to accomplish. This is the primary reason for specifying objectives in performance terms. If we can specify ahead of time what the learner is to be able to do after the instructional experience, there is a good chance that we can choose or design instruction that works. Specifying the outcomes of instruction serves other important purposes; it makes the instructional curriculum "visible." This allows the student to know what is expected of him or her; it lets the designer know if the instruction he or she is producing is effective; it lets the teacher know how to evaluate the progress of the student; and it lets the parent know what the school is trying to accomplish. If all instruction were based on performance objectives, there would be much less mystery about what education is trying to achieve.

Types of Learning Outcomes

Gagné (1977b) and Gagné and Briggs (1979) describe five domains of learning outcomes. These domains are:

(1) verbal information;
(2) intellectual skills;
(3) cognitive strategies;
(4) motor skills; and
(5) attitudes.

The first three domains may be seen to be components of what Bloom (1956) referred to as the Cognitive Domain—that dealing with knowledge, or knowing. The Attitudinal Domain is somewhat equivalent to what has been called the Affective Domain (Krathwohl, Bloom, and Masia, 1964), and motor skills is equivalent to what has also been called the Psychomotor Domain.

Sub-Domains of Learning Outcomes

The first two domains of outcomes listed above will be treated here as having sub-domains—three sub-domains for verbal information and five sub-domains for intellectual skills. These, along with the remaining three domains, comprise 11 types of learning outcomes, as shown in Figure 5.

Also shown in Figure 5 are standard *capability verbs* to be used when writing objectives, along with typical *action verbs*. The significance of these two kinds of verbs will be made clear in later portions of this Chapter. Figure 5 reflects many

Domains and Sub-Domains of Learning Outcomes	Standard Capability Verbs	Typical Action Verbs
Verbal Information Learning		
1. Verbatim learning: names, labels, poems	list, recite	orally; in writing
2. Non-verbatim learning: facts	state	orally; in writing
3. Substance learning: organized information	summarize	orally; in writing
Intellectual Skills		
4. Making sensory discriminations among objects or positions or qualities of objects	discriminate	pointing; sorting; underlining; matching
5. Concrete concepts	identify	sorting; pointing; underlining; matching objects
6. Defined concepts	classify	sorting correct and incorrect examples by *use* of a definition (not giving a definition)
7. Rules (Rule Using)	demonstrate	by applying the rule orally, in writing or by performing
8. Higher-order rule using (problem solving)	generate	orally or in writing a product requiring use of several rules
9. Cognitive strategies	originate	by speaking, writing, or constructing a *novel* solution to a problem
10. Motor skills	execute	by a manual performance of *new* series of movements
11. Attitudes	choose	by engaging in an activity voluntarily

Figure 5. Eleven types of learning outcomes and verbs used in writing objectives for these outcomes.

distinctions made earlier (Gagné, 1977b; Gagné and Briggs, 1979), and some that are new.

The 11 types of outcomes listed in Figure 5 will be discussed in turn along with a sample objective for each. These sample objectives employ the two kinds of verbs listed in Figure 5. After you have read the entire chapter, see if you can write an objective for each of the 11 categories in a subject area of your own choice.

Learning of Verbal Information. Information learning has been described as knowing *that* something is the case, whereas intellectual skills learning is learning *how to do something.* The former makes us *knowledgeable,* and the latter makes us *competent.* We can learn information from a book, but we have to do something with the information to convert it to a skill. We might read everything in a chapter in an algebra text, and be able to pass an *information test* on its content, but we may not be able to solve linear equations as a result. Also, information can be *looked up* if forgotten, but a skill must be *relearned* if forgotten. Note that the chapter information tests in this book can be answered by careful reading and by looking up the answers in the chapter, while the performance objectives require you to *generate* a design plan by *applying* what you learned from the chapter. The latter is clearly the more challenging task. We will now discuss the three types of information learning listed in Figure 5.

1. **Verbatim learning.** This term, of course, is the equivalent of rote learning, in which the exact words, names, symbols, or poems must be recited or written as they were encountered. Examples would include learning of names and telephone numbers of friends; lists of chemical symbols and their equivalents expressed in words; Spanish words and their English equivalents; lists of steps in procedures; or verbatim memorization of poems or other materials. An example of an objective would be: "Upon request, in a classroom situation, recite orally the poem 'Old Ironsides' without prompting." A teacher might add, in directions for this test situation, "without error or hesitation" or "in a striking tone of voice." (Criteria of performance in a test situation for the objective.) Note that both meaningful and non-meaningful, or arbitrary, material may be memorized. The telephone numbers are arbitrary—there is no "meaning" in them to the learner unless he or she employs memory devices or "bridges" (mnemonic devices). (Of course, the telephone company may have a ration-

ale for how the number was chosen.) The poem, on the other hand, is meaningful, but not a word may be changed in the recitation of it. Other examples would include memory of formulas, lists of items, etc.

2. **Non-verbatim factual learning.** Facts and other isolated bits of information may be meaningful to the learner who may state them in his or her own words. The fact, "Water freezes at 32° Fahrenheit," may be recalled verbatim (making it Type 1 learning, above), or it may be expressed in one's own words. The event, signing of the Declaration of Independence on July 4, 1776, may be restated in a number of ways (although the truth of the "fact" may be challenged by some historians). Lists, such as printed steps in a manufacturing process, are also facts, but are often confused by learners in instructional design courses with intellectual skills. Facts are distinguished from substance learning by their isolation, simplicity, and lack of organization or relatedness to other information. A sample objective: "In response to a written test item taken in a closed-book, classroom test situation, the student will list in writing the five causes of the Revolutionary War" (as listed in the textbook). In other objectives, the student could be asked to give dates of events but not to recite the events verbatim as given in the book.

3. **Substance learning.** When a student is asked to give a brief summary in his or her own words of a chapter in a book, or a lecture, or a film, we are dealing with *organized* information. Note that *interpretation* or *application* of the information is not involved, although skill in organizing and paraphrasing will assist in the expression of the substance recalled. A sample objective: "In a classroom oral test situation, the student will summarize Chapter 3 in the textbook without assistance." If that chapter discussed the protections provided by the Bill of Rights, the student would be asked only to *summarize* them, not to say when and how these protections have failed in practice; this latter could be a separate intellectual skills objective.

In all three types of information learning just discussed, the learner's task is to recall information, not to *apply* the information in any way. For example, a student would be asked to recall the standard deviation formula, but he or she is not asked to calculate a standard deviation for a set of numbers. In learning a definition of "democracy," the student is not asked to classify anything as democratic or nondemocratic. The characteristic of nonapplication seems to separate verbal information from the other domains where the information is applied in some way.

Teachers who have had experience writing objectives generally consider verbal information objectives trivial. Obviously, there is so much information that specifying all the verbal information objectives associated with a course would quickly become a tedious and seemingly meaningless task. Specifying verbal information objectives becomes much more meaningful if the function the verbal information will be serving in other types of objectives becomes clear. Verbal information serves an important function in the attainment of intellectual skills, motor skills, and attitudes. It might also serve an important role in the attainment of cognitive strategies. A figure showing how learnings in the various domains "interact" to be mutually supporting is presented in a later chapter (Figure 15, Chapter 6).

Verbal information is probably one of the least complex types of learning, but since there are such great quantities of verbal information to be learned, it often occupies a significant portion of the learner's time. Although not complex, verbal information learning can be quite difficult, and unless it is learned in a meaningful context or used regularly, it is easily forgotten. Attention to instructional conditions that facilitate verbal information learning deserves careful consideration in the instructional design process.

Intellectual Skills. One of the more common curricular goals is to have the students become "problem solvers." This is a noble goal, but before students can attain the skills for solving problems they must attain less complex, lower level capabilities that are used in the process of solving problems. With problem solving at the apex, Gagné (1977b) and Gagné and Briggs (1979) have identified four other intellectual skills that are subordinate to and prerequisite for problem-solving capabilities. These sub-domains of intellectual skills, shown in Figure 5, are listed again here, along with abbreviations used in Figure 6.

1. Discrimination Skills (D.S.)
2. Concrete-Concept Skills (C.C.)
3. Defined-Concept Skills (D.C.)
4. Rule-Using Skills (R.U.)
5. Problem-Solving Skills (P.S.)

These sub-domains have a hierarchical relationship to each other as shown in Figure 6.

This is not to infer that all learning structures look like Figure 6, but in general a problem-solving skill requires the use of two or more rules, a rule the use of two or more concepts, and a concept the use of two or more discriminations. The remainder of this section will be devoted to looking at each of the sub-domains that comprise the intellectual skills.

1. **Discriminations.** The ability to discriminate relates to the performance of being able to tell if two stimuli are similar or different. Discrimination may include visual, auditory, olfactory, tactile, or taste stimuli. Examples of discrimination objectives include:

a. Given cards containing drawings of circles, rectangles, and triangles, the student will be able to discriminate among their geometric shapes by sorting them into separate groups, with no assistance.

b. Given several pots of soil, the student will be able to discriminate degrees of soil moisture among the pots.

c. When hearing pairs of notes struck on a piano, the student will be able to discriminate musical pitches, by saying whether the two notes in each pair are the same or different.

Note that each objective describes the *test* performance, not the method of learning, nor what the teacher presented during instruction. In order to be sure that the learning "generalizes," one might construct "generalizing" test items like these:

a. Draw a line connecting the figures that look the same:

b. Find the note on the piano that sounds most like the one the teacher plays on the xylophone.

There are other formats for discrimination tests, but notice that in the examples given above the student is not asked to give the name, or any verbal information about the discrimination; he or she is actually asked to perform it by matching two stimuli. For instance, the student is not asked whether sample "A" has the correct amount of moisture for growing plants—that objective is a different, higher order, skill. Nor is the student asked to name different shapes, or to name the note being played.

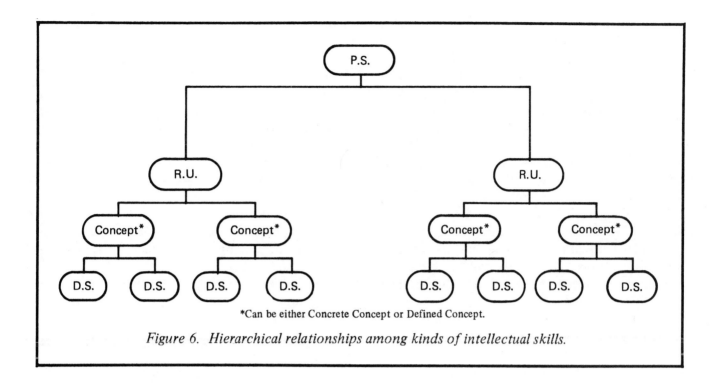

*Can be either Concrete Concept or Defined Concept.

Figure 6. Hierarchical relationships among kinds of intellectual skills.

2. **Concrete Concepts**. The concrete concept is something that has physical attributes and can be touched, pointed to, or "identified." The best examples of concrete concepts would be things like chairs, tables, sports cars, or horseshoes. Each has a set of physical attributes that separate it from other physical objects. The nature of a concept is that it represents a "class" of items. These items may be different in some ways, but all items in the class will exhibit the same critical attributes. It may be apparent that some items, in fact, most items, can belong to more than one class of items. For instance, both Datsun 280Z's and Ford Pintos belong to the class of items called automobiles; however, only the Datsun 280Z would be considered a member of the class "sports cars."

Some examples of objectives that typify concrete concepts are:

    a. Given a variety of kinds of beans scattered on a table, and the direction to set aside all the kidney beans, the student will be able to separate the kidney beans from the others.

    b. Given pictures of several persons, the student will be able to identify human physical characteristics as "endomorph," "mesomorph," or "ectomorph."

    c. The student will be able to identify the proper laboratory set-up for displacing oxygen by heat.

Notice that the name of the objects is used in the directions to the test; the directions do not say "Point to those that are alike," as in discriminating. Notice also that in all cases the student must make a choice, based on physical attributes, as to what class something will be assigned.

3. **Defined Concepts**. Defined concepts, like concrete concepts, call for an assignment of something to a class of things based on whether or not it possesses the attributes of the concept. Defined concepts, unlike concrete concepts, do not possess physical attributes, or at least not critical physical attributes. For instance, the concept "family" would contain people (physical entities), but there is nothing in the physical attributes to make the decision as to whether a particular grouping of people are in fact a family. In this case, information about the unobservable relationships or parentage of the individuals is needed for correct categorization. The student may use a definition in order to classify the items, but merely reciting the definition is information learning. The student must *use* the definition.

Some examples of defined concepts are:

    a. Given several newspaper editorials, the student will be able to classify them by writing either "conservative" or "liberal" on each one.

    b. Given descriptions of the relationship among several groups of persons, the student will be able to classify persons as either members or non-members of a given "nuclear family."

   c. Given a list of words, the student will be able to classify them as synonyms or antonyms, by writing the correct label next to each word.

Defined concepts must be tested with items that call for classification tasks. In other words, simply asking the student to give the definition of conservative or liberal does not tell us if the student could recognize a conservative newspaper article if he or she saw one. But the student needs to "understand" the definitions in order to make the classifications. Thus, the student "uses" the definition but does not "recite" it either verbatim or in his or her own words.

   4. **Rule Using**. Rule-using behaviors are characterized by the demonstration of procedural operations involving two or more concepts. Some examples of rule-using objectives are:

   a. Given pairs of integers, the student will be able to demonstrate the calculation of the quotient of each two integers in writing, showing both the procedure and the answer.

   b. Given a series of words pronounced by the teacher, the student will be able to demonstrate spelling rules involving I and E by writing each word correctly.

   c. Given several temperature/pressure "problems," the student will be able to demonstrate the application of Boyle's Law in writing, showing each step in arriving at an answer.

   d. Given several pairs of fractions, the student will demonstrate the addition of two fractions by use of the lowest common denominator, showing his or her work in writing.

Notice that in these objectives the student is not asked to state the rule but rather to apply it. Most arithmetic operations involve rule using, as do other operations, like writing a theme using correct grammar.

   5. **Problem Solving (Higher-Order Rule Using)**. Problem solving involves the use of two or more rules in combination in order to arrive at a conclusion (solution). Problem solving may permit more than one path to the solution. The gaining of problem-solving capabilities means that the student can determine which rules to use, and to apply the rules together in combination. The power of rules used in combination is far greater than rules used alone, and allows the generation of solutions to problems that are unique (have never before been taught as specific procedural operations). "Solutions" to problems may include arriving at a correct answer by "discovering" a higher-order rule, based on simpler rules, as the method for arriving at the solution.

   Some examples of problem-solving objectives are:

   a. Given the need for a new item of information, the student will be able to generate a business letter, requesting information about a company's product, by typing the composed letter.

   b. Given relevant (and irrelevant) data, the student will be able to generate orally a prediction of how many Congressional seats will be Republican after the next general election.

   c. On a written, closed-book test, the student will be able to generate a hypothesis with regard to the transmission capabilities of fiber optics on a 50 megahertz band.

It is more difficult to evaluate problem-solving skills than it is rule-using skills, since generally there are a number of acceptable solutions, or routes for arriving at the same solution. One way to evaluate problem-solving skills is to use a criteria sheet that lists the attributes of a "good" solution. This approach is used in some of the exercises included in this handbook. This serves two purposes: to give the reader a guide as to what is important to the evaluator, and to serve as a check sheet for the evaluator when reviewing the solution. It also enables the students to evaluate their own performances, and serves as a guide in arriving at the performances.

Problem-solving skills are the highest or most complex in the intellectual skills hierarchy. This should be remembered when a unit of instruction has problem-solving objectives. It means that a task analysis (learning hierarchy) should show the rules, concepts, and discriminations that the learner will have to possess in order to succeed at the task. More will be said about the task analysis process later.

Cognitive Strategies. Cognitive strategies are placed here because they are most like capabilities in the intellectual skills domain. When engaging in cognitive strategies, the student originates a strategy for the manipulation of information. Gagné also refers to cognitive strategies as executive subroutines. These subroutines are learned, and they govern the manner in which the student will approach a performance task. It is possible that cognitive strategies are gained through a variety of experiences, both formal and informal, and that they control a major proportion of new learning that takes place. A "slow" learner may be one who possesses relatively fewer cognitive strategies than does his or her peer group.

Some examples of cognitive strategy objectives are:

a. Given a list of names and pictures of these persons, the student will be able to originate a system for remembering the names, as tested by the pictures without the names.
b. Given written case descriptions of behavior problems of students, the learner will be able to originate behavioral control strategies, and to give a written description of his or her solutions.
c. Given a series of geometric figures and questions about them, the student will be able to originate a method for deriving geometric theorems, and explain the method orally.

In all cases, the cognitive strategy enables the student to look at information in a new way. Bruner, Goodnow, and Austin, in their book, *A Study of Thinking* (1962), describe three types of concept behavior, convergent, divergent, and relational. It appears that certain "cognitive strategies" are used in the three types of concept tasks. This raises the question of how "learning to learn" may be taught. We know little about cognitive strategies, but they may be one of the most fruitful areas for educational research.

It may be noted that in the above examples, the student develops a strategy for a specific problem or purpose. Students may employ more general habits of thinking which guide the strategies they employ to invent novel solutions to specific problems.

Motor Skills. The learning of motor skills involves the physical execution of a specified behavior. For example:

a. On a city street with moderate traffic, the student will be able to execute the parallel parking of a car.
b. In an actual game situation, the student will be able to execute a forehand return in tennis.

c. In a speech class of 30 students, the student will be able to execute the delivery of an emotional speech.

The attainment of motor skills is often facilitated by the attainment of other types of behaviors, such as verbal information, rules, and problem-solving skills, but the attainment of the motor skill must be tested through the direct observation of the student performing the skill. Probably one of the most serious violations of test validity is assuming from a verbal report that a student can in fact perform the motor skill that is to be attained. Likewise, the methods that are needed to teach motor skills are more diverse than those needed for cognitive or affective skills.

Attitudes. Attitude behaviors are characterized by choices made by the individual with regard to persons, places, things, and ideas. Attitudes represent a disposition (positive, negative, neutral) that will govern the choices the student makes. Many theorists believe that these dispositions are the result of information the student possesses about the consequences or probable consequences of a particular choice behavior in a given situation.

Typical attitude objectives might include:

a. When given the option, the student will choose to attend class.
b. When given a free period and several alternate activities, the student will choose to read for pleasure.
c. When free time is available for any desired activity, the student will choose to be politically active as indicated by engaging in such activities.

In attitude type learning, the measurement of the behavior must be unobtrusive. The wording of attitude objectives is thus somewhat different from other objectives. The choice behavior on the part of the student should not be governed by a punishment contingency (if the choice is to continue voluntarily after instruction). It is probably safe to say that very little attitude instruction is consciously designed—if it were, the nature of instructional materials would likely be quite different from materials typically produced.

Writing Objectives

In the preceding section of this Chapter, some examples were given of objectives for various types of learning outcomes. In some instances, tests for the objectives were presented.

In moving on to the matter of how to write objectives, and to make tests that are congruent with the objectives, we need to point out first the reason for considering objectives and tests together in this Chapter. This reason is that objectives describe what learners will be doing *after study*, not *during study* of the objectives. Objectives define the test to be designed to measure attainment of the objectives. Objectives do *not* describe the content of the learning materials, nor what the teacher says or does. Objectives do *not* describe what the student *receives* from instruction but rather what the student can *do* after the instruction *that he or she could not do before the instruction*. Hence, good objectives do not refer to the content or nature of the *instruction* but to the *new capability* that the learner has acquired as a *result* of the instruction.

For the above reason, objectives describe the performance of learners in appropriate test situations; they do not describe the learning and teaching situation which precedes the tests.

Some criteria for judging the adequacy of performance objectives are as follows:

1. Objectives describe the test behavior of learners which is used as an *indicator* that the desired *performance capability* has been acquired.
2. Objectives need to be *unambiguous*, because they need to communicate clearly the essential features of the test situation in terms of both the *indicator* action of learners *and* the *capabilities* that the indicators signify.
3. Test situations designed to measure the learners' attainment of the objectives must be *congruent* with the objectives. Tests must measure the *capabilities* described in the objectives, not some other capabilities.

The accomplishment of the above three criteria is demonstrated in examples of objectives and their corresponding tests given in the other sources cited at the opening of this Chapter, especially Chapter 3 in Briggs (1977) and Chapter 7 in Gagné and Briggs (1979). These same criteria will also be illustrated later in this Chapter in sample objectives, some written by students and some written by the authors.

Before discussing the separate elements or components of objectives, when written in the five-component form recommended here, we now illustrate several ways of stating an objective to show why the five-component method is preferred.

Suppose a teacher is asked what he or she is going to teach during the next meeting with his or her class. Suppose the teacher says, "mathematics." This is not specific enough, obviously, to indicate *what* mathematics is to be taught. If asked to be more specific, the teacher might say "adding fractions." This is a definite improvement in specificity and clarity of communication. However, suppose that a substitute teacher must come in for that particular lesson. The substitute teacher might not know whether the addition of fractions is to be taught by the least common denominator method with the answer to examples to be expressed as mixed numbers, or whether the method to be taught is to change the fractions to decimals, and then express the results as whole numbers and decimals. So writing "adding fractions" might be well enough for the teacher as a reminder to himself or herself, but it would not be specific enough for the substitute teacher not familiar with the intent. If the teacher had left the following objective for the substitute teacher, matters would have been clarified: "Given pairs of fractions such as 3/4 and 5/8, the learner will demonstrate the addition of fractions using the least common denominator method by writing the steps in the solutions and the answers in the form of fractions and mixed numbers."

Such objectives as the one just given are more unambiguous than the other, briefer forms of the illustrated objective. Just as the latter form would guide the substitute teacher's actions more adequately, such clear objectives also help in team situations in curriculum and course design. Design teams and teacher teams often need to communicate at this degree of specificity if the team effort is to result in unified and coherent plans.

In order for you, the reader, to be able to write objectives meeting the criteria stated earlier, we next describe the components to be attended to in the recommended five-component method of writing objectives proposed by Gagné and Briggs (1979).

The five formal components of the recommended method of writing objectives are:

1. In what environment (situation), and given what kind of test item(s),
2. for what type of learned behavior (learned capability) the
3. student does what (object)

4. in what observable way (action verb)
5. using what tools, with what constraints, or under what special conditions (tools, constraints, and special conditions).

Each of these components of objectives is discussed next.

Situation

The Test Environment. Under the situation component, the objective writer describes the environment in which the student will demonstrate the new behavior he or she has acquired. This component is often overlooked and taken for granted, but it is important when the testing situation is likely to be different from the real-world performance situation. For instance, let's take the objective, "the student executes the changing of a car tire." This objective does not specify the environment in which the student will be changing the tire. After the instruction, he or she may be asked to execute the changing of a tire in the school parking lot. However, faced with the situation of changing the same tire on a busy highway, in 10° weather, with a 20 m.p.h. wind, the student may not be able to execute the performance. It would look, to the unbiased observer, that this person could not change a tire, while the results of the school performance would say that he or she could.

For some tests, specification of the environment would seem unnecessary, since the conditions under which the behavior is performed in the real world are very similar to the conditions that exist in the classroom. For such cases, saying "when given 10 linear equations to solve," may be more important than specifying "at home" or "in a classroom," although this can, of course, be indicated.

Noise and other distractions may change the psychological environment. Suppose an objective reads: "The student will generate a letter of reply to a customer's inquiry, and execute the typing of that letter in a period of no more than 10 minutes." Again, this objective does not specify the environment or situation in which this performance will take place. It is likely that the student will be working in an office where there are many other things going on at the same time that he or she is trying to compose and type the letter. The exact performance that the student demonstrated in the classroom is no longer displayed, given this different environment.

The situation component of the objective allows the designer to determine the external validity of a testing situation. The more like the real-world situation, the greater the external validity of the testing situation. One point might be noted here: the situation does not specify what the learner does before exhibiting the performance. For example, "after reading the text" does *not* describe the situation or the environment in which the behavior will be displayed, nor does it specify the problem presented by the test. The reading of the text may be the teacher-designated means of attaining the objective, but it is possible that the student has learned the behavior in a different way. The demonstration of the performance is the purpose of the test. It does not matter when or how the student learned to do the performance.

The Test Stimulus. The situation component of an objective often includes two separate elements: designation of the test environment (just discussed) and description of the test stimulus to be presented to the student.

A description of the test stimulus often includes two components: directions to be given, and the nature of the test item(s) to be presented.

> 1. *In a classroom situation, cubes of different colors will be placed in a random arrangement on a table. With other pupils watching, the learner will be asked to "put all the red ones together and all the blue ones together."*

To be sure, a teacher for his or her own purposes may simply call this "sorting objects by color." But in a team planning situation, where one person plans the lessons and another person plans the tests, the objectives must be clear enough for the two persons to work somewhat independently.

Note also that since the words "red" and "blue" are specified, we are testing for these *concrete concepts*. If discrimination only were to be tested, we would not use these two words in the directions. Instead, we would specify "put the ones that are the same together." The two performances might be taught either simultaneously or separately (discriminations first).

> 2. *In a take-home, open-book assignment, the learner will generate a previously unencountered five-component performance objective in writing, for each of the 11 types of learning outcomes.*

47

This situation allows reference to the text, but it requires *new* objectives to be generated. This eliminates writing a copied or memorized objective seen previously.

Note also that the learned capability, *generate,* is a complex objective requiring the prior mastery of many rules, the *production* of new objectives, and the use of the learner's own language—a new capability has been acquired! But this capability is *indicated* by use of a very familiar, previously mastered skill—*writing.* Thus the *action* (indicator) verb is chosen because the learner is *known to be able to write,* while the capability to be judged by *what* is written is the *new* capability to be inferred from the writing—generating five-component objectives.

In this example, it was recognized that it will take considerable time for the learners to generate their first five-component objectives, even though they have studied the rules and read many examples of such objectives. We may judge that this performance is complex and time-consuming the first time, but otherwise it is not necessarily *difficult.* At least our own students have been able to do this at the end of the third week of class in our design courses.

In the first example above, we used two sentences to express the objective. This seemed less awkward than putting it all in one sentence. There is nothing wrong with this, if it improves the clarity of the communication. In general, however, the five-component objectives often do result in less than elegant prose! It is often possible to improve and simplify the wording by departing from the standard order of placing the five components. Notice, however, that students manage to write understandable objectives when placing the components in the usual order, as shown in the student-produced examples presented later in this Chapter.

Learned Capability

The second component of an objective is a statement of the learned capability inferred from the performance of a student in a test situation.

In the examples of objectives given earlier in this Chapter, and in Figure 5, a standard single verb was used to refer to a single new capability representing a specific type of learning outcome. Thus, there is a different standard capability verb for each of the 11 domains and sub-domains of learning outcomes. Many of these were originally suggested by Gagné

and Briggs in their First Edition of *Principles of Instructional Design,* and were retained in their Second Edition (1979, p. 125). Figure 5 adds some new ones along with examples of appropriate *action* verbs for each standard capability verb.

These standard capability verbs, if used by all designers, could remove much of the confusion and ambiguity about the intent of objectives. By using them, the designer *automatically* informs others of the type of outcome being referred to. If the standard verbs are used correctly, the step of classifying objectives is already accomplished. If the standard verbs are not used, others may not agree on the type of outcome intended.

In the writing of objectives, the learned capability verb categorizes the type of learning which the designer is intending the objective to represent. Learning is the changing of an internal state of the learner, and we can only infer its existence through external activities or performances. The learned capability verbs are descriptive of the different types of learning, but they do not depict how these inferred behaviors will be exhibited. For instance, the learned capability verb for one type of learning called *facts* is "states." So, when we write this type of verbal information objective, we say the student will be able to "state" something. However, there are at least two ways of stating something, orally or in writing. The verb *state* simply describes a new capability to be gained by the learner; *how* he or she will do the stating is described later in the objective in the form of an *action verb.*

Object

The object of the objective is a description of the content of the learned capability—a description of *what* has been learned. For example, the student will be able to state "the names of the planets in the solar system." "The names of the planets in the solar system" is descriptive of the verbal information that is to be learned. Notice that the objective was not written, "The student will be able to state, Mercury, Mars, Earth, Venus, etc.," even though this is the answer to the question, "What are the names of the planets?" As long as the intent of the object is clear, the objective should be written in as brief a statement as possible. The objective does not and should not contain the content of the instruction that will be designed to elicit the desired behavior. The nature of the *object* should become clearer in the examples given later.

Action Verb

The action verb describes the observable behavior the learner will exhibit from which the learned capability will be inferred. The action verb is therefore the *indicator* of the *capability* inferred from the action. As in the example given previously, two ways of showing the learned capability of "stating" is to report orally or in writing. With regard to another type of learning, the concrete concept, the student might "identify" something by *touching* it, *circling* a picture of it, *pointing* to it, etc. Whereas there are only 11 learned capability verbs, one for each type of learning outcome, there are a great number of appropriate action verbs. Some action verbs are more appropriate for certain types of learning than others; for example, one would not be able to "state" by "matching"; the two behaviors are not congruent. This means that certain types of test items are more appropriate for certain types of behavior than others.

When writing five-component objectives, it is *not* desirable to use learned capability verbs as action verbs. The reason is that when used in the five-component context the learned capability verbs take on a very specific meaning, whereas the action verbs may be used as indicators for several capabilities. Using synonyms for the learned capability verbs or using them as action verbs becomes confusing to both the reader and the writer of the objective. Appropriate action verbs for each standard capability verb are shown in Figure 5 and in the numerous examples of objectives in this Chapter.

Tools, Constraints, and Special Conditions

The tools, constraints, and special conditions further delimit or qualify the situation. The tools may include a special machine, e.g., using an IBM Magnetic Card typewriter, or using a HP 2121 calculator. The constraints may include time constraints or criteria of performance. The special conditions might include other environmental factors that govern the acceptable demonstration of performance.

Mager (1962) includes the criterion for acceptable performance in his three-component method of writing objectives, just as he often specifies the number of items for the test ("the learner must answer correctly six of the eight items"). We prefer to separate these two elements from the objective, leaving them to be decided when developing the test. Some others concur in this preference (Kibler and Bassett, 1977).

Examples of Five-Component Objectives

We have given some examples of objectives earlier in this Chapter for the purpose of showing their relevance to domains of outcomes and to illustrate our discussion of the function of each of the five components in an objective.

Now we turn to examples of completed objectives arranged and labelled to correspond to the 11 types of outcome, illustrated for a variety of subject-matter areas.

The objectives in Figures 7 to 9 were prepared by three students in a first course in instructional design at Florida State University in the fall quarter of 1979. These students prepared these objectives at the close of the third week of the course, following a unit on needs analysis and overall course description. They were instructed, in so far as possible, to write an objective for each of the 11 types of outcomes intended for the courses of their own choice which were the subjects of their needs analyses and course descriptions. If a chosen course would not include discriminations and concrete concepts, for example, they were instructed to turn to any subject area for demonstrating ability to write objectives in such outcome categories. You will notice this change in subject area for this reason in the three sets of student-produced examples.

The three sets of student-prepared objectives in Figures 7 to 9 were chosen to illustrate three different subject-matter areas. These objectives were considered to be among the best examples prepared by the class of 19 graduate students. The format used was suggested by Amy Ackerman (1977) when she was a student in the design course. These three students gave permission for their objectives to be reproduced in this book; we thank them for this permission. Their objectives have not been edited; they are reproduced here as they were submitted. The students' names are shown in the three figures.

Notice that capabilities mastered earlier were specified by one student. There are also four lapses from the rule not to specify the method of learning. Can you find them? Also notice the left column in Figure 9. You might wish to use this format at first.

Situation	Capability	Object	Action	Tools/Constraints
Given written summaries of a cancer patient's admission interview, physical exam, and lab data,	the student will *originate*	an individualized nursing care plan to include nursing diagnoses, nursing actions with rationales, and evaluation criteria	in writing.	The *ANA Standards of Nursing Care* and the textbook may be used.
Given one of the five categories of cancer chemotherapeutic agents,	the student will *list*	the names of three drugs which are examples of that category	in writing.	Reference materials may not be used.
Having read literature on the pathophysiology of cancer,	the student will *state*	the characteristics of malignant neo-plasms	in writing	within 15 minutes.
Given the chapter to read on the psycho-social aspects of cancer,	the student will *summarize*	the impact of cancer on the patient and family	orally	within 15 minutes.
Given a prefilled sterile syringe, an alcohol wipe, and a medication card,	the student will *execute*	the administration of an intramuscular injection	by injecting the medication into the dorsogluteal site of a patient simulator	using sterile technique.
Given readings, discussions, and exposure to learning experiences in oncology nursing,	the student will *choose*	to give care to persons with cancer	by selecting patient assignments on the oncology unit	without prompting from the clinical instructor.
Given a tennis ball and drawings of a square, a circle, and a triangle,	the student will *discriminate*	the drawing which looks like the tennis ball	by matching by pointing to the drawing	without assistance.
Given a drawing of a syringe and needle,	the student will *identify*	the plunger, barrel, shaft, hub, and bevel of the syringe unit	by labelling the drawing	within five minutes.
Given a list of ten side effects of cancer chemotherapy,	the student will *classify*	the side effects which are a result of myelosuppression	by placing an "X" in front of the appropriate terms.	A dictionary or other reference may not be consulted.
Given pictures of a 22g 1 1/2" needle, a 25g 5/8" needle, and a 20g 2" needle,	the student will *demonstrate*	the needle to use for a subcutaneous injection	by drawing a circle around the needle	within one minute.
Given a pediatric nomogram, a child's height and weight, the recommended dosage of a drug in mg/m^2/day, and a vial labelled '100 mg/cc,'	the student will *generate*	the correct dosage of the drug to be given in cc q. 6h	by calculating the amount.	The answer and the calculations done to derive the answer will be shown on the test answer sheet.

Figure 7. Student-prepared sample objectives by Nina Entrekin.

Situation	Capability	Object	Action	Tools/Constraints
Given successful test performance on problem solving and naval capabilities, and on being presented with a hypothetical politico/military contingency,	the learner will *originate*	a plan for the maritime defense of Australia	by preparing a service paper for consideration by higher authority.	Stenographic assistance provided. Specialist officers will be available for advice. The task to be completed in 10 hours and in the format of JSP(AS)102.
Given successful test performance on Australian Fleet organization and a general statement of New Zealand and Indonesian task force organizations,	the learner will *generate*	an appropriate task force organization for a combined, Australian/New Zealand/Indonesian task force	by producing an operation order.	Unassisted except for stenographic support. Task to be completed in 2 hours and in format of JSP (AS) 102. (Remainder without human assistance.)
Given age, years of service, and salary of three officers,	the learner will *demonstrate*	the method of ascertaining pension entitlements	by calculation of their respective benefits.	Calculator may be used. Task to be completed in 15 minutes.
Given a list of 10 aircraft and their weapon systems,	the learner will *classify*	the antisubmarine aircraft	by checking only those aircraft on the list that qualify.	The list must include all types of aircraft. Task to be completed in 10 minutes.
Given a military organization wiring diagram (organization chart),	the learner will *identify*	the 'staff' and 'line' positions	by marking them with an 's' or 'l,' respectively.	The wiring diagram is to be limited to one command, or Branch if in head office, and displayed on one page.
Given one unknown silhouette and 10 known silhouettes of destroyers,	the learner will *discriminate*	the known which matches the unknown	by pointing to it.	Task to be completed in one minute.
Given that it is August,	the learner will *list*	the steps to be followed in preparation of the Military budget	by writing them on paper.	All steps to be included. Task to be completed in 10 minutes.
In response to a question,	the learner will *state*	three technological trends which will affect the future capabilities of navies	in an oral answer.	Answer to be completed in three minutes.
Following a guest lecturer's presentation,	the learner will *summarize*	the important points of the lecture	by writing a paragraph.	Task to be completed in 10 minutes.
In a platoon of marching men on parade on the order 'eyes right,'	the learner will *execute*	a salute to the reviewing officer	by inclining his head and eyes to the right.	Salute to be executed when right foot next hits ground after order 'eyes right' is given.

Figure 8. Student-prepared sample objectives by Haydn Daw.

Category of Capability	Situation	Capability	Action	Object	Tools/Constraints
I. Intellectual Skill					
A. Discrimination	Presented a number of tastes and several taste categories (sweet, sour, bitter, etc.),	the student *discriminates*	by placing the food item	under the proper taste category	without assistance and within two taste test trials.
B. Concrete Concept	Given a diagram of the reproductive organs,	the student will *identify*	by writing next to the associated arrow	the proper name of the structure	within 45 minutes.
C. Defined Concept	Given role-played examples of intervention techniques for parents (reinforcement, punishment, effective communication, deprivation),	the student must *classify*	by writing next to the number of the example	the type of intervention used	within one minute following each presentation.
D. Rule	Given a list of unacceptable behaviors exhibited by a child and a list of effective management interventions,	the student will *demonstrate*	by matching in writing	the effective consequence to the inappropriate action	within 45 minutes.
E. Higher-Order Rule (Problem Solving)	Given a series of conflict-situations requiring effective communication skills,	the student must *generate*	in writing	the appropriate communication intervention in each situation	within one hour.
II. Cognitive Strategy	Given the current contributors to ineffective parenting and the rise in social ills,	the student will *originate*	by discussion (oral presentation)	the interrelationship between these two social influences	within a 15-minute presentation to the class.
III. Information					
A. Names, labels, or poems	Given a copy of the poem, 'Children Learn What They Live,'	the student will *recite*	by oral verbatim reproduction	the poem	within ten minutes.
B. Facts	Given a list of the important developmental milestones of childhood,	the student must be able to *state*	in writing	in appropriate communication intervention in each situation	within one hour.
C. Meaningful or Substance Learning	Given the "Cardinal Rules" of effective parenting,	the student will *summarize*	in his or her own words by writing in a few paragraphs	the essence of good parenting	within 45 minutes.

Figure 9. Student-prepared sample objectives by Sandra Quesada.

IV.	Motor Skill	Given prior verbal instruction and demonstration on how to bathe an infant and given a doll and the needed supplies,	the student will *execute*	a bath	cleansing the doll	with the prepared supplies within 15 minutes.
V.	Attitude	Given a number of written situations of an acting-out child, in which a clear choice exists between physically punitive (positive punishment) and deprivational consequences (negative punishment),	the student will more frequently *choose*	by writing a letter associated with the action,	deprivation rather than physical punishment	within 20 minutes.

(Figure 9 Continued)

Converting Incomplete Objectives to the Five-Component Format

Often an instructional designer begins work as a consultant on a project after the needs analysis is finished and after the courses have been outlined in some form.

In the event that objectives have also been written for course units and lessons, they are likely to be defective in communicating the intent of the writers of the objectives. The designer then would often need to confer with the writers as to their intent, or to rewrite the objectives and ask the original writers to review them.

Often the original objectives are either too broad (referring to goals rather than to objectives) or they are couched in vague terms, like "appreciate," "know," "understand," etc., thus providing no basis for designing either instruction or test items.

In Figure 10, we start with objectives that are not as defective as those just described, but they are incomplete, and not written in the five-component form. Read each objective to see which components are absent or faulty; then read the completed objective and note the improvement in clarity.

Examples of Incomplete and Complete Objectives

After each number there appears an incomplete objective. Below it the objective is rewritten in the five-component format.

Verbal Information: Factual Information

1. The student will be able to recall the definition of "normal distribution."

Situation —	In a typical classroom test situation,
Learned capability —	the student will be able to *state* (either verbatim or paraphrased)
Object —	the definition of "normal distribution"
Action —	in writing
Tools/Constraints —	without the use of references; the definition may be given in the learner's own words.

Figure 10. Examples of incomplete and complete objectives.

Motor Skill

2. The student will be able to change a car tire.

    Situation —   Alongside of a highway,
    Learned capability —   the student will be able to *execute*
    Object —   the changing of a flat tire
    Action —   by removing the flat from the car and replacing it with the spare,
    Tools/Constraints —   observing safety rules specified for this operation.

Problem Solving

3. The student will determine how much stock should be ordered to cover holiday buying.

    Situation —   Preparing a summer order form for winter goods,
    Learned capability —   the student will be able to *generate*
    Object —   an estimate of how much stock of various items will be needed in order to cover increased demands due to holiday buying habits
    Action —   by writing on paper his or her estimate and explanation of how he or she deduced it
    Tools/Constraints —   and explaining why this estimate is not unreasonably high.

Rule Using

4. The student will apply Boyle's Law.

    Situation —   In a laboratory experimental situation,
    Learned capability —   the student will be able to *demonstrate*
    Object —   the relationship between pressure and temperature as expressed by Boyle's Law
    Action —   by recording the pressure increase over a temperature range of 100 to 110°C,
    Tools/Constraints —   using the Smith pressure chamber with a safety setting of 40lbs/sq. in.

Defined Concept

5. The student will know the difference between judging mode and regular mode in a computer program.

    Situation —   When looking at a printed computer program,
    Learned capability —   the student will be able to *classify*
    Object —   the state of the program execution as regular or judging mode
    Action —   by drawing a line between line statements where the modes change
    Tools/Constraints —   for the PLATO Program Author's Language.

Concrete Concept

6. The student will sort resistors and capacitors.

    Situation —   Given a bin of assorted electrical components, and requested to "sort out the resistors from the capacitors,"
    Learned capability —   the student will be able to *identify*
    Object —   resistors and capacitors
    Action —   by selecting them from the bin and putting them into separate piles
    Tools/Constraints —   without references, and at a rate of 15 pieces/minute.

Discrimination

7. The student will be able to use a job performance aid to sort electrical components.

(Figure 10 Continued)

Situation —	Given a bin of assorted electrical components,
Learned capability —	the student will be able to *discriminate*
Object —	the various types of components while using a job performance aid that shows pictures of the various components (without the names given),
Action —	by selecting the components from the bin and placing them on their respective picture
Tools/Constraints —	at the rate of 15 pieces/minute.

Attitude

8. The student will enjoy statistics.

Situation —	In normal everyday non-formal settings when students are talking about courses,
Learned capability —	the student will *choose*
Object —	to express his satisfaction with statistics and report enrolling in a second course,
Action —	verbally, when conversing with other students
Tools/Constraints —	as observed in an unobtrusive situation.

Cognitive Strategy

9. The student will discover a new way to subtract numbers.

Situation —	Given the stimulus "Find a new way to subtract numbers,"
Learned capability —	the student will *originate*
Object —	a new procedure for subtracting numbers
Action —	by writing the procedure and giving examples
Tools/Constraints —	so that other students could apply it.

Information: Memorized Verbatim

10. The student will know the poem, "Old Ironsides."

Situation —	Given the request, "Recite 'Old Ironsides,' "
Learned capability —	the student will *recite*
Object —	that poem
Action —	orally
Tools/Constraints —	within five minutes, with no errors, prompting, or pauses.

Information: Substance Learning

11. The student will know the Bill of Rights.

Situation —	On a written test in the classroom,
Learned capability —	the student will summarize
Object —	four protections mentioned in the Bill of Rights
Action —	in writing
Tools/Constraints —	within 10 minutes, using no references.

Note: The readability of objectives may often be improved by departing from the order in which the components are shown above. For example, in the last objective, one could say "Summarize in writing at least four protections. . . ."

(Figure 10 Continued)

Classifying Objectives Not Written in
the Five-Component Format

Now that you have seen many objectives written in five-component form, and have seen incomplete objectives converted to complete objectives, perhaps you should try your hand at *classifying* relatively clear objectives which are not, however, written in the five-component format.

Do Exercise No. 1, and check your answers with the key at the end of the book.

Exercise No. 1: Classifying Objectives
Not Written in the Five-Component Format

Often we need to interpret (and later rewrite) incomplete objectives that we encounter. Classify each of the following types of performance according to the domain or sub-domain of behavior represented (all 11 types are included). You may wish to use abbreviations, such as "R.U." for rule using, etc.

.... 1. The student will be able to write a paragraph using a topic sentence, developmental sentences, and a transition or concluding sentence.

.... 2. The student will be able to "select the wingnuts" from a bucket of assorted nuts and bolts.

.... 3. The student will be able to sharpen a pencil.

.... 4. The student will be able to do a back dive in pike position.

.... 5. The student will listen to popular music.

.... 6. The student will be able to recall verbatim the names of the Presidents of the United States in the order in which they served.

.... 7. The student can tell where to obtain auto license tags.

.... 8. Before changing lanes, the student glances in the rear mirror to see if the lane is clear.

.... 9. The student can select articles about segregation from newspapers or magazines.

.... 10. The student can match paintings with the names of their painters.

.... 11. The student helps other students with their work.

.... 12. The student can select socks that match the color of his pants.

.... 13. The student puts different shaped blocks in similar shaped holes.

.... 14. The student uses electrolysis to convert water to oxygen and hydrogen.

.... 15. The student designs a traffic plan for Tallahassee.

.... 16. The student can use a city map when he or she is unfamiliar with the area.

.... 17. The student develops a way to keep salt water fish alive in fresh water.

.... 18. The student can detect loopholes in contracts.

.... 19. The student determines the composition of a chemical compound by collecting appropriate data.

.... 20. The student develops a new semiconductor material that produces an electric current when touched.

.... 21. The student supplies the symbol for chemical elements.

.... 22. The student gives the meaning of the Declaration of Independence.

Rewriting Incomplete Objectives

Now that you have *classified* incomplete objectives in Exercise 1, do Exercise 2, in which you *rewrite* incomplete objectives into the five-component format. Then check the answer key for this exercise. If necessary, re-read earlier portions of this Chapter.

Exercise No. 2: Rewriting Abbreviated
Objectives into the Five-Component Format

Rewrite the following objectives into the five-component format. Notice that the type of learning is indicated at the end of the sentence.

1. Shown pictures of rattlesnakes and copperheads, the student will properly label the snakes. (This labelling is to be done by noting the appearances of the snakes, not by use of definitions or a classification system.) (concrete concept)

2. The student will be able to make bibliographic entries using APA format. (rule using)

3. The student will be able to pick a paint color that matches the color on a sample of cloth. (discrimination)

4. The student will treat others as he or she wants others to treat him or her. (attitude)

5. The student will give the Spanish equivalent to a list of English words. (names, labels: information)

6. The student will deliver an impromptu speech about beanbags. (problem solving)

7. The student will use a crosscut saw properly. (motor skill)

8. The student will develop a new method of teaching reading to children. (cognitive strategy)

9. The student will determine which variables in a research study are the independent variables. (defined concept)

10. The student will tell what Chapter 4 in this book is all about. (substance learning: information)

11. The student will know given dates and the events they stand for. (facts: information)

Practical Short-Cuts in Writing Objectives for Students

So far in this Chapter, we have advocated the five-component method of writing objectives because it results in precise, unambiguous objectives. This method is worth the trouble when each member of a design team is to perform a different function in planning the instruction and the evaluation of learner performance. It is easier to coordinate team effort when objectives are written in this form. In the past, students have learned to write this form of objective with less instruction and fewer exercises than found in this Chapter. The speed of writing them comes with practice once the method is learned.

When preparing objectives to give to the learners, there are many ways to short-cut the procedure without destroying the intent of the original five-component objectives prepared for use by the design team.

When communicating the objectives to a group of learners, it is economical to take advantage of the major types of test situations applicable to the course, and to group the objectives accordingly.

For example, look at the *performance objectives* at the opening of this Chapter. They are known to the students in our classes to be "take-home, open-book" objectives, to be handed in after completing study of the relevant chapter or group of chapters. The students also know that these assignments are to be submitted *in writing*, and that they are to do their own design work (the honor code as applied to this situation allows them to confer with fellow students, but not to have somebody else do their written assignments). Thus, four of the five components of objectives are taken care of once and for all at the beginning of the course. For *performance objectives* for the course, the *situation, action verb, tools and constraints,* and *capability verb* (generate) need only be stated once by the instructor. It is only the writing of *what* (object) that needs to be described in the objectives. Notice, therefore, in the chapter performance objectives in this book, that the *what* (object) is explained in more detail than in most five-component objectives, and the language is simpler and less "technical."

For the *information* tests for each chapter in this book, the *what* (object) is supplied by the test items, and the *action verb* is supplied by the direction to *write* the answers. Since these tests are labelled "information tests," the *capability* verb is obvious. The directions for the test, given by the instructor, define the situation and the tools and constraints.

Just as we can minimize the number of words needed in the objectives as given to the students, so we can structure written tests to minimize the number of directions to be given. This is done by grouping items, both as to capability verb and form of test question.

For example, on a written test, these kinds of situations could be utilized.

1. "For the following four questions, each of which contains lists of words (defined concepts) for you to classify, match the examples in the right-hand column and labelled A, B, C, etc., with the concepts listed in the left column. Write the appropriate letter in each space in the left column." (This takes care of a number of objectives represented in the corresponding test items.)

2. "For the next four questions, generate the answer in your own words, in writing. Do not exceed the space allowed on this sheet."

3. "Show the difference between two types of shapes (discriminate) by marking an 'A' on each picture that is like this picture (*picture here*)."

While the capability verbs need not always be named in objectives and tests given to students, older students may be interested in learning the different ways in which they are responding to the course content.

Writing Test Items

In this Chapter, we deal with the need to design *appropriate* tests and test items to measure the performance of students following the completion of the instruction relevant to groups of objectives. We are concerned primarily here that the test items are in *agreement* with the objectives—that they are congruent with the objectives, and hence are *valid* measures, in the context of objective-referenced teaching and testing. (See Gagné and Briggs, 1979, Chapter 12, for an analysis of the difference between objective-referenced—often called criterion-referenced—tests and norm-referenced tests.)

In objective-referenced teaching and testing (which is what this book is about), the purpose of objectives is to guide the design of both the instruction and the testing. Any lack of congruence among objectives, teaching, and testing is a violation of the design principles discussed in this book (with due allowance for "unexpected outcomes," which are of interest in "goal free evaluation").

In preparing test items for an objective, we need to attend to each of the five components of objectives. That is, the test items must attend to the situation, the capability verb, the action verb, the object, and the tools and constraints specified in the objective.

The question of *how many* test items should be included in each test is a matter of the *reliability* of testing, which is discussed in Chapter 10.

It may be noted that each sample five-component objective presented in this Chapter describes the appropriate test situation so clearly that the objective *almost is the test*! Often by simply rearranging the words, the "test" is prepared for administration.

Process and Product Measures

In this Chapter, the word "test" has a generic meaning. That is, a test may consist of a conventional written essay or short-answer format, or the test may require actions to be observed while they are taking place (process measures like acting in a play), or the test may consist of evaluation of a finished piece of work (product measures like painting a picture). In the objectives in Figure 10, the various test situations would require learners to do many different things. Some of these performances could reasonably be evaluated by either process or product measures, as indicated:

Objective Number	Action (Performance)
1-	Write in own words a definition (product).
2-	Change a flat tire (process or product).
3-	Write an order for stock (product).
4-	Use a pressure chamber (process or product).
5-	Draw a line in a computer program (product).
6-7-	Place objects into separate groups (process or product).
8-	Talk with fellow students (process).
9-	Write a procedure (product).
10-	Recite orally (process).
11-	Write in essay form (product).

In a written test, there is no need to observe the process of writing, as the resulting answers would be evaluated after the writing of the test is finished.

In the case of painting a picture, the instructor may choose to observe the student at work to evaluate techniques, or the instructor may wish to evaluate the finished product, or both. In making a speech or acting in a play, recording by tape or videotape could be used for evaluation and feedback to the student. Recording such performances would permit playback, corresponding to the ability of the instructor to look back while evaluating a written test. This also permits study of reliability of evaluation among two or more instructors.

Unobtrusive Measures

Attitudes are best measured while observing a student or a record of his or her actions (such as records of books checked out of the library). These unobtrusive data are gathered without the student being aware that he or she is being evaluated, since such awareness could bias the choices made. Some teachers may not choose to measure any attitude objectives concerning choice behaviors they *hope* their students will make. They may prefer to *model* desirable behavior to set a good example for their students, but they may not deem it appropriate to intrude upon privacy by making unannounced evaluations. Of course, we all observe other people's choice behavior, and we may evaluate it in our own thinking even when we do not communicate the evaluation to anyone else.

Some tests attempt to measure attitudes by self-report measures, in which the student is asked what he or she does or likes to do. Written tests of this nature are more convenient than directly observing the choice behaviors in a real-life situation, but their validity may be questioned, depending on the circumstances.

The Verbs in the Objectives

While all of the five components in objectives must be considered when making the tests over the objectives, the two *verbs* are especially important, as they are more likely to be distorted in the test than is the *object* in the objective. That is, a kind of behavior different from that described by the two verbs is likely to be introduced, due to our prior habits about teaching and testing, and due to our experiences as students. Also, it is tempting to adopt a convenient and preferred form of test item that is inappropriate for the objective on which performance is to be measured. Lack of time for evaluating papers tends to lead teachers to adopt an inappropriate (invalid) form of test item in order to make the test comprehensive rather than making the other obvious choice—to *measure properly as many of the objectives* as is feasible.

Information Objectives. Suppose an objective says, in part: "the student will *list* (meaning from memory) five causes of the Revolutionary War." But to save time because the class is large, the teacher lists on the test five "correct" and five "incorrect" causes, and asks the student to put a check mark opposite each "correct" cause. This would, indeed, save scoring time for 100 test papers (and even more time if separate answer sheets and electronic scoring were to be used), but the item is *invalid* for this objective. The teacher has changed from a recall process to a recognition process, which would also *distort* the evaluation because the scores are usually higher on a recognition than on a recall test. True, this objective may not be important, relative to other objectives, and the compromised test may save time, but the teacher needs to realize with open eyes that the test is invalid for this objective, although valid for a different objective phrased to require only recognition rather than recall. This may seem to be a trivial, hair-splitting matter, but it may remind the designer of the choice between making valid tests measuring few objectives or invalid tests "measuring" many objectives.

If one prefers *some* "measurement" of each objective, even if the test is invalid because it departs from the intent of the objective, it would be wise to either decide to change the objective and announce the change to the students, or to foresee the problem and write an objective that differs from the objective that the teacher would *like* to teach and measure.

The above example of the information objective concerning the Revolutionary War could be classified as either verbatim or non-verbatim recall, depending on whether the student is to give an answer in his or her own words or the words of the text. In the case of memorizing a poem or famous speech, the performance must be verbatim.

In substance learning, where it is understood by all that the learner is to *summarize* briefly in his or her own words the major theme but not the specifics of a passage read, fewer problems are encountered concerning test validity. Still, one must be careful to observe the *object* in the objective—to not ask the student to summarize something not specified in the objective. Students properly resent such a violation, and it can undermine the trust relationship one wishes to maintain. A stated "objective" to be ready to summarize "anything in the book" is not really an objective, and it is seen by the authors to be an unreasonable demand.

Intellectual Skills. The observation of the two verbs in an objective is especially important when making tests for intellectual skills objectives. If the students are told by the objectives that they will be asked to classify correct and incorrect examples of a defined concept, it is downright unfair (and invalid) to give a test that requires them to use the concepts in rule using or problem solving (unless there are *other* objectives that so specify). It would be equally invalid to make it "easier" by asking for definitions of the concepts (an information objective). The height of invalidity occurs when the *objective*, the *instruction*, and the *test* refer to three different types of outcomes. If the instructor presents problem-solving objectives to students, but teaches only concepts, and tests for only information, we have an example that may be worse than not even giving any objectives to students. There they would *know* they are in the familiar "guessing game" situation when it is time to prepare for the test.

If a designer or teacher is to violate the objectives in the test, it seems less unjust to test for a *lower* rather than a *higher* intellectual skill. While equally invalid, it seems ethically worse to lead the students to expect to be tested for concepts but on the test to be asked to solve problems, *than vice versa.* This is because the concepts are presumably essential prerequisites for problem solving, and hence the task asks *less* rather than *more* than the students were led to expect. Of course, if no provision for learning of either concepts or problem solving are made in the instruction, we have poor teaching as well as poor testing, in the above example.

For objectives in all domains of outcome, then, a good practice is to write an objective, then its test item, then another objective and its test item, etc. This avoids later problems in testing.

With all the above matters in mind, do Exercise No. 3, and check your answers.

Exercise No. 3: Classifying Valid and Invalid
Test Items for Objectives

Directions: Classify the following situations as valid or invalid test items by placing a "V" or "I" in each space. The objectives and test items are abbreviated for this purpose.

1. Objective: "Generate a paragraph in writing."
   Test items:
   .... a.   copy this paragraph
   .... b.   summarize this page
   .... c.   which of these two paragraphs is correct?
   .... d.   write a paragraph about cats

2. Objective: "Find the area of circles."
   Test items:
   .... a.   write the formula for areas of circles
   .... b.   what is the value of "pi"?
   .... c.   what is a radius?
   .... d.   what is the area of this circle?
   .... e.   what is the radius of this circle?

3. Objective: "Classify nouns and verbs."
   Test items:
   .... a.   here are 10 words: place a "V" by each verb and a "N" by each noun
   .... b.   here are 10 words: give the meaning of each
   .... c.   define "noun" and "verb"
   .... d.   write two sentences and underline the verb and the noun in each
   .... e.   write a paragraph containing nouns and verbs
   .... f.   define "adverb"

4. Objective: "Discriminate squares and rectangles."
   Test items:
   .... a.   place an "S" in each square and an "R" in each rectangle:

   .... b.   put a check mark in each shape that is like this one:

   .... c.   what is a rectangle? how does it differ from a square?
   .... d.   draw a square and a rectangle
   .... e.   name an object that is square and one that is rectangular

5. Objective: "Identify squares and rectangles."
   Test items:
   .... which alternative in 4, above, is correct?

6. Objective: "Summarize the Bill of Rights."
   Test items:
   .... a.   where is the Bill of Rights found?

(Continued on Other Side)

.... b. list things not guaranteed in the Bill of Rights
.... c. write from memory the first paragraph in the Bill of Rights
.... d. tell what the Bill of Rights says

7. Objective: "Memorize designated parts of the Bill of Rights."
   Test items:
.... which answer in 6, above, is correct?

8. Objective: "List 5 parts of speech."
   Test items:
.... a. define 5 parts of speech
.... b. explain 5 parts of speech
.... c. write the names of 5 parts of speech
.... d. give an example for each of 5 parts of speech
.... e. discriminate 10 nouns and verbs
.... f. classify these 10 nouns and verbs
.... g. write a paragraph using 5 parts of speech

9. Objective: "Originate a novel method for adding fractions."
   Test items:
.... a. tell how to add fractions
.... b. write 5 fractions
.... c. write 2 fractions, then add them by using the least common denominator
.... d. find a new way to add fractions

10. Objective: "Execute parallel parking of a car."
    Test items:
.... a. drive this car into this parking space
.... b. steer this car into this driveway
.... c. explain the rules for parallel parking
.... d. who has the right of way when a car is parking into a parallel space?

11. Objective: "Choose to read as a leisure activity."
    Test items:
.... a. read this book by Friday
.... b. do you like to read?
.... c. have you checked out a biography from the library this week?
.... d. you have a free period; do anything you want as long as you stay in the building

12. Objective: "State the formula for finding areas of triangles."
    Test items:
.... a. what is the meaning of "area"?
.... b. find the area of this circle:
.... c. find the area of this triangle:

.... d. write a rule for finding areas of triangles
.... e. what is a triangle?

Writing Valid Test Items

Now that you have learned to write five-component objectives, and you have distinguished valid from invalid test items in Exercise 3, you should be able to generate your own valid test items. This is the purpose of Exercise No. 4.

Remember, when doing Exercise No. 4, to first describe the *environment* (situation) in which the test will be given, such as in a classroom, in a laboratory, alongside a highway, at a computer terminal, etc. This description includes what tools you will give the learner being tested. In other words, describe where you and the person(s) to be tested are, and what equipment or resources are available for use on the test.

Then write the *directions for the test* as you will give them to the learner, and indicate whether these directions are given orally or in writing.

Then write the test items, or tell what the learner is to do, if other than *write* answers to the test item(s). If it is a conventional written test, such as in algebra, tell how many "problems" (like the sample ones you saw for Exercise No. 3) are to be given in the actual test situation.

Remember that some tests require only one "item"—like "write a 500-word theme about your favorite hobby, making no errors in grammar or punctuation." Other one-item tests could include: singing a song; making a speech; painting a picture; changing a tire; writing a dissertation; performing a motor skill.

Examples of objectives requiring several items for a valid test include: discriminating shapes; identifying and discriminating objects and defined concepts; demonstrating a rule in science. Chapter 10 discusses further the matter of how many items to include on tests of various kinds.

Now, take Exercise No. 4.

**Exercise No. 4: Writing Valid Test Items, or
Preparing Tests That Are Congruent with Objectives**

For each five-component objective in Figure 10, prepare a test item.

a. If necessary, give the "directions" for the item, just as they will appear on the test.

b. If a "performance test" is required, describe the setting, the directions to the student, and how the performance will be observed and recorded.

c. If materials not referred to directly in the objective are required, specify them.

See the answer key in the back of the book, and compare the two sets of answers.

Evaluate yourself. Did you do satisfactorily on the test, or do you need to do further study?

Chapter 5
Organizing the Course

Chapter in This Book	Recommended Readings		
	Briggs, L.J. (Ed.) *Instructional Design: Principles and Applications*. Englewood Cliffs, N.J.: Educational Technology Publications, 1977.	Gagné, R.M., and Briggs, L.J. *Principles of Instructional Design*, 2nd ed. New York: Holt, Rinehart, and Winston, 1979.	Gagné, R.M. *The Conditions of Learning*, 3rd ed. New York: Holt, Rinehart, and Winston, 1977.
4	Chapter 3 Pages 158-170	Chapter 2 Chapter 3 Chapter 7	Chapter 2
⑤	**Chapter 4**	**Chapter 8**	
6	Chapters 4, 5	Chapter 6 Chapter 8	Chapter 11

Introduction

The word "course" means different things to different people. In formalized "credited" educational settings, a course generally relates to a specific content area, and to a specific period of instructional time. For instance, college and university courses are generally designated by a course title that describes the content, and a "credit hour" designation that indicates how many hours of formal instruction will occur. A three-credit-hour course generally meets for three hours of instruction per week (whether it is "quarter hours" or "semester hours" depends upon the number of weeks). In typical secondary public school settings, a student is awarded a certain number of "graduation points" depending upon the length of the courses he or she takes and the frequency of classes.

In non-formal educational settings, the relationship of time to a course becomes less clear. Although courses are generally scheduled to meet a certain number of hours, there is no credit-hour designation. There often is a certificate of proficiency or a certificate of attendance awarded at the completion of the course, and through experience the instructors know how long it will take students to reach proficiency, but the course is not designed, necessarily, to fit into a specific time slot. Therefore, we are more likely to encounter a greater variety of types of courses in the non-formal situation. A six-hour workshop on recreational sailing, for instance, might be considered a course or mini-course.

In summary, there are long courses and short courses. When a designer is working within certain types of institutions, there are pre-established expectations to be met. Very often the content of a brief course might be included elsewhere in a large course, so the designation becomes a matter of scope. Perhaps it is not necessary to arrive at an exact definition, but generally courses have two recognizable characteristics:

1. They have a recognizable start and finish point.
2. They deal with an organized set of content.

Within these parameters, there may be many configurations (not necessarily exclusive or parallel), such as self-paced courses, lecture courses, seminars, audiotutorial, television, mastery based, etc. This Chapter will use the six-level model of course design suggested by Briggs (1977).

Chapter 5 Information Test

1. *Name the two recognizable characteristics of a "course."*
    a. ....
    b. ....

2. *Name three levels of Instructional Curriculum Maps which represent designing "from the top, downward."*
    a. ....
    b. ....
    c. ....

3. *Name four characteristic differences among the successive levels of subordination represented by the different kinds of ICMs.*
    a. ....
    b. ....
    c. ....
    d. ....

4. *Why do we use life-long objectives in this model?*
    ....
    ....

5. *Name three different kinds of course structure.*
    a. ....
    b. ....
    c. ....

13. Generate some possible course objectives for a specific content area.

14. Generate a subdivision of the course objectives into a feasible unit structure.

15. Generate a course-level "Curriculum Map" that shows the relationship among units.

The end product of these three objectives is a course-level "Instructional Curriculum Map" (ICM). In this Chapter and in Chapters 6 and 7, you will encounter three "levels" of such maps:

(1) the course ICM,
(2) the unit ICM, and
(3) the lesson ICM.

An example of the course-level map is presented later in this Chapter (in Figure 12). In the following Chapters (6 and 7), you will encounter the other two maps; these three maps are drawn up, in the order named, in the model of instructional design presented in this book.

Background

The six-level model of course design described by Briggs (1977) represents designing "from the top, downward"—that is, from general to specific. The levels of design in Briggs' procedure consider the following stages:

(1) needs analysis,
(2) goals definition,
(3) lifelong objectives,
(4) end-of-course objectives,
(5) unit objectives, and
(6) specific behavioral objectives and their supporting prerequisite objectives.

It is essential to realize that the *scope* of objectives is broad for the course, narrower for a unit, and still narrower for a lesson. Sometimes a lesson, in turn, will contain several subordinate, enabling objectives. These levels of subordination are comparable to making an outline which reveals levels of subordination in content instead of skills. Differentiating among the levels is a matter of organizing different degrees of scope and complexity.

Although the amount of instructional time is typically associated with the definition of "course," we are going to ignore that for now and concentrate on defining a course as "that organization of instructional activities, resources, and evaluation activities which leads to a prespecified directional change in the learners' behavior." This includes consideration of the types of outcomes in a taxonomy (Chapter 4) that constitute a course.

From the first level of course design, needs analysis, we obtain a statement of discrepancy between what *is* and what is desired. This has been elaborated in Chapter 2. The next level, goals definition, relates to a general statement of desired outcomes at different levels of responsibility, i.e., national goals, state goals, local goals, school goals, and course goals. At the national level, a goal might be "To produce better informed citizens." This is a very broad goal, and it becomes meaningful only in terms of the smaller component behaviors of "informed citizenry."

Goals are generally global in nature, and so they must be operationalized by defining more specific behaviors before the design of instruction to attain them can begin.

Lifelong objectives relate to goals, and they tend to put goals and the more specific behaviors that we will call "course objectives" into context. For example, a national goal might be to produce a more informed citizenry, a state goal might be to improve teaching effectiveness, a "lifelong goal" of an instructional program might be "to apply established psychological principles to the practice of teaching." A related course goal might be to "enable teachers to use diagnostic tests to ascertain the entry level of students in an instructional program."

In an entire curriculum or program of studies, the lifelong objective also serves to relate courses in a sequence to each other. In other circumstances, courses stand alone as having a "practical value or terminal value in themselves." That is, after taking an auto mechanics course a student may be able to fix his or her own car if it breaks down. However, many courses do not have an immediate practical value. That is not to say that they are unimportant or irrelevant, but that their value lies in their relationship to future courses or other experiences. For instance, persons taking a Basic Spanish course would not be very conversant in Spanish at the end of the course, but they would have the entry skills for the next course in Spanish, where they might become conversant. In this sense, lifelong objectives give perspective. It would not be appropriate to state, as a course objective in Basic Spanish, that the students will become conversant in Spanish, but that is one of the "lifelong objectives," given subsequent completion of the next course. The course objectives themselves would be more specific, relating to the exit skills of the first course that are the entry skills for the subsequent course that the students would be taking.

In some cases, the lifelong objectives and the course objectives might be the same. That is, the course is sufficient to impart the skills desired without follow-up courses. This might be true in the case of the previously mentioned course on recreational sailing, in which the purpose is to teach enough techniques so that the student could enjoy himself or herself safely on the weekend. However, there are very few courses in education that exist in isolation of other courses and broader goals, and consideration of these relationships might be cause for reevaluation of the course curriculum and/or scope. In military and industrial training, however, a course might prepare the learner to perform at an entry level of skill in a specific job. In short, lifelong objectives show the ultimate value either of a course alone, or of a course followed by other courses or practical experiences.

Course Level Objectives

Most designers center their activity around the course and subordinate-level objectives. The design model in this handbook is oriented toward changing the learner in some measurable way, and generally this change is made within the context of a course. The designer's problem becomes one of how to state the outcomes of a course in a meaningful way, and how to identify the subordinate unit and lesson competencies needed to achieve the course objectives.

Other design models (Kaufman and English, 1979; Tyler, 1949) focus on curriculum design for a whole series of related courses. Thus, one could think of "curriculum design" as the setting of an overall curriculum scope and sequence, and then of design of a single course within the curriculum.

In this Chapter, we focus on design of the single course, which in the public school setting could consist of one semester or one year of instruction in a single subject or in combined subjects.

How to Do It

In refining the course objective so that it reflects some learner change, the designer can ask the questions, "What will learners be able to do after taking this course that they could not do before?" "How will the learners be different after taking this course?" These questions, when related to the needs analysis, assume that consideration will be given to the entry skills and attitudes of the student. By asking these questions, the designer is committing himself or herself to the assertion that one could measure the difference in relevant performance between a person who has had the course and a person who has not. This means that the outcome behaviors will have to be specific, observable, and measurable.

In the case of the College Teaching course that we have been using as an example in earlier chapters, the course objective was written as follows: "Students (trainees) will be able to plan instruction, to demonstrate the presentation of instruction, and to apply criterion-referenced models of evaluation of student learning." The broader course goals might be stated as: "The graduate will be able to plan, design, and deliver criterion-referenced instruction based upon psychological principles of learning and teaching."

The difference between the course goal and the course objective might be viewed as the degree of measurability. The course objective, through the use of simulation techniques such as micro-teaching, is more focused and measurable than is the goal statement.

Unit Objectives

The next step in course organization is to break down the course objective into manageable units. One way of doing this is to break down the course objective into manageable content units, and then to express these units in the form of performance objectives. These terminal unit objectives are established, again, by asking the question, "What will the student be able to do after finishing this unit?" The question might be expanded to capture possible attitude objectives by asking, "What will this student choose to do after instruction?"

Relationships among units. Unit objectives may or may not be needed, depending on the course structure. If the course has a "flat" structure, course objectives are simply the sum of lesson objectives and could be diagrammed as follows:

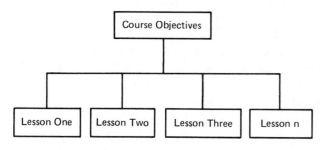

Even in a lengthy course requiring unit objectives, the units might be relatively independent of each other. In this case, the unit objectives would be diagrammed the same way.

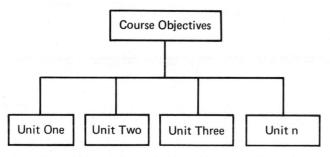

The "flat" unit structure shown above would not be appropriate in a course which required a particular fixed sequence of objectives, either because there is transfer from one objective to another in a direct linear fashion, or because the series of objectives represents steps in a procedure to be performed in a fixed sequence. To show transfer among objectives or to show procedural sequence, a vertical course structure might be employed and diagrammed as follows:

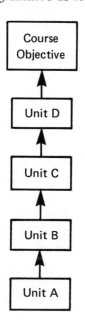

The sequencing of instruction is from A to D because that is the direction of the assumed transfer of learning, or it is the order in which a procedure must be performed.

There is also the possibility of a combination of the flat and vertical structures, as would be the case for the hypothetical course diagrammed below.

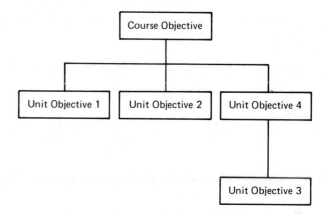

In the above example, unit objective 3 transfers to the learning of unit objective 4, and hence 3 needs to be taught before 4. However, units 1, 2, or 4 may be taught in any order. Units 3 and 4 are said to be "hierarchical" in nature because of the transfer needed. Less is known from the experimental research literature on such hierarchical relationships among units than is known for hierarchical relationships of objectives at a more specific level. These latter relationships will be dealt with later. Some of the pertinent research has been reviewed by Briggs (1968b), and examples of hierarchies are found in all three texts cited at the opening of this Chapter.

For a hierarchically structured course, one could present the structure for the entire course in one Instructional Curriculum Map (ICM). However, in practice such diagrams would be very complex and difficult to produce. Thus by producing a number of ICMs at different levels of course organization (course, unit, and lesson), the task becomes much more manageable.

Examples of Course Structure

Following up with the two courses which were used as examples of needs assessment and selecting delivery systems (Chapters 2 and 3), we now show the course structure and units of instruction for these two courses.

Example No. 1: The College Teaching Course

The relationships among the unit objectives for the College Teaching Course are diagrammed in Figure 11. You may notice that while the units are relatively independent in a cognitive sense, they are more dependent in an attitudinal sense. As shown in Figure 11, the attitude objective specified for the student evaluation unit, the teaching skills unit, and the classroom management unit all relate to the attitude objective specified for the media and methods unit.

Unit One. Student Evaluation (Criterion-Referenced Measurement, CRM).

Intellectual Skills. The student will be able to (SWBAT) generate an evaluation program based on the criterion-referenced measurement model.

Attitudes. The student will choose to evaluate his or her students' classroom performance using the CRM model where appropriate.

Unit Two. Media and Methods.

Intellectual Skills. The SWBAT generate hypotheses about task, learner, and media interactions with regard to the selection of effective and efficient delivery systems.

Attitudes. The student will choose to use effective modes of instruction for the accomplishment of stated instructional objectives; i.e., an effective environment.

Unit Three. Teaching Skills.

Intellectual Skills. The SWBAT generate and deliver an organized lecture type presentation and a discussion session according to prestated standards. The SWBAT generate inquiry type questions spontaneously during a discussion type presentation.

Attitudes. The student will choose to solicit and use student and peer feedback for the purpose of improving "teaching skills."

Unit Four. Classroom Management.

Intellectual Skills. Given a course definition, and hypothetical student population, the SWBAT generate and support hypotheses about the effectivenesss of various classroom management systems.

Attitudes. Given a course to teach, and a defined student audience, the prospective teacher chooses to select a classroom management system based on theoretical considerations as to its probable effectiveness, appropriateness for the learner, and the task within the environment.

Figure 11. Terminal unit objectives for the College Teaching Course.

The process of diagramming the relationships among objectives is called "instructional curriculum mapping," and the resulting diagrams are instructional curriculum maps (ICMs). ICMs may be constructed for different levels of curriculum complexity. The map in Figure 12 would be considered a "course-level map" as it shows the relationships of objectives at the course level. The following two chapters in this handbook will address the construction of unit-level maps and lesson-level maps. These three levels of maps are like drawing separate maps for a Nation, a State, and a City. The first map in each case gives the overall picture, and the other two show increasing detail.

Example No. 2: The Instructional Design Course

The final example of a course objective and unit objectives is the Instructional Design Course, originally designed by the senior author. The course goal was to produce designers who could apply psychological principles and empirically derived procedures to the design of instructional materials. The course goal might be stated as: "The student will be able to generate prototype instructional materials by applying the model of instructional design taught in this course."

Obviously, this is a rather complex course (in terms of the number of subordinate competencies), so the course was divided into four manageable units. These units are shown in Figure 13. Notice, in Figure 13, that the four unit objectives are shown in a hierarchical (vertical) course structure. This is not because the type of unit outcomes differ in nature, since all four are problem-solving objectives, as shown by the standard verb, *generate*. The unit sequence is as shown because the assignment for each unit builds upon work done in the previous unit. While the separate skills comprising each unit could be taught in a different unit sequence, this would be inadvisable, because it would not follow the design sequence called for by the model and because it would require students to prepare lesson materials before the lesson objective was justified by analyzing the course "from the top, downward," as recommended by the model.

It may be noted that the course outlined in Figure 13 is an earlier version of the skill kind of course for which this book has been written. The choice of assignments for the four units represents a somewhat different approach from that outlined in this book; but the course goal is the same. The

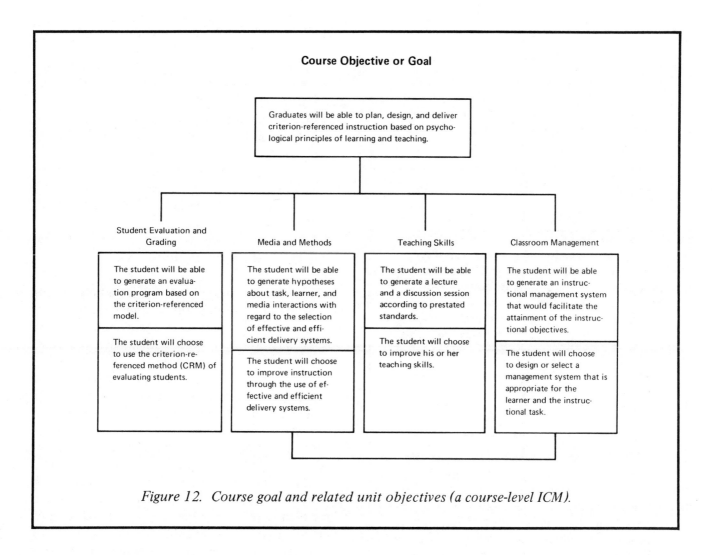

Course Objective or Goal

Graduates will be able to plan, design, and deliver criterion-referenced instruction based on psychological principles of learning and teaching.

Student Evaluation and Grading

The student will be able to generate an evaluation program based on the criterion-referenced model.

The student will choose to use the criterion-referenced method (CRM) of evaluating students.

Media and Methods

The student will be able to generate hypotheses about task, learner, and media interactions with regard to the selection of effective and efficient delivery systems.

The student will choose to improve instruction through the use of effective and efficient delivery systems.

Teaching Skills

The student will be able to generate a lecture and a discussion session according to prestated standards.

The student will choose to improve his or her teaching skills.

Classroom Management

The student will be able to generate an instructional management system that would facilitate the attainment of the instructional objectives.

The student will choose to design or select a management system that is appropriate for the learner and the instructional task.

Figure 12. Course goal and related unit objectives (a course-level ICM).

major differences lie in how instructional maps are approached, and the absence of "time-line charts" discussed in a later chapter.

Summary of Course Structure

In summary, after determining the course objective and the unit objectives, the designer creates an instructional curriculum map in order to diagram the relationship among these objectives. This map will show a flat structure if the course objective is simply the cumulation of the unit-level objectives or of the lesson-level objectives. It will show a vertical structure if the attainment of the course objective is dependent upon the successive attainment of the unit objectives, in a fixed sequence; some course maps may show a combination of the flat and vertical structures. After constructing the "course-level" ICM, the designer would construct a "unit-level" ICM, and then "lesson-level" ICMs.

It may be noted that the chapter objectives stated at the opening of each chapter in this book are a restatement of unit and lesson objectives for the instructional design course (Briggs, 1977, pp. 464-468) shown in Figure 13.

Exercise in Classifying Objectives

Before you undertake to generate a course-level curriculum map, for the course you will design in order to develop and demonstrate design skills, you might check your skills by doing Exercise No. 5.

Remember that you organize a course "from the top, downward." This is done so that you work from superordinate to subordinate levels of objectives, e.g., from lifelong to course to unit objectives. The ultimate reason for doing this is to be able to justify each lesson as supporting a unit objective, and to justify each unit as supporting the

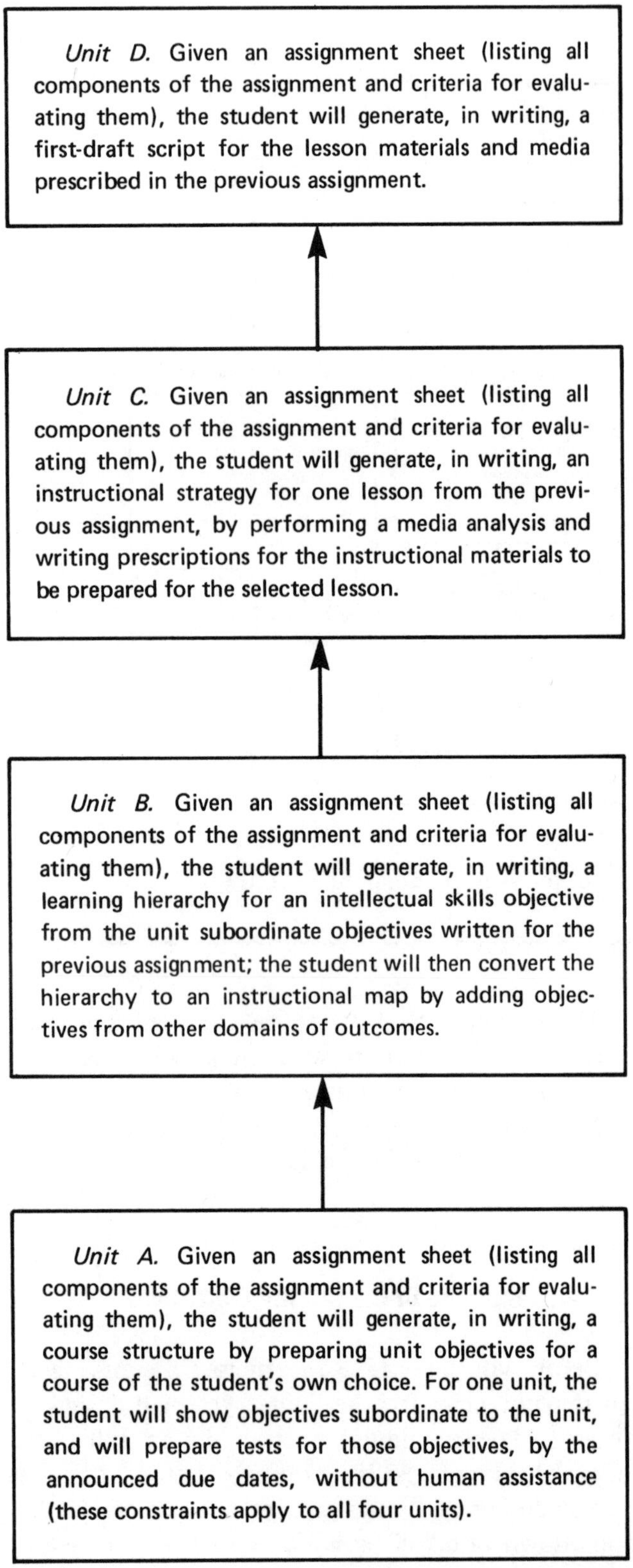

Unit D. Given an assignment sheet (listing all components of the assignment and criteria for evaluating them), the student will generate, in writing, a first-draft script for the lesson materials and media prescribed in the previous assignment.

↑

Unit C. Given an assignment sheet (listing all components of the assignment and criteria for evaluating them), the student will generate, in writing, an instructional strategy for one lesson from the previous assignment, by performing a media analysis and writing prescriptions for the instructional materials to be prepared for the selected lesson.

↑

Unit B. Given an assignment sheet (listing all components of the assignment and criteria for evaluating them), the student will generate, in writing, a learning hierarchy for an intellectual skills objective from the unit subordinate objectives written for the previous assignment; the student will then convert the hierarchy to an instructional map by adding objectives from other domains of outcomes.

↑

Unit A. Given an assignment sheet (listing all components of the assignment and criteria for evaluating them), the student will generate, in writing, a course structure by preparing unit objectives for a course of the student's own choice. For one unit, the student will show objectives subordinate to the unit, and will prepare tests for those objectives, by the announced due dates, without human assistance (these constraints apply to all four units).

Figure 13. Units (assignments) in the course, Design of Instruction (course-level ICM).

course objective, etc. This procedure keeps "dead wood" from creeping into the instruction.

The different levels of subordination and the three levels of ICMs dealt with in Chapters 5, 6, and 7 have these features:

(1) going from broad to narrow objectives;
(2) going from problem solving down to supporting skills such as rule using;
(3) going from lifelong outcomes to lesson outcomes; and
(4) going from lengthy curricula to short lessons.

Alternative Course Designs

Designers are often prone to have an entire unit of information learning, followed by concept units, and ending with a problem-solving unit. Usually this is a mistake at the course level of ICM, although it may be reasonable for a unit or lesson ICM. Usually it would be better to have each unit contain both information and intellectual skills objectives. This tends to avoid boredom and information overload. So a general rule of thumb is to present some information on a topic, then develop the skills, attitudes, or cognitive strategies related to that block of information. Then move on to another unit, repeat the cycle of information, then skill development. An example of this type of sequencing would be the training of maintenance technicians for a complex radar-computer system. One could first learn information about the low-voltage power supply, followed by learning the parts (concrete concepts), then learning fixed, routine check procedures, then how to troubleshoot the power supply. Similar sequences could follow for major functions (e.g., transmitting) or for each major part of the equipment (the synchronizer). Thus, the learner gets quickly to the highest skill level (troubleshooting, or problem solving) for a small unit, then builds up to this for other units. This provides motivation and avoids trying to learn too much information (which is hard to recall) at once.

Also, one may "spiral" the instruction so as to teach some parts of units A, B, and C, and then return to more instruction on A, B, and C in a second cycle. An example would be the learning of a foreign language. In each lesson, the learner acquires some vocabulary, some sentence structure, and some practice in listening, speaking, reading, and writing.

Exercise No. 5: Classifying Objectives
as Lifelong, Course, or Unit Objectives

Label the following objectives as either
(a) lifelong objectives
(b) course objectives
(c) unit objectives

I. **Course Title: Aerobics**
..... 1. The student will be able to execute ten sit-ups in a period of one minute.
..... 2. The student will choose to participate in a schedule of exercise that will keep him or her fit.
..... 3. The student will be healthier as a result of proper exercise, weight control, and diet.
..... 4. The student will be able to generate a program of exercise that corresponds to his or her body weight and caloric intake.
..... 5. The student will demonstrate the calculation of the number of exercises necessary to burn up 3,000 calories.

II. **Course Title: Television Production**
..... 1. The student will generate a script for a television program.
..... 2. The student will write and produce a 20-minute television program designed to meet certain instructional objectives.
..... 3. The student will demonstrate the operation of a television camera.
..... 4. The student will direct the production of an instructional program.

Chapter 6
Organizing the Unit

Chapter in This Book	Recommended Readings		
	Briggs, L.J. (Ed.) *Instructional Design: Principles and Applications.* Englewood Cliffs, N.J.: Educational Technology Publications, 1977.	Gagné, R.M., and Briggs, L.J. *Principles of Instructional Design,* 2nd ed. New York: Holt, Rinehart, and Winston, 1979.	Gagné, R.M. *The Conditions of Learning,* 3rd ed. New York: Holt, Rinehart, and Winston, 1977.
5	Chapter 4	Chapter 8	
⑥	**Chapters 4, 5**	**Chapter 6** **Chapter 8**	**Chapter 11**
7	Chapter 5 Chapter 7 Pages 179-193	Chapter 6 Chapter 8	Chapter 11

Introduction

Earlier chapters discussed the gross structure of curricula and of courses, and the implications of structure for sequencing among the units of instruction in a course. In this Chapter, attention is focused on the detailed structure of units in terms of their component individual behavioral objectives encountered in single lessons. Previous chapters have also discussed a "taxonomy of learning outcomes"—a system for categorizing performance objectives and their enabling objectives into domains of learning and learning outcomes, and a "learning hierarchy"—a relationship between an objective and its prerequisites in the intellectual skills domain.

The sub-domains of learning in the intellectual skills domain and the idea of learning hierarchies both have important implications for sequencing of instruction. If there is a hierarchical relationship among either (a) the major units of a course, (b) the specific objectives that make up a unit, or (c) the subordinate competencies of an objective, this suggests, at least in part, the appropriate sequencing of instruction. In this hierarchical form of structure, sequencing implies that transfer of training occurs from the bottom to the top of the hierarchy in an upward direction; i.e., the learning units placed early in the course facilitate the learning of later units. This does not necessarily mean that learning (at least for some students) couldn't take place if the sequencing were different; it merely suggests that learning, on the average, will occur more rapidly and more easily if a hierarchical task is sequenced according to the inferred direction of transfer. This general hypothesis is discussed in more detail in your reference texts.

In Chapter 5 you encountered instructional curriculum maps (ICMs) for showing course structure, e.g., the relationship among units of the course.

In this Chapter, we will investigate the process of instructional curriculum mapping as it relates to the structure of a unit of instruction. This is basically the process of instructional curriculum mapping applied at a more specific level than was shown in the course-level curriculum maps in Chapter 5. Then, in Chapter 7, we go on to see greater detail in the construction of curriculum maps for individual lessons. The purpose of these three levels of curriculum mapping is to justify lessons as needed to reach unit objectives, and to justify units as needed to reach course objectives.

Chapter 6 Information Test

_1._ _A learning hierarchy is relevant to only one of the five major domains of learning outcomes; which domain is it?_ ....
....

_2._ _How many sub-domains may be represented in learning hierarchies?_ ....

_3._ _Three levels of curriculum maps are used in course design. Name them._
  _a._ ....
  _b._ ....
  _c._ ....

_4._ _How does an ICM differ from a learning hierarchy?_ ....
....
....
....

_5._ _Name at least four aids in drawing an ICM._
  _a._ ....
  _b._ ....
  _c._ ....
  _d._ ....

_6._ _When does one stop when drawing a hierarchy or an ICM?_ ....
....

_7._ _Why do we recommend designing from the top, downward?_ ....
....

_8._ _Should an attitude or an intellectual skill in an ICM be taught first?_ ....
....

_9._ _When several objectives are on the same level in an ICM, how is the planned sequence among them shown?_ ....
....

_10._ _Why are some intellectual skills and information omitted from ICMs?_ ....
....
....

```
┌─────────────────────────────────────────────┐
│   Chapter 6 Performance Objectives           │
│                                              │
│     16. Specify the specific performance     │
│   objectives that relate to and comprise a   │
│   unit objective.                            │
│     17. Produce an ICM that diagrams the     │
│   relationships among the objectives that    │
│   comprise a unit. Check your ICM to fill    │
│   any gaps or to eliminate "deadwood"        │
│   objectives from the unit structure.        │
└─────────────────────────────────────────────┘
```

The end product of these objectives is a unit-level ICM which shows all necessary objectives in all domains of learning. Intellectual skills objectives in this map may not go below the level of problem solving or rule using. However, in a complete *lesson-level* ICM (see the next chapter), each such intellectual skills objective would be further analyzed into its component parts, down to the level of assumed entry skills.

Background

Please refer back to Figure 12 in Chapter 5. Note again the course objective at the top of the Figure; then note the unit objectives for the unit called "Student Evaluation and Grading." You will note further that there are "twin" objectives for each unit—an intellectual skills objective paired with an attitude objective. You can easily imagine, for the intellectual skills objective, ". . . generate an evaluation program based on the criterion-referenced model," that much information and many subordinate skills would have to be learned before a student could demonstrate mastery of this objective. How would one decide just what the needed information and subordinate skills are? What, specifically, would have to be taught before the learners could demonstrate that they can perform this unit objective? Such questions are by no means easy to answer, but doing so represents one of the crucial parts of successful course design.

In this Chapter, we will present the unit-level ICM as a *vehicle for displaying* all the objectives (in all domains of learning outcomes) that need to be learned in order to achieve the unit objective. But the unit-level ICM *is only the result* of the analysis of the unit objective. How is this result arrived at?

How does one determine the specific objectives which must be learned in each lesson making up the total instruction for the unit objective?

Essentially, there are seven possible aids in determining which specific objectives need to be learned in order to reach the capability of performing the unit objective. These same seven aids also can be applied to the next stage of design—identifying what must be taught in each lesson (Chapter 7). Thus, these seven aids are appropriate for arriving at both the unit-level ICM and the lesson-level ICM. These seven aids are:

1. Hierarchical analysis—drawing a learning hierarchy to show the direction of transfer from simpler intellectual skills to more complex ones (see Gagné, 1977a; 1977b).

2. Information-processing analysis—showing the sequence of the mental operations (decisions, actions, and stimulus inputs) needed to perform a task (see Gagné, 1977a; 1977b).

3. Procedural analysis—showing the separate manual or mental operations to be performed in a linear, step-like manner for a task (see Gagné, 1977b).

4. Teaching experience—recalling and listing in order the separate components taught in prior successful teaching experience for the unit objective (or lesson objectives).

5. Consideration of domain interactions—how the objectives in different outcome domains may be expected to support each other.

6. Recording of one's own performance—simply recalling and listing how you perform the objective.

7. Experimental (empirical data)—from research comparing different teaching sequences of the various parts of the total learning.

Some of the above aids are more closely related to how a task is *learned*, while others have to do with how it is *performed* after it has been learned. Both kinds of information may be useful, since the purpose is to *identify* the separate elements to be *taught*, and to sequence the elements in an effective teaching plan.

Throughout this Chapter and the following chapter some of the above seven aids for arriving at ICMs are discussed. For more detail, see the chapters in the recommended readings at the opening of these chapters.

In Chapter 5 it was shown that the units of a course may represent either a flat (non-hierarchical) structure, a vertical (hierarchical) structure, or a combination of the two. In a similar fashion, these same structures may be found for objectives making up a *unit*, and for objectives and their sub-objectives making up a single lesson within the unit.

Learning Hierarchies for Intellectual Skills

One useful aid in arriving at the components for an intellectual skills objective is the learning hierarchy. A hierarchy for such an intellectual skill can thus help in deriving any of the three levels of curriculum maps, but it is most likely to help with unit and lesson maps. Remember, however, that it applies only to intellectual skills objectives, not to objectives in other domains.

Identifying the competencies. The process of identifying subordinate competencies for a unit or lesson objective parallels the process of identifying objectives for a unit of instruction in a course. Looking at a particular behavioral objective one asks, "What would the learner have to be able to do or to know before he or she could perform this entire objective, given only instructions as to what he or she is to do on a test over this objective?" Immediately it is possible to identify two or three rather general skill or knowledge components that comprise the abilities needed to perform the specified objective. These are then examined, asking the same question, and each is reduced from complex to increasingly simple skills and knowledges.

For a hierarchical objective in which analysis moves downward toward more and more simple components, generally the types of learning involved also run down to more simple types of learning; e.g., moving from problem solving, down toward rules, concept learning, and discriminations, the lowest type of intellectual skill, depending upon the objective. For illustrations of this ordering of "layers" of learning in the hierarchy, see Gagné (1977a).

When has an objective been analyzed in sufficient detail? According to the present model, this occurs when the description in each box in the diagram represents a single type of learning, as defined by Gagné, and when entry skills are thus encountered.

Stated another way, it is possible to determine that analysis of an objective is complete and correct if the behavior identified in the next higher box can be performed as a single act, when all preceding learning implied in the diagram has been accomplished. The chart demonstrates one way of checking the completeness of the analysis of an objective. If the teaching or presentation is done well, but the student fails at any point, this indicates either that a step is missing from the hierarchy, or, that the student has not mastered the earlier steps. Of course, it is possible that the teaching was poorly conducted.

Gagné's experiments (1977b) have shown that, even in moderately effective teaching programs, most failures to learn an objective in a hierarchically structured task are due to failure to master some subordinate competency. Identifying reasons why a teaching program failed is a complex matter; but given the fact that it is relatively difficult to change student aptitudes, it is deemed practical to check the student's entering competencies before he or she begins work on a new objective. This is one way to identify deficits in learning and acquiring skill or knowledge components required to master the objective of a given unit or course.

Some hierarchies contain layers of rule-using skills at different levels of complexity (Gagné and Briggs, 1979, p. 109). Other hierarchies contain several sub-types of intellectual skills, as illustrated in the following diagrams. (A learning hierarchy could be called an ICM composed of intellectual skills.)

Complete and empirically tested hierarchies for intellectual skills objectives appear to illustrate the following set of rules:

1. Problem-solving (P.S.) skills require the use of two or more rules (R).
2. Rule-using skills require the use of two or more concepts (C).
3. Concept behaviors require two or more discriminations (DS).

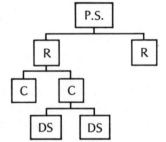

A hierarchy containing only one type of learning, e.g., rules, differing in generality, would

1. Have the most complex rule at the apex.
2. Have other rules related directly as prerequisites.
3. *Or* indirectly as subordinate rules to the prerequisites.

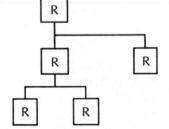

Different rules may have the same concepts as prerequisites (or share many of the same concept components); likewise, some concepts may share common discriminations. This factor makes it very tedious and probably unnecessary to diagram complete hierarchies for every intellectual skills objective in a unit, because many skills low in the hierarchy may have been learned previously. Also, it is probably safe to say that most instructional curricula contain objectives from more than one domain of learning. For instance, it is very likely that a course objective such as "The student will be able to apply rules relating to consumer economics to effectively conserve depletable resources" would be accompanied by an attitudinal objective such as "The student will *choose* to conserve depletable resources." In this case, the course will consist of both intellectual skills and at least one attitudinal objective. Thus, an ICM for a unit of instruction can contain intellectual skills objectives and their principal prerequisites as well as objectives from other domains of outcomes.

Curriculum Maps

When one takes the trouble to construct both learning hierarchies and ICMs, the probability is increased that the goals of a curriculum will be accomplished because all the component behaviors can be identified and the relationships among the component behaviors understood. Constructing an ICM would lead one to ask: "How does the intellectual skills objective (in the example above) relate to the attainment of the attitudinal behavior (or vice versa)? What subordinate behaviors are going to lead to the attainment of each?"

The instructional curriculum map is derived from an analysis of the functions that component objectives serve in the learning process. Diagramming these relationships provides a visual, analytic tool for instructional sequencing, and makes evident the need for instructional strategy decisions based upon the functions being served by the performance objectives. How learning in each domain may support learning in other domains is summarized in Figure 15.

An Example of a Unit-Level ICM

An understanding of how the ICM process works is illustrated by analyzing an attitudinal objective from the College Teaching Course (see Figure 12, Chapter 5). Taken from Unit one, "Student Evaluation and Grading," the objective states:

"The student will choose to use the criterion-referenced method (CRM) of evaluating students."

The above objective can be observed; i.e., one could follow a student into the classroom after graduation and determine whether or not he or she was indeed using CRM.

The question is, what other behaviors are necessary (or will have to be developed or changed) for a student to leave the course with a positive attitude toward CRM? There are probably a number of things. First, one would expect that the student would require some facility in applying CRM techniques (basically intellectual skills objectives). Second, the student would need some information as to the value of CRM (or would have to come to value its application). It is possible that the teacher could create in the student a positive attitude towards CRM before teaching him or her to apply the model. Some of the recognized techniques of attitudes change include the use of verbal reports (Hovland, Janis, and Kelley, 1953), hence verbal information objectives may facilitate the achievement of the intellectual and affective objectives. In addition, it is probably true that if we can develop in students a positive disposition toward CRM, they will take less time to master the intellectual skills necessary to apply the model.

Figure 14 represents an ICM for the unit on "Student Evaluation and Grading" in the course on college teaching.

The attitudinal objective previously mentioned is represented in the upper right-hand corner of the ICM and is identified by the verb "choose." Instructional Curriculum Mapping makes use of the 11 standard capability verbs for the five domains and their subdivisions (Figure 5, Chapter 4). The use of these "standard verbs" makes the ICM more easily understood, since each type of learning can be easily identified. The objectives in the ICM shown in Figure 14 employ these verbs.

One can see from Figure 14 that the attitudinal objective has connected below it two verbal information objectives. The assumption is that if students are asked to perform these two behaviors, they will be more likely to have a positive disposition toward CRM than if they were not.

The value of the ICM to the course developer in this case derives from the realization that achievement of the attitudinal objective is to be effected through the achievement of some verbal informa-

Student Evaluation and Grading

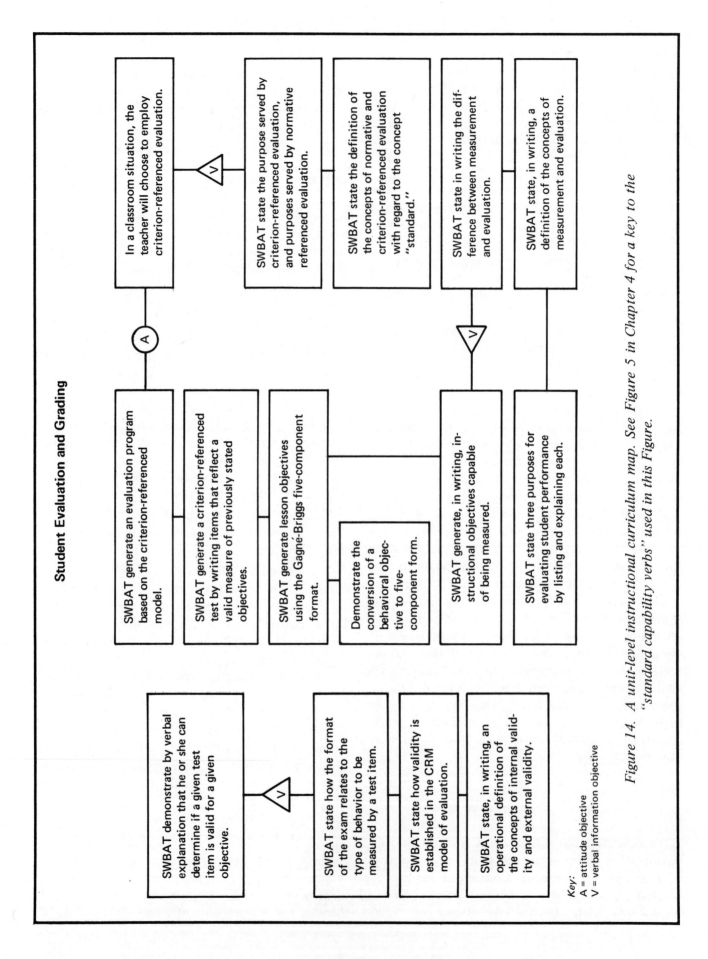

Figure 14. *A unit-level instructional curriculum map. See Figure 5 in Chapter 4 for a key to the "standard capability verbs" used in this Figure.*

Key:
A = attitude objective
V = verbal information objective

tion objectives requiring different learning strategies than, say, concept learning tasks.

Within the intellectual skills domain, the objectives take on the true hierarchical relationship. The lower level skills, such as concept learning, lead into rule-using skills, which lead into problem-solving skills. The ICM is not, however, a pure intellectual skills hierarchy. Rather, the ICM is a graphic representation of the performance objectives of each domain and their *relationships* both *hierarchical* and *functional* to each other for a defined instructional "unit" or "lesson." That is, both essential prerequisites and "supporting" prerequisites are listed (Gagné, 1977a).

Implications of Interdomain Relationships

Much instructional methodology recognizes interdomain relationships. For instance, the driver education student learns "the steps" in pulling away from a curb. Whereas the experienced driver probably does not think of the independent steps, the learner can facilitate behavior acquisition by "talking it through." In this case, verbal information serves as an "input" for the desired learning outcome, a motor skill. The function served by the verbal information is one of providing a cognitive routine for sequencing the motor performances to be learned. If we observe how other domains of educational outcomes facilitate motor skills learning, we can see that attitudes probably play a role, in that they affect the perseverance of a student with regard to the work requisite to becoming proficient.

Interaction also exists between types of learning from other domains. These interrelationships are diagrammed in a matrix form in Figure 15, showing the inputs or enabling objectives along one dimension and the outputs or behaviors to be learned along the other. In order to see what function "attitude behaviors" might play in learning "intellectual skills," find attitudes on the "input" side of the matrix (top) and intellectual skills on the output (left side), and follow the column and row to where they intersect. That is, the function served by developing positive attitudes would seem to be motivational in that changing an attitude held by a majority of the target audience would lead to better acceptance of subsequent intellectual skills instruction. The relationship between the attitude and the intellectual skills

(course-level) objective might be diagrammed as shown in Illustration 1.

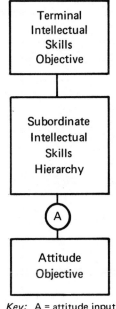

Key: A = attitude input.

Illustration 1

This diagram implies that attitude change precedes attainment of the intellectual skills, and therefore the instruction should include methods and content aimed at attitude change in the orientation stage of the course, i.e., before "skills" instruction.

Diagrammed differently, as in Illustration 2, the attainment of intellectual skills is seen to be the input or competency preceding attitude change. In this case, according to the matrix, the learner attains a more positive attitude due to the development of a skill with reinforcing potential.

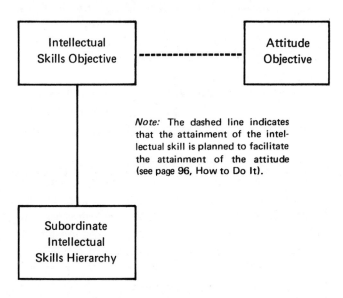

Note: The dashed line indicates that the attainment of the intellectual skill is planned to facilitate the attainment of the attitude (see page 96, How to Do It).

Illustration 2

93

In Illustration 3, a new dimension is added to the curriculum.

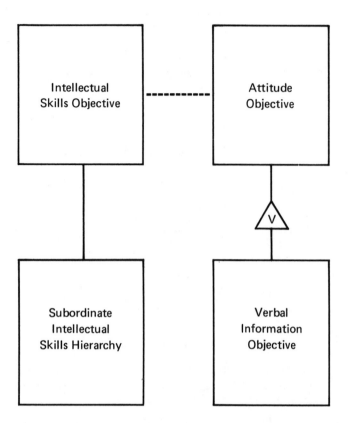

Key: V = verbal information input.

Illustration 3

The designer has added another competency to be attained by the learner, i.e., the verbal ability to state something. With regard to changing an attitude, the learner may be stating the value of something, the rationale for something, etc. The attainment of the attitude is to be facilitated by two factors, the verbal information behavior and the intellectual skills behavior. The most efficient instructional decision would be to elicit the verbal information behavior first, since a more positive attitude should facilitate attainment of the intellectual skills, and it takes far less time for the learner to attain the verbal information objective.

Probably one of the most common interdomain relationships encountered by the instructional designer is that between verbal information and intellectual skills. It is improbable that a designer is interested in the complete hierarchy of intellectual skills necessary to attain even a modest problem-solving competency. One reason might be that there are many ways to solve most problems (or classes of

problems), and instructionally we generally focus on only one or a few approaches at a time. Therefore, the course curriculum is but one example of what "might be possible." Secondly, many problem-solving competencies involve the use of previously learned problem-solving skills, concepts, etc. In this case, it is not necessary to diagram the entire hierarchy of intellectual skills, but rather to recognize how they are being recalled and related through the use of verbal information. As an example, if the problem-solving skill is to "generate hypotheses with regard to the efficiency of two different instructional methodologies," the learner must know the relationship between concepts, efficiency, effectiveness, and cost. He or she can learn this relationship as verbal information, and we would expect that would be enough to allow him or her to solve the problem (if he or she has previously learned the rules and concepts expressed by simple functional relationships). The ICM for relating the intellectual skills and verbal information objectives would look like Illustration 4.

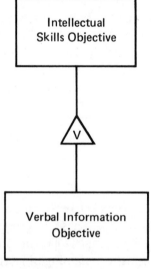

Key: V = verbal information input.

Illustration 4

In Illustration 4, a verbal information objective is replacing a portion of an intellectual skills hierarchy, not because it doesn't exist, but rather because it has been learned previously and is now being applied in a new context with the facilitation of the newly acquired verbal information.

Often it is the case that a few new intellectual skills, and intellectual skills from previous instruction, are linked in the instructional curriculum, as shown in Illustration 5.

Inputs

	Cognitive Strategies	Verbal Information	Motor Skills	Attitudes	Intellectual Skills
Cognitive Strategies	One might develop strategies for developing new strategies. (speculation)	Verbal information may mediate a transfer of learning, allowing learner to adapt old strategies to new situations.		Dogmatism, field dependence, etc., may affect learner's ability to perceive new strategies.	A repertoire of I.S. probably leads to a generalized "strategy" for solving similar problems (Gagné, 1977b).
Verbal Information	Strategies for memorizing work strings, facts, or organizing meaningful knowledge, e.g., megamemory research by Rohwer (1975).	A number of studies show that the learning of one set of information influences the learning of a second set (Ausubel, 1968). Many theories imply organization into propositions "associative" in nature.	Reading may be dependent upon motor coordination (Wilson and Geyer, 1972, p. 160). Clinical application (directional orientation).	Attitudes about source affect perception and probability that information will be learned (Hovland, Janis, and Kelley, 1953).	Appreciation of classification routines may lead to ability to make relational or associative "propositions" enhancing verbal learning (Klausmeier and Davis, 1980).
Motor Skills	Strategies for learning new motor skills may exist, e.g., patterning, faded cues, successive approximation, cognitive routines.	Provides cues for the sequencing of a motor performance.	Developed in a progressive manner so that part skills may be combined to form more complex skills.	Probably affect effort learner will put into learning new skill or improving an existing one.	Executive subroutine which governs the pattern of responding is an intellectual skill that may be previously learned (Gagné, 1977b).
Attitudes	The ability to self-analyze one's attitudes may be facilitated by learning a cognitive strategy, e.g., strategies for resolving dissonance.	May input directly into some attitude objectives; gives learner expectation of reinforcement available for making certain choices.	The attainment of a skill leads to a more positive attitude towards the use and value of that skill.	Attitudes towards persons, places, or things are mutually supportive; changing one may necessitate changing many (cognitive consistency theory).	The attainment of I.S. may lead to a more positive attitude if their practice is reinforcing to the learner.
Intellectual Skills	Affects ways learner can approach task of learning new skills.	Input into I.S. at any level; serves to clarify terminology and mediate learning transfer; also may serve as advance organizers. Defined concepts may first be learned as verbal information.		A positive attitude probably facilitates motivation needed to make work of learning worth doing. A negative attitude probably serves as a perceptual screen.	A hierarchy exists within the intellectual skills domain so that learning a higher level skill is facilitated by recall of previously learned simpler skills.

Outputs

Figure 15. A domains/function matrix summarizing how learning in various domains may interact.

95

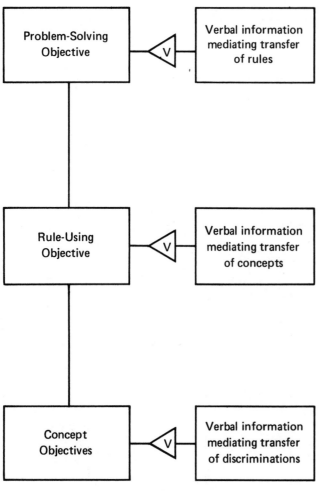

Key: V = verbal information input.

Illustration 5

Diagramming these relationships makes the assumptions of the curriculum or instructional developer more obvious, i.e., what skills are and are not being taught, and what skills are being transferred. The verbal information objectives are generally derived from asking the question, "What should the students be able to say or remember about this problem, rule, concept, etc.?" If having the student memorize something serves as an input to an intellectual skill, it may be serving a transfer function, in which case it is being assumed that a portion of the intellectual skills has been previously acquired.

The process of constructing an ICM resembles the process of writing a computer program. There are many ways to accomplish the same ends, but some are more efficient than others, some are easier to construct than others, etc. It is not only possible, but probable, that two persons, given the same objectives, would map them differently; for, as the reader can see, the process is more a set of guidelines than a scientific procedure.

How to Do It

After the interrelationships among the major unit objectives have been established, it is possible to describe subordinate "specific" objectives. These are behavioral objectives (learned capabilities) the student will acquire in order to perform the major unit objectives. To facilitate interpretation and development of the ICM, some diagrammatic conventions have been adopted:

1. When different domains intersect, a symbol designates the change:
    (a) ─▷ is used to show a verbal information input;
    (b) ─Ⓐ─ shows an attitude input;
    (c) ─M─ shows motor skills input; and
    (d) ──── shows intellectual skills input.

2. Relationships *among objectives in the same domain* are shown with straight lines in a conventional flowcharting manner. If the standard verbs are used to describe the learned capabilities, the developer will have little subsequent trouble in determining the type of learning being represented, and he or she can then start diagramming the relationships. The intellectual skills hierarchy remains relatively the same, as described by Gagné (1977b), where problem solving is recognized as the highest order skill, followed by rules, concepts, and discriminations, respectively. By looking at the major intellectual skills for a unit, the designer can begin a "task analysis." One procedure for constructing this hierarchy is to ask the following set of questions:

    (1) To define "problem-solving" objectives: "What problems will the student be able to solve at the conclusion of this unit?"
    (2) To define "rule-using" objectives: "What set of rules must the learner apply (learn) in order to solve the subsequent problems?"
    (3) To define "concept" objectives: "What concepts (categorizations) must the student apply (learn) in order to use subsequent rules or procedures?"
    (4) To define "discrimination" objectives: "What discriminations must a student make (learn) in the process of differentiating between attributes of different concepts?"

The answers to these questions will provide the objectives for the intellectual skills domain, and these objectives can be diagrammed in a hierarchical manner. Notice the use of the word *learn* in parentheses above. In the process of doing a task analysis, there are many discriminations, concepts, rules, and other types of behavior that the learners, for whom the instruction is being designed, are assumed to possess. For instance, if we are teaching intermediate algebra, we assume that the student can add, multiply, subtract, and divide; he or she can solve simple arithmetic problems in a base ten system; he or she can count; etc. The task analysis will not dissect the task all the way down to performing simple arithmetic operations because we expect that the students can recall and use these operations, since they used them in the previous course, "elementary algebra." Likewise, we do not expect to have to teach the student to read, or to write numbers on paper. The task analysis looks at the behaviors we expect to teach in order to enable the student to perform the particular terminal behaviors we have described.

The task analysis for intellectual skills, then, seldom contains a complete, pure hierarchy of all the subordinate intellectual skills. The starting and termination points are usually described by the level of the learners, and many assumptions are made about previously acquired behaviors that will affect the learning to take place.

The Procedure

A procedure used by Wager is described in the following paragraphs.

Starting with a pack of 3 x 5 cards, the designer and the subject-matter expert begin generating specific behavioral objectives that both feel relate to the unit being mapped. If the subject-matter expert is not accustomed to specifying behavioral objectives, or for some reason is opposed to starting in this manner, the designer might ask to see the unit test or the items on the final examination that relate to the unit being developed. The objectives can then be deduced from the test items. If the course is new, and there are no tests or previously established objectives, the objectives can be generated by asking the question, "What would the learner have to be able to do or say in order to be able to accomplish the terminal objective?"

Following the above process, you will have a handful of 3 x 5 cards that represents behaviors you will expect students to exhibit at some point in this unit. The next step is to relate the intellectual skills to each other, following the rules for hierarchical organization explained earlier in this Chapter. That is, the specific problem-solving objectives (if any) would be related to the larger, unit problem-solving objectives, cognitive strategies, or attitudes. In turn, the rule-using objectives would be related to the problem-solving objectives, the concept objectives to the rule objectives, and the discrimination objectives (if any) to the concept objectives.

It is not uncommon to find students of instructional design generating objectives for a unit map that are broader than the originally stated terminal unit objective. If you find this to be the case, you may have to reevaluate the terminal unit objective to determine if, in fact, it might be subordinate to the broader objective, which in turn might become the terminal unit objective. The rules regarding the hierarchical relationships between levels of intellectual skills objectives should not be violated, and all of the intellectual skills objectives should fit into the unit somewhere. (Wager does this step by physically taping the 3 x 5 cards to a piece of Kraft paper with masking tape.)

The next step is relating the objectives from other domains to the intellectual skills objectives. The objectives, such as verbal information, should relate to the intellectual skills objectives in some functional way as described by the function-domains matrix. If they do not relate to the intellectual skills objectives in any identifiable manner, put them aside for future review.

If the unit has a terminal attitude objective, then the other objectives functionally related to it should be mapped. It is most often the case that an attitude will be functionally related to an intellectual skill. It is also common to see one (or more) verbal information objective(s) related to the attitude.

There are basically two approaches in the literature that may be used in designing instruction to change attitudes (or establish new ones). One is based on the information approach described by Estes (1972); the other is based on the "behavior change" approach described by Bem (1970). With regard to interrelationships between objectives from the different domains, Estes' approach would make use of verbal information, and Bem's approach would interface with intellectual or even motor skills.

Estes (1972) found that information about the magnitude and probability of reinforcement (even though the information may be false) can facilitate attitude change. In this case, the learner could be supplied with verbal information presented in a logical manner by a credible source, and if he or she "learned" this information an attitude change would probably accompany it. Bem theorizes that attitudes should follow behavior (1970, p. 57). Although this is not inconsistent with Estes' approach, this implies that attitudes of certain types, e.g., towards the subject matter being studied, are likely to be more positive after the student has mastered that subject matter. This makes intuitive sense, since we would expect that someone who could "do" statistics would be more positive towards it than someone who could not "do" it. If we were trying to facilitate attitude attainment or change by this approach, we would wish to design our instructional system so that the intellectual skills are attained under the most reinforcing conditions. Then the subsequent use of the skills is designed into the program so that a high degree of facility with the new skills is attained and maintained. The relationship between motor behaviors and attitudes would seem to follow the same model of reinforced incremental learning, successful performance of the terminal skill, and maintenance of the skill.

At this point in the procedure you have the basic map, but more than likely there are gaps. Remember, you generated the original set of objectives from memory, or from materials that were not necessarily complete. You have also eliminated for the time being the objectives that do not seem to relate to any of the other objectives in your present map. The problem is to determine which objectives are missing by asking, from the top objective, downward, "Could the learner do this after performing the objective(s) I have related to it?" If the answer is *no*, the needed objectives should be generated and added. The final step is to review the objectives that had been set aside earlier, to see if they now relate to any of the newly generated objectives in the map. If not, perhaps the objective belongs in another unit, or relates to an entry skill, or perhaps it is irrelevant. Resist the temptation to "stick it in," just because it would be nice to know.

Your map should look like the one in Figure 14, in that:

1. The map will contain objectives from two or more domains.
2. The intellectual skills objectives will follow the rules for learning hierarchies.
3. The objectives from other domains will be related to one or more objectives in a "functional" (supporting) way.
4. Learned capability verbs will automatically classify the objective (this tells the reader the type of objectives in the map).
5. Diagramming conventions will show the reader which objectives are "inputs" to other objectives (this has sequencing implications for instructional presentation).

As stated earlier in this Chapter, probably no two persons, given the same terminal unit objective, would produce the same map. The ICM produced offers only one instructional solution, and there are probably many. The question of the adequacy of the map is not fully determined at this point; the map will later be reviewed after the first tryouts of the instruction. The map might be checked with other subject-matter experts for "face validity," but it represents simply an estimate of the needed curriculum based on the application of a systematic procedure, following guidelines based on psychological principles. The two exercises on the following pages have the same purpose. You may wish to choose the one for which you have the most knowledge of the subject matter.

Summary

The procedure outlined above for arriving at a unit-level ICM applies generally also for constructing maps at the other two levels: (a) the course map (Chapter 5) and (b) the lesson map (Chapter 7). Research on the validity of these procedures is more extensive for the unit and lesson levels than for the course level. In short, we know more about design of small units of instruction (lesson level) than we do about courses and entire curricula.

Exercise No. 6: Constructing a Unit ICM

Below are objectives for a unit-level ICM. Write each on a 3 x 5 card, and follow the procedure outlined in this Chapter to produce an ICM. Some of these objectives may be irrelevant; some needed objectives may be missing. Compare your map to the one shown in the answer key at the end of this book.

Objectives

1. The student will be able to generate a monthly budget.
2. The student will be able to demonstrate calculation of the average of a set of numbers.
3. The student will be able to classify costs as either fixed costs or variable costs.
4. The student will be able to demonstrate calculation of interest on loans.
5. The student will choose to budget his or her money.
6. The student will be able to state the advantages of budgeting.
7. The student will be able to define the term "budget."
8. The student will be able to state examples of fixed costs.
9. The student will be able to state examples of variable costs.
10. The student will be able to define the term "savings."
11. The student will be able to define the term "opportunity costs."
12. The student will be able to calculate a mean variable cost for a specified number of billing periods.
13. The student will be able to state three ways of saving money.
14. The student will be able to state the rules for budgeting variable costs.
15. The student will be able to state a definition of the term "escrow."
16. The student will be able to state the rules for budgeting fixed costs.
17. The student will be able to demonstrate the rules for using an assets-liabilities sheet.

Alternate Exercise No. 6

Copy the objectives below onto 3 x 5 cards, and construct an ICM according to the procedure described in this Chapter. Check your map with the answer key at the end of this book.

1. The student will be able to (SWBAT) generate a straight lecture and a "lecture-discussion" type lesson according to preestablished guidelines for each, as evidenced by delivery of the lesson to a group of students.
2. SWBAT generate a short (7-10 minute) lecture type presentation by teaching a group of students something they don't already know.
3. SWBAT generate a short (7-10 minutes) "lecture-discussion" (inquiry) type lesson by teaching a group of students something they don't already know, and including the asking of leading or opening and probing type questions.
4. SWBAT generate a set of inquiry type statements relating to a given specific objective.
5. SWBAT generate an objective capable of being taught in a short inquiry type lesson.
6. SWBAT classify inquiry and recitation type objectives.
7. SWBAT define the term "inquiry."
8. SWBAT generate an objective capable of being taught in a lecture type presentation.
9. SWBAT state the components of a lecture type presentation.
10. The student will choose to elicit feedback from students and peers for the purpose of improving classroom presentation skills.
11. SWBAT state the importance of developing lecture and/or discussion skills.
12. SWBAT generate behavioral objectives (entry skill).
13. The student will choose to use an instructional delivery technique appropriate for the topic (objectives) being taught.
14. SWBAT demonstrate lecture outlining by preparing an outline for a lecture that he or she will subsequently deliver.
15. SWBAT demonstrate reinforcement of a student's response by providing positive feedback.

Chapter 7
Organizing the Lesson

Chapter in This Book	Recommended Readings		
	Briggs, L.J. (Ed.) *Instructional Design: Principles and Applications*. Englewood Cliffs, N.J.: Educational Technology Publications, 1977.	Gagné, R.M., and Briggs, L.J. *Principles of Instructional Design*, 2nd ed. New York: Holt, Rinehart, and Winston, 1979.	Gagné, R.M. *The Conditions of Learning*, 3rd ed. New York: Holt, Rinehart, and Winston, 1977.
6	Chapters 4, 5	Chapter 6 Chapter 8	Chapter 11
⑦	**Chapter 5** **Chapter 7** **Pages 179-193**	**Chapter 6** **Chapter 8**	**Chapter 11**
8	Chapters 8, 9	Chapter 10	Chapter 12

Introduction

Chapter 6 discussed the procedure for showing the relationships among objectives comprising a unit by constructing what was called a unit-level ICM. To the best of our ability, the objectives that would be taught were generated and related to one another in a hierarchical or functional manner. By looking at a map, a designer can obtain a quick picture of the instructional task ahead. Instruction generally takes place in a given period of time, and the instructional activity that takes place in that period of time is called a lesson. Lessons may vary in length from 15 or 20 minutes up to, perhaps, three hours. The length of a lesson will depend upon the type of learner—and very often upon the constraints of the instructional environment in which the lesson is to be given. Within reasonable parameters, the authors believe that lesson length should be such that the learners do not become either bored or overwhelmed by the instructional presentation. This means adjusting the length of the lesson to the audience and the objectives to be attained, or adjusting the objectives to be attained to fit within the time constraints of the instructional situation. Since time is usually a constraint (the teacher or trainer does not have unlimited time to teach the student), the designer is most often doing the latter.

In this Chapter, we will investigate the process of breaking down a unit map into manageable "lesson" structures. A lesson-level ICM can be produced that will show how objectives taken out of the unit map will be grouped for the purpose of designing the instructional materials the learner will encounter in each single lesson. Also, while drawing the lesson-level ICM, more detailed information about subordinate skills for an objective may be added—details which were omitted from the unit-level ICM.

Chapter 7 Information Test

_1._ What is the source of lesson objectives? ....
....

_2._ What factors determine how much to include in the lesson?
  _a._ ....
  _b._ ....
  _c._ ....
  _d._ ....
  _e._ ....

_3._ Terminal objectives for lessons were .... objectives in the unit ICM.

_4._ How many lessons are to be planned for a unit of instruction? ....
....
....

_5._ What learning theory is consistent with our design model? ....
....

_6._ What principle is to be utilized in deciding how to sequence instruction within lessons and among lessons? ....
....

_7._ What important kind of capability is likely to be revealed by drawing a hierarchy that may be missed by an information-processing analysis? ....
....

_8._ How does a prerequisite skill differ from supportive objectives? ....
....
....

_9._ What two factors should be kept in mind when clustering objectives in the unit map to form maps for individual lessons?
  _a._ ....
  _b._ ....

Background

One of the products of the instructional design process is the set of instructional materials from which the student is to learn (acquire a new behavior or "learned capability"). Gagné (1977b) describes the process of learning in terms of an information-processing model. Physiological and mental processes within the learner sense, store, process, and act on stimuli in the environment. Instruction is the process of arranging the environment so that learning is facilitated. This means developing and arranging the stimuli so that they support the internal information-processing events of the learner.

Our model works on the assumption that learning is cumulative. That is, intellectual capabilities are learned as rather specific skills; however, they are related to previously learned skills, and they will be used in learning new skills later on. The model engages the notion of learning generalization and "learning transfer" where previously learned skills may be used in learning to solve new, previously unencountered problems. This all implies that a maximally effective learning environment depends in part upon the learner and the competencies he or she already possesses.

Another consideration in the arrangement of the learning environment is the structure of the learn-

ing task. For instance, before demonstrating the rule for long division, the student will have to be able to multiply numbers, since multiplication is a component of the process of long division. In this case "long division" might be considered our terminal objective, and "multiplication" a prerequisite competency that the students will have to learn (if they do not already possess it) because it will be called upon in learning long division.

At this point it might be appropriate to make a distinction between what Gagné (1977a) calls supportive objectives and prerequisite skills. There are many learned capabilities that are supportive of learning new capabilities; for example, a positive attitude towards mathematics will be supportive in learning intellectual skills associated with mathematics. Cognitive strategies related to reading might be supportive of learning verbal information (although not necessarily so, as there are other modes of learning). Prerequisites, on the other hand, are necessary with regard to learning a particular skill, because they are components of what is to be learned. "The true meaning of prerequisite is a capability of prior learning which is incorporated into new learning" (Gagné, 1977b, p. 268). Prerequisites are considered to be "enabling objectives"; that is, objectives that must be learned to enable the learning of other objectives. Enabling objectives define the requirements for learning the terminal objective. The enabling objectives for a particular learning task may have been learned long ago, or they might be components of the current lesson. If they were learned prior to the lesson in which they are needed, they would be referred to as *entry skills*, and if they are to be learned in the current lesson, they would be referred to as *subordinate competencies.*

The task of the designer in constructing an instructional curriculum map for a lesson is to define the terminal objective(s) of the lesson, and then to define the prerequisites in terms of the subordinate objectives, the entry skills, and the supportive objectives that will be used in facilitating learning and transfer. The lesson map is a subset of the unit map and often an elaboration of the unit map. That is, the terminal objectives of the lesson map will be subordinate objectives of the unit map. These "subordinate objectives" will then be analyzed for their enabling objectives (both entry and subordinate), and they will be related to one another in a functional manner as they were in the unit map.

Of the seven kinds of aids which can be used to identify the components to be displayed by a lesson-level ICM (as mentioned earlier in Chapter 6), we will now refer to two. The *hierarchical* analysis has been discussed previously with regard to the relationships among intellectual skills. The *information-processing* approach analyzes a task in terms of its procedural requirements. For instance, the procedure in calculating the mean (average) of a set of numbers would include the following steps:

1. List the numbers to be averaged.
2. Add these numbers to obtain a sum.
3. Count the number of numbers.
4. Divide the sum of the numbers by the number of numbers.

This analysis is useful from the standpoint of determining the skills that will be needed at each step in the final objective, but it is not detailed enough to define the enabling competencies needed in the lesson. For example, nowhere in the information-processing analysis is there a mention of the skill of multiplication, yet multiplication is prerequisite to division. So, although helpful in an initial analysis of the learning task, the procedural or information-processing type of analysis is not enough for defining the necessary enabling objectives that will have to be considered in the construction of the lesson map.

The purpose of the lesson-level ICM is to provide a basis for the selection and sequencing of what Gagné and Briggs (1979) call "external events of instruction," as discussed in Chapter 9. These external events to facilitate the new learning will be sequenced so that prerequisite competencies are learned and recalled at the appropriate times for learning the new and more complex competencies.

How to Do It

The ICM below (Figure 16) represents an analysis of the enabling competencies for one of the subordinate objectives in the unit-level map shown in Figure 14, in the previous chapter.

The lesson ICM identifies, to the best of our ability, those enabling skills that must be possessed by the learner before entering this specific lesson (entry skills), and skills that will be taught in the lesson (subordinate objectives). The entry skills may have been learned in a previous lesson, or

through adjunct instruction, e.g., homework readings, but regardless of when or how learned, they are prerequisite to the objectives to be attained in this lesson.

Another way to arrive at a lesson map is to first draw a learning hierarchy for each intellectual skills objective to be included in a lesson, and then to add the supporting objectives from other domains—information, attitudes, motor skills, and cognitive strategies. An example of this by Ackerman is found elsewhere (in Briggs, 1977, p. 483).

The unit-level map may be broken down into smaller segments that you as a designer feel constitute lessons. This may be done from either past experience or upon the advice of the subject-matter expert. The total instructional time for the unit should be kept in mind; that is, if there are five units in the course (each being essentially equal) and there are approximately two weeks for each unit (six total instructional hours per unit), each unit would consist of two three-hour lessons, six one-hour lessons, etc.; so the unit map has to be segmented accordingly.

The lesson map in Figure 16, for example, is expected to take approximately two hours of instructional time. Looking back at the unit map (Figure 14), it might be noted that a large number of objectives are of the verbal information type that are supportive of the learning of intellectual skills. However, these information objectives are not complicated to learn, and they may be taught in a relatively short period of time, perhaps among the events used for the teaching of the intellectual skills objectives. Exactly how the designer divides the unit ICM into lessons is not important as long as sequencing rules are not violated (prerequisites are taught first); however, the efficiency of the instruction might depend on other factors, such as time between lessons, amount of practice, etc., so that essentially the same materials used in a different arrangement could be differentially efficient.

Any particular unit map should be capable of being divided into a number of lesson maps that represent the subordinate objectives in the unit map. Furthermore, the lesson maps should include entry skills that are identified as "prerequisite" to the skills to be taught in the lesson. These skills are differentiated from the subordinate "lesson objectives" by a dashed line, as shown in Figure 16. All other conventions for the ICM, as described in the previous chapter, remain the same.

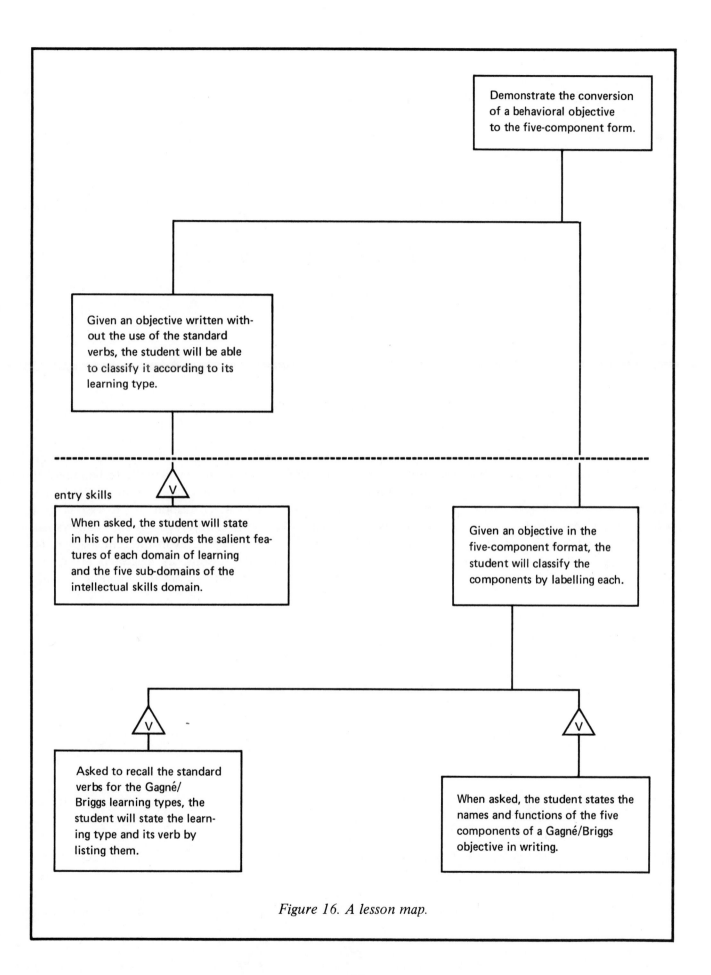

Demonstrate the conversion of a behavioral objective to the five-component form.

Given an objective written without the use of the standard verbs, the student will be able to classify it according to its learning type.

entry skills

When asked, the student will state in his or her own words the salient features of each domain of learning and the five sub-domains of the intellectual skills domain.

Given an objective in the five-component format, the student will classify the components by labelling each.

Asked to recall the standard verbs for the Gagné/Briggs learning types, the student will state the learning type and its verb by listing them.

When asked, the student states the names and functions of the five components of a Gagné/Briggs objective in writing.

Figure 16. A lesson map.

107

Planning a Series of Lessons

In the case of the lesson map shown in Figure 16, the terminal lesson objective was simply one of the 15 objectives which constituted the unit map (Figure 14, in Chapter 6). As indicated above, some of the information objectives in the unit map could be incorporated into the actual lesson for some of the intellectual skills objectives in the unit map.

In the unit map (Figure 14), one could draw lines around the "boxes" which are to be included in single lessons. Or, one could number the boxes in the unit map to correspond with lessons in a series. Whatever coding system is used, one needs to show how the objectives in the unit map are to be clustered into lessons, as suggested in performance objective No. 18 at the opening of this Chapter. Now do Exercise No. 7.

Exercise No. 7: Designing a Lesson Map

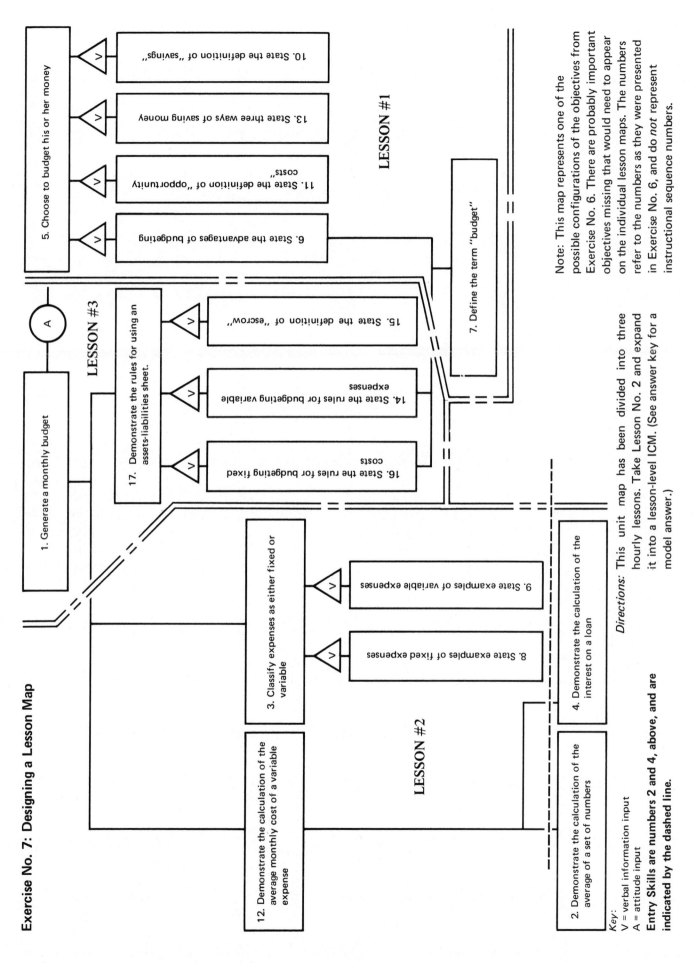

5. Choose to budget his or her money

10. State the definition of "savings" V

13. State three ways of saving money V

11. State the definition of "opportunity costs" V

6. State the advantages of budgeting V

LESSON #1

7. Define the term "budget"

A

LESSON #3

1. Generate a monthly budget

17. Demonstrate the rules for using an assets-liabilities sheet.

15. State the definition of "escrow" V

14. State the rules for budgeting variable expenses V

16. State the rules for budgeting fixed costs V

3. Classify expenses as either fixed or variable

9. State examples of variable expenses V

8. State examples of fixed expenses V

12. Demonstrate the calculation of the average monthly cost of a variable expense

4. Demonstrate the calculation of the interest on a loan

2. Demonstrate the calculation of the average of a set of numbers

LESSON #2

Note: This map represents one of the possible configurations of the objectives from Exercise No. 6. There are probably important objectives missing that would need to appear on the individual lesson maps. The numbers refer to the numbers as they were presented in Exercise No. 6, and do *not* represent instructional sequence numbers.

Directions: This unit map has been divided into three hourly lessons. Take Lesson No. 2 and expand it into a lesson-level ICM. (See answer key for a model answer.)

Key:
V = verbal information input
A = attitude input

Entry Skills are numbers 2 and 4, above, and are indicated by the dashed line.

Chapter 8
Factors in Media Selection

Chapter in This Book	Recommended Readings		
	Briggs, L.J. (Ed.) *Instructional Design: Principles and Applications*. Englewood Cliffs, N.J.: Educational Technology Publications, 1977.	Gagné, R.M., and Briggs, L.J. *Principles of Instructional Design*, 2nd ed. New York: Holt, Rinehart, and Winston, 1979.	Gagné, R.M. *The Conditions of Learning*, 3rd ed. New York: Holt, Rinehart, and Winston, 1977.
7	Chapters 5, 7 Pages 179-193	Chapters 6, 8	Chapter 11
⑧	**Chapters 8, 9**	**Chapter 10**	**Chapter 12**
9	Chapters 7, 8, 9	Chapters 4, 5, 9, 10, 11, 13, 14	Chapters 3-10 Chapter 12

Introduction

This Chapter represents a turning point in our account of how instruction may be designed. Up to this point, we have dealt with methods for deciding *what* to teach in curricula, courses, units, and lessons. Now we turn to the matter of *how* to teach.

Stated differently, Chapters 1 through 7 outlined a procedure for identifying needs, deriving goals, then planning a course or series of courses to reach the goals. Each course was analyzed, in part, by drawing instructional curriculum maps for the course, then for units, then for individual lessons. These maps state the objectives, and they depict how the objectives may be sequenced to achieve the goals. This is the process for deciding and justifying *what* to teach.

Turning to the matter of *how* to teach, we are opening our account of how to design lessons. These lessons may be taught by a human instructor, or by a variety of materials presented by many non-human media, or by a combination of teachers and other media. By saying "*other media*," we are saying that the teacher is a medium of instruction. This is not to detract from the importance of the teacher's role, but to introduce the important idea that *instruction* consists of accomplishing several *external instructional events*. These events may be performed by the teacher, by other media, or by the learners themselves when interacting with the instructional materials (stimuli). The purpose of the "external events," which can be conveyed by the various media, is to stimulate the "internal events" that comprise learning—events accounted for by an information-processing theory of human learning (see Gagné, 1977b, and Figure 17, Chapter 9, in this book).

The "external instructional events" are listed in Chapter 9; they consist of such familiar teaching activities as "presenting the lesson objective," "presenting stimulus material," "guiding thinking," and "providing feedback." Depending on the characteristics and age of the learner, these events are presented by many sources. At an early age, events tend to be provided by the teacher or by real objects in the environment. Later on, classroom activities provide more of the events. After the learners become good readers, books provide more of the events.

In the model of lesson design presented in Chapter 9, you will learn to *design lessons* by selecting and using appropriate media of instruction. An unusual aspect of our model of lesson design is that *media selection* first takes place, separately, *for each external instructional event* planned for a lesson. Then the media selections for the entire series of events for a lesson are reviewed, and final choices are made. The purpose of this "two-step" process of media selection is to induce you to consider first the *theoretically best* medium choice for each lesson event, and then to teach you to review this theoretically best choice by considering the *practicality* of that choice. This latter step is to result in an effective, easy-to-arrange total sequence of media utilization for the lesson.

Size of Chunk

This introductory explanation has been made to introduce the concept of "size of chunk" in media selection models. Our model may be called a "small chunk" model, because we ask you to consider media selection for each of the individual events of a single lesson. This may appear to be an unnecessarily detailed way of going about media selection. It is believed worth the time it takes, especially when design teams are to develop new materials for a course to be used by many learners over a period of time. Our model may not be equally cost-effective for only a few learners, but it can pay off handsomely for larger numbers. We have previously shown how media selection by this model can be used not only by teams who develop new materials but also by teachers who plan lessons by *selecting* from available materials (Briggs, 1977, Chapters 8 and 9).

Whereas our model asks you to consider media choices for each of the external instructional events in a lesson, the more common practice is to make these selections in "large chunks"—such as making one selection for an entire lesson or unit, or even for an entire course. We have good theoretical reasons for preferring our model, but we lack empirical evidence as to how size of chunk is related to the effectiveness of instruction.

Another difference between our model and others is that we teach you to give a *rationale* for the choices made, rather than leaving you to make the choices on only an intuitive basis. For this reason, this Chapter gives you a variety of information that you can use when making media choices. This information can provide a better rationale for the choices made.

The details of our media selection model are

given in Chapter 9, in the form of procedures and formats for recording decisions made when planning instructional materials for lessons.

In this Chapter, we present a variety of kinds of information that should be helpful to you when you study Chapter 9.

The Bases for Media Selection*

As a summary of factors to be considered in media selection, whether following a "large-chunk" or a "small-chunk" model, we list factors discussed further either in this Chapter or in Chapter 9. It should be noted that this list is intended for an "open" media selection model, in which the designer wishes to consider all media, not just a few conventional or "preferred" media. Our reason for adopting an "open" model is that we do not believe there is any evidence that *any* single medium is always best for all learners or all courses. Therefore, our model is "unprejudiced" as to any favorite media. We do favor preplanned, replicable media ("replicable" is discussed in Chapter 9), and we favor assigning as many of the instructional events as possible to the materials, when suitable materials can be located or developed. We thus favor "self-instructional" media when appropriate for the learners and for the course being designed. While we think that much of our model can be used by teachers who *select* media (Briggs, 1977, Chapter 8), we are addressing most directly the circumstance in which teams design and develop materials for a course (Briggs, 1977, Chapter 9, and Chapter 9 in this book).

With this introduction, we now list types of factors to be considered in arriving at a rationale for media selection.

1. *Media characteristics.* It is necessary, of course, that a designer be aware of the features of a variety of media. Both their features as usually employed and the features that *could be* employed need to be known. In this Chapter, we present a description of a range of media and how they are or could be utilized.

2. *Learner characteristics.* The nature of the "target audience" is an important factor in media selection. In this Chapter, we present Dale's con-

*Since this is a background Chapter to prepare you for the work on Chapter 9, we have *not* included an information test, nor performance objectives, nor exercises.

cept of the "Cone of Experience," which is helpful in media selection. This Cone relates age of learners to appropriate media.

3. *Task characteristics.* In Chapter 9, we show how the types of learning outcomes desired for a lesson should influence both media selection and media utilization. Of greater importance than the medium itself are the conditions of learning that are incorporated into the prescriptions and scripts showing how the events of instruction will be designed.

4. *The assumed learning environment.* Media choices vary for home, school, or laboratory learning situations. Thus the choice of "delivery system" influences the specific medium selected. Gagné and Briggs (1979, pp. 176-177) have listed possible media, learner activities, and teacher roles for a variety of delivery systems.

5. *The assumed development environment.* Media choices will vary according to the resources of the teacher or of the design team. The amount of time and money for materials and media development must be taken into account, as well as the kinds of expertise possessed by the personnel available. In fact, the *design model employed* will vary according to the training and experience of the people already available or to be made available for the materials design, development, and production effort (Carey and Briggs, 1977).

6. *The economy and the culture.* Overlapping somewhat with paragraph No. 5, above, is the broader consideration of media as viewed by the users of the course and by their "sponsors." Some schools or other organizations have biases for or against particular media, apart from their cost, as do the public or other sponsoring groups. The idea of "intermediate technology" (*The Futurist*, 1979) as more appropriate for developing countries than is advanced technology should be considered. A culture that has few technicians or scientists is probably not ready for sophisticated electronic equipment, unless it is prepared to rely upon foreign technology or to mount a sizeable training program for its own people. The economy of the country is linked to plans for the rate of using advanced technology.

7. *Practical factors.* Later in this Chapter we provide information on many practical factors in selection and utilization of media.

Some of the above types of factors in media selection and utilization are discussed next in more detail.

Media and Their Characteristics

In order to select appropriate media, it is useful to review, in a general way, the features of various media.

The *function of media* is to present the *kinds of stimuli* the course designer deems appropriate for *specific learners* for achieving the *instructional events he or she chooses for the competency.* Media are *physical means* for presenting stimuli to the learner. The entire set of stimuli in a continuous sequence of instruction in a given medium is often termed "the message" or "the content." These stimuli, conveyed by the media, and the learner's responses to them, accomplish the instructional events. Thus, "media" here includes all of the following and any other similar or related mechanisms: books, charts, tape recordings, slides, motion pictures, the teacher's voice and gestures, programmed texts, teaching machines, instructional television (ITV), and videotape recordings (VTR). These media stimulate the eye and the ear. Other media, such as field trips and laboratory exercises, may stimulate other senses (taste, touch, and smell) and muscle response.

Programmed Instruction

Some writers have defined programmed instruction as any form of systematically designed and validated instruction.

Here, the more narrow, more conventional usage is adopted. Booklets, or printed matter, or filmstrips presented by a teaching machine, using programmed instruction, provide the following:

1. *Type of stimuli.* Printed words, drawings, or stationary pictures, as in a textbook. One type of teaching machine utilizes motion picture sequences.

2. *Arrangement and format.* Small segments of printed information interspersed with required student responses (free responses such as "fill in," or multiple-choice). Feedback is provided after each response.

3. *Size of step.* Small step size is most often used. There are many meanings of step size:

    a. Only a sentence or two of reading materials is presented before a response is required.

    b. The steps (or "frames") are arranged intentionally in a sequence that makes correct responding highly probable; the feedback, given after previous responses in the series, also helps form new correct responses.

    c. Each frame represents only a small learning increment towards a total learning objective.

    d. The responses are made rather effortlessly; the answers are "easy" for the learner.

    e. When a response to a new concept or principle is first required, there are "formal prompts" (cues, hints) to help the student make the correct response.

    f. Later, successive frames over the same concept have less and less prompting ("vanishing" or "fading" of prompts) until the final frame on the concept is a test frame (unprompted; prompts completely withdrawn or "vanished").

    g. Much repetition of new concepts tends to produce "overlearning" (continued practice after the first correct response to the new concept), and hence enhances retention (ability to recall after a prolonged period of no further practice).

4. *Branching.* A type of program that permits the learner to skip over material to which he or she can respond correctly already, and that provides either more repetition or a more detailed, simpler instructional sequence when he or she fails to respond correctly.

5. *Reading ability.* Since most programs employ printed words plus graphical illustration, some reading ability is required. (However, there are pictorial, non-verbal programs for young children, and some programs teach learning and discrimination of the letters of the alphabet.) But many studies show that poor readers do better with programs than with conventional texts, since feedback informs the learner when he or she responded incorrectly, whether this was due to poor reading or poor thinking. It is conceivable that programs make for more *careful* reading, perhaps at a slower reading rate.

6. *Generalizing experiences.* Most programs are weak in providing opportunities to generalize, but they could be improved if after the first correct response to a new concept the program included a variety of examples. In a series of examples of a given concept, it is important to change the exact responses required as well as to change the stimuli to which the learner responds. It is also desirable to exercise "S-R reversal"—if the student responds to "big = ?" (large), also have him or her respond to "huge, great, not small," as well as to respond with "big" to these other stimuli. Otherwise, the stu-

dent's knowledge will be limited and will not be functional, e.g., he or she will be either "response bound," "stimulus bound," or both. (Recall William James' famous example of the boy who would say "vertical" if a pencil were held in a vertical position as the chosen stimulus, but would respond with "knife" if a knife were used in the vertical position as the stimulus.)

7. *Self-instructional.* Because programs not only present stimulus material (words and pictures to represent ideas), but also require responses and provide feedback, this medium is "self-instructional" if properly programmed for the type of learner using it. That is, *if printed words and still pictures are proper forms for presenting the stimuli for the competency and instructional events being designed, it is possible to provide practically all instructional events that one might specify.* Programs are also self-paced, and thus lend themselves to individualized instruction.

Motion Pictures

Type of stimuli. Films can provide printed words, drawings, and still pictures, as can programmed instruction, but they have the added advantage of showing actions and objects in motion. When objects in motion cannot be filmed "live," animation can be used (but it is very expensive). Even though expensive, animation of theoretical objects or processes could be effective (speed of movement of molecules as a function of temperature; action of electrons as related to voltage, amperage, and resistance; lines of force in social dynamics; lines of force in physics, motives, or perception; pressure build-up; etc.).

Another stimulus characteristic of motion pictures is the capability for altering normal time-place relationships. Movement can be speeded up (to show a year of movement of stars or an hour of movement of clouds in five minutes) or slowed down (to show a golf club compressing the ball at the moment of impact). This medium can help to indicate relationships of objects or events across the continent or world, or space can be compressed to show more closely the correlation of action effects, such as the moon and the tides.

Film splicing and editing makes it possible to reshoot ineffective motion sequences, and to collect shots from all over the world to make a brief, effective overview or kaleidoscopic presentation of events far apart in space or time.

Sounds which cannot be produced by voice or equipment in the classroom can be recorded at another location with audio equipment, and introduced alone or with video, as desired.

In short, sound motion pictures can present many auditory and visual stimuli which cannot be presented by a teacher, a book, a teaching machine, or programmed instruction. Even local laboratories cannot match the stimulus range of film. Special lenses can make microscopic or macroscopic pictures that classroom resources cannot produce, thus providing useful *distortion of real life for instructional purposes.* "Simulation" may have more instructional value than real-life pictures for some purposes, but distortion may not be desirable for others. "True to life" is not a safe criterion to apply to all instructional stimuli. (A flight simulator *acts* like an airplane, but it cannot kill the pilot; a student needs to know the current beliefs about electrons, but he or she can't see them, unless by simulated animation.)

Other characteristics. While films are relatively expensive to produce (perhaps $1,000 per minute of running film), this expense, when converted to rental or purchase price, places film within the budgets of most schools. *Low-cost cameras for amateur productions can yield many educational values. School usage of film may be somewhat hampered by the need to move projectors and screens about, the need to darken the room, etc.* Increasing the number of "media-designed" classrooms can minimize these mechanical problems, and increasingly good media services are being provided by the schools.

Since films require mechanical equipment, they are usually presented to entire groups; they do not fit in easily with individualized instruction, at least in conventional classrooms. But with proper space arrangements, films can be feasible for individual and small-group instruction, as are filmstrip projectors, which even small children can operate.

Cartridge-loading film projectors are easy to operate, and many available devices can project brief (five-minute) "single-concept" films.

Conventional films are strong in the range of stimulus characteristics, and *deficient* in requiring explicit responses. Since explicit, overt responses are usually not required, neither is explicit feedback. But a film designed for a specific objective, when used with adequate preparation, follow-up discussion, and evaluation, can be made to serve an instructional purpose.

The motion picture projector was designed for a

continuous presentation. It lacks the response-receiving and feedback features of the teaching machine. However, in one project (Markle, 1977), the film runs only five or ten minutes before the sound track tells the instructor, "now turn the projector off so the students can next study the programmed material" (or practice the manual procedures, or have a group discussion—or do whatever is listed next in the instructor's guide). Also, films can be made to contain pauses for covert responses to questions, with the right answers provided following the pause in each case. Although unconventional uses of film, which borrow techniques from other media, have not caught on with professional film producers, you, as a course designer, could still prescribe them.

Commercially available devices can serve as "master control devices" for operating multiple projectors and recorders, making possible an automatic, preprogrammed, multimedia sequence of instruction. Some devices make an automatic tally of learners' responses to questions, permitting the instructor to "override" the presentation in order to correct errors made by a large number of the students.

Educational technology needs various machine combinations which would capitalize upon the richness of films in stimulus characteristics combined with the ability of the teaching machine in student response and feedback, and self-paced, individualized procedures.

One disadvantage of films compared to videotape recordings (VTR) is the lack of immediate rapid playback, an important feature of VTR used in micro-teaching and in critiques of other simulated performance situations.

Conventional films have no features corresponding to the small step size or the branching of programmed instruction. Nor can one easily scan, as in a book.

Videotape Recording (VTR) and Instructional Television (ITV)

Stimulus characteristics. In general, these two media share many of the advantages of motion picture film in richness and range of stimulus features. However, VTR and ITV are normally restricted to "live" action, for groups of people, a teacher at a chalkboard, people in a laboratory, etc. Not much animation is used. Sometimes VTR and ITV use "talking face" presentations. They differ from a lecture primarily in that the lecturer is not physically present; he or she is "recorded" for "playing" at other times and places. Even so, an expert lecturer can thus reach more students than in the live lecture situation, and the recorded lecturer is often better prepared—even to the point of being "programmed" through previous presentation and formative evaluation of the effects of the lecture in terms of student performance. Also, the "props" are usually more elaborate than in most live lecture situations, since most TV studios have facilities for the production of visuals. Typically, there is no posing of questions with pauses for students to respond, followed by feedback. But experimental efforts in ITV (Gropper, 1963) have essentially converted some ITV presentations to "teaching machine presentations." Thus, VTR and ITV are not normally used for distortions of real-life stimuli, as in film animation, slow motion, or fast motion. However, for showing ongoing events in real time, any TV has the advantage of instant communication. Quick playback is possible with VTR, while films require longer processing time.

Evaluation uses. VTR is ideally designed for use as an evaluative technique for students performing in a trainee capacity in a job-simulation circumstance. It has been employed to evaluate brief lesson presentations of teachers in training; to provide a basis for self-evaluation of lectures by professors; and as a "way to see yourself as others see you" for other "performers."

Student Response-Equipped Classrooms

Several mechanical and electrical devices are available for an instant tally of responses of a group of students to questions posed by the teacher during a lecture or demonstration. These tallies enable the teacher to provide feedback, and to decide whether to go on to the next topic, or to backtrack, to review, or to re-explain something that many students have missed. Some devices provide feedback automatically to the individual student; some leave this to the teacher. It is likely that group-conducted instruction could be improved substantially by equipping more classrooms with such devices.

Teaching Machines

Many teaching machines have been described as "program holders." Machines of the type developed for the small-step linear programs (nonbranching programs) are essentially that. One such plastic device has two rollers; the "program" is printed on a long, continuous strip of paper, rather than on pages in a booklet. The strip is advanced frame by frame by the student, who simply turns a knob until the entire new frame is in view in a window. The student reads the frame, writes his or her response in another window, then turns the knob until the "correct answer" (feedback term) appears in the window. Other machines require the student to press buttons labelled to correspond to multiple choices in test questions, or to rotate cylinders to show answers, as in an arithmetic machine.

This type of machine keeps the student from "cheating" or from skipping around in the (linear) programmed text presented by machine. Some machines will not present the next frame until the student has responded to the previous frame; some keep a mechanical tally of correct responses.

Except for these mechanical controls over the action of the student, the program presented by machine is not essentially different from the same program in programmed booklet form. *If the student follows directions*, there is no reason why a machine of this type should be more effective than a booklet format, unless the fun of "pushing buttons" serves as a "pin ball" effect in motivating the student.

The advent of the "student station," consisting of a cathode ray tube (CRT) and computer keyboard, permits whole "pages" of printed, graphical, or pictorial data to be presented to the learner. Visual questions are answered by the student touching a particular area on the surface of the tube with a pencil-like "light gun," or by typing the response. The computer responds to the answer by displaying another "frame," saying "right," "wrong," or presenting a remedial explanation of the error made by the student.

Modern CAI Programs

Modern computer-assisted instruction (CAI) programs can be compared to simpler teaching machines in the following ways.

1. They provide a greater variety of stimulus displays.

2. They avoid the awkwardness of the teletypewriter printout and typed responses, and are now capable of spoken response.

3. They can select "branching sequences of instruction" that are especially relevant for the error history recorded in a series of students'

responses. Such "branching programs" potentially can present a totally different series of instructional content for each learner, depending on his or her entering competencies and the specific nature of the type of error reflected in the learner's answers. This "adaptive" style of CAI can result in more effective instruction for each learner, and often does so in less time than a fixed, "linear" program for all. But, at present, CAI systems are often faulty in construction, entailing delays for "down time" due to hardware or software malfunctions. Yet CAI is promising, particularly since remote terminals can serve students located miles away from the computer itself, yielding rapid data-gathering for achieving high quality, validated programs. "Time-sharing" circuits permit many students to work at their own rates, using pathways within branching programs at any given time.

One added potential bonus of CAI is the use of student history data. Theoretically, at least, a computer could not only "branch" on the basis of errors made on the particular program being studied, but also on the basis of a long history of student performance on past programs. Branching could be based on competencies previously mastered, types of stimuli to which the learner responded well, or the degree of terseness the learner can typically handle.

Of course, the computer can only present material it has been programmed to present; its matching of lesson style to learner characteristics is no better than the matching planned by the designers of instruction. Yet, in long-term overall potential as a tool for individualized instruction, CAI has much promise for the future, especially with the development of low-cost, high-power microcomputers now on the market in rapidly increasing numbers.

Filmstrips

This medium is becoming more feasible for widespread use as projection devices become easier to load and operate. Filmstrips lend themselves to both group and individualized instruction, since reliable, low-cost projectors can be located for easy access on a personalized schedule of student activities under a "contract" type arrangement for individual progress. Instruction can be self-paced, so that the learner advances from frame to frame as he or she chooses. Usually, it is also easy to backtrack, or to view the entire strip a second time. There is no reason why the content of the strips cannot be programmed to utilize the same characteristics contained in programmed-instruction booklets. Slide projectors wedded to audio-tapes can produce programmed instruction.

Adjunct Auto-instruction

Oddly enough, this simple technique has never "caught on" to the extent that programmed instruction has. It may be that it is regarded as a testing procedure, thus overlooking its teaching value. Yet the procedure, first developed by Pressey (1926), lends itself to study by almost any means of presentation. One simply prepares a list of multiple-choice, self-test questions over a unit of material—a chapter in a book, a lecture, a field trip, a demonstration, or a film. The questions can either parallel the sequence of the material in the book, or they may be chosen primarily to empha-size the most important points. Still another alternative is to sequence the review in accordance with the learning structure of the objectives.

Feedback for responses to such sets of questions can be provided by separate "key sheets," by use of the "slider" technique employed in some programmed-instruction booklets, or by a small mechanical device now marketed commercially to provide feedback immediately after each response; the student stays with each question until he or she finds the correct answer before going on to the next one.

As implied above, such practice tests can *sequence the review by the student* over materials which actually were not prepared or sequenced to achieve stated objectives. If some core information (missing from the study source) is needed for the defined objective, often a single sentence or two added between the sequenced review questions will bridge the gap. This economic procedure is usually less expensive because it permits one to program the review responses as compared to rewriting the text to follow the learning structure of the objectives. (No known data show the relative merits of sequenced study in relation to sequenced review.) Essentially, this technique helps the student to sort the core materials from other material in the text. This is one way to use existing material more effectively to achieve stated objectives, even though objectives may not have been provided originally, and none of the material was actually sequenced to meet identified objectives.

An increasingly large body of research data indicates that a terse text accompanied by such self-test review items is an economical and effective mode of learning and is often a less expensive way to achieve results than to prepare new material in other media. Evidence also indicates that adjunct methods achieve equal results in less time than programmed instruction.

These concepts suggest a way to improve text-books; e.g.,

(a) state objectives;

(b) sequence materials to match the learning structure of the objectives; and

(c) intersperse the self-test items at appro-priate intervals in the text. How does one determine what an "appropriate" interval would be? One study suggests that for the adult student, about 2,000 words of text should be followed by a set of questions. Perhaps this interval of interspersal should be more frequent for younger students or more difficult ma-terial. Less is known about the adjunct techniques with information sources oth-er than printed text.

Lectures

This extensively used, much maligned, and often joked-about medium of instruction has not been the subject of nearly as much empirical study as have films and programmed instruction. Thus, little of a scientific nature is known of the value of lectures or of the features which make them more effective.

Perhaps Ausubel (1963) has been the most systematic in describing how learning may take place as a result of lectures. According to his analysis, the amount learned depends heavily on the listener's ability to incorporate the main ideas into his or her personal "cognitive structure." Except for such characteristics as techniques to add emphasis, to show relatedness, to provide contiguity and redundancy, and the like, perhaps Ausubel's most concrete suggestion for how the lecturer may improve his or her presentation is by the use of "advance organizers"—brief, introducto-ry remarks which summarize the content to follow in the most general, abstract form, as an aid to forming a cognitive structure or framework upon which to hang the various details to be learned. Most of the evidence for the "advance organizer," however, has been adduced from research with printed rather than spoken content.

But Ausubel considers both reading and listening

to be "reception" learning, as distinguished from learning by laboratory experiences or other discovery methods. He identifies *reception learning* as that received by didactic methods in which the entire content of what is to be learned is presented to the learner in final form. The message transmitted can contain either rote or meaningful learning materials. In rote learning, the content is arbitrary (that is, the learner can't figure out the matter by logic or discovery). Meaningful material is non-arbitrary material, consisting of relationships which can be figured out by the listener. In non-reception or discovery learning, the entire content is not given directly to the learner; rather, under guidance, he or she is led to derive new ideas for himself or herself. Discovery, like reception learning, can consist of either rote or meaningful materials. It is under this pair of dichotomies (reception/discovery and rote/meaningful) that Ausubel subsumes other specific kinds of learning, such as conditioning, motor skills, perception, and discrimination.

Lectures, like other media, can be improved by requiring explicit student responding, with immediate feedback (knowledge of results; reinforcement). Explicit response is student response to definite questions posed purposefully, rather than to unplanned (implicit), private reactions of the listener to the lecture. Explicit responses may be overt (written down or spoken aloud) or covert (just thought, but not expressed for public scrutiny and recording). Thus, lectures could be improved using student response devices discussed earlier, or using outline handouts, printed questions, or other simple means.

Other Media

Discussions among students represent a medium of learning that has received almost no attention by researchers, but which graduate students believe to be important in achieving objectives. The maturity in self-evaluation of strengths and weaknesses makes it possible for graduate students to improve in achievement through discussions with their peers. Their ability to identify what they need to know but must yet learn (deficits) is another facet in the success of this educational medium. It is likely that providing students with prepared questions for discussion could enable them to achieve more through this medium.

Class discussions usually have more value for generalizing upon knowledge than for acquiring new information as a first instructional step. Books and programmed instruction are thus often employed to start both learning and directed discussion under teacher guidance for concluding a unit of learning. One value of discussion is to learn what applications other students make of the new learning. Particularly where value judgments are to be made, hearing the views of others may accomplish more than the author of a text could plan to do without research among groups of students. Discussion also provides exercise of some of the more "general" educational objectives, such as skill in oral communication, respect for the rights of others, courtesy, and listening to both sides of controversial issues before reaching conclusions.

Laboratory exercises serve as vehicles for discovery learning as well as for reviewing, sorting, and testing knowledge first acquired by verbal presentations. They help develop specific research skills relating to hypotheses formation, experimental design, handling of equipment, and observing, researching, organizing, and reporting of observed events. They also provide an early experience on which one may judge his or her intellectual and temperamental suitability for a pursuit of a laboratory science. They may have more general value in forming one's concept as to how dependable knowledge in some fields may be generated, and how to weigh opinion, belief, theory, and empirical observation.

Conferences with teachers, which loom especially important in graduate and professional training, also may have great impact for younger learners in both academic and personal areas of life. Conferences on a one-to-one basis are more flexible than other forms of individualized instruction, which depend heavily upon prepackaged content. Teachers often can diagnose difficulties and identify missing competencies which can result in effective remedial study, clearly focused on individual need. Conferences, no doubt, often result in dissipating (or increasing) anxiety, reformulation of goals, reassessments of progress, or revision of academic plans. A few minutes of private consultation often can clear up problems which the teacher cannot identify in the classroom. Also, conferences offer the teacher occasions for greater insight into student needs, and both the time and opportunity to develop personalized prescriptions of what the student should do next, in contrast to what normally can be accomplished using group-administered diagnostic tests and group assignments.

The more problem-solving work a student must do for a unique kind of (productive learning) project, the greater the value of student/teacher conferences. Conferences may be useful in defining the task, identifying features of a successful solution, providing feedback to first solution attempts, suggesting a model of performance, and for appraisal and guidance of thinking. And, no less important, they provide recognition and reinforcement of unique attacks upon the problem and encouragement of the student in the further development of special aptitudes.

Finally, the self-organizing ability of the learner's brain has been recognized not only as the locus of the learning that does take place, but as the most important of all the media of instruction (Melton, 1960). Only inside the learner do both the *internal events* of instruction and the *external events* of instruction provided through other media meet, interact, and become organized into ideas, actions, habits, beliefs, competencies, and values. For the unusually gifted this is the locus of success or failure, whatever the quality of the external events of instruction. To some extent this is true for all learners; but it is *especially for the less-than-gifted learner that the quality of the designed instructional events* may well tip the balance between success and failure. This is the major role of the other media of instruction. How well they are chosen and used, or programmed may well determine, for many learners, the probability that their own brains can handle the vast organizing chore to be accomplished.

While some students succeed despite poor teaching, the majority will doubtless suffer serious losses. Because our present knowledge of how to select and use the external media of instruction is so imprecise and imperfect, compared to knowledge in the physical sciences, if learners are soon to achieve their own educational "man on the moon," they must rely heavily upon their own resources—their brains—while scientists try to learn more about using the other media of instruction.

Media Selection Strategies

In the beginning of this Chapter, we characterized our media selection model as a "small-chunk, open" model, and we explained the meaning of these terms. The details of how our model operates are presented in Chapter 9.

In this section of the Chapter, we review some procedures that have been used in the past in selecting, developing, and producing media, and we present some practical guidelines that can be helpful in either a "large-chunk" or a "small-chunk" media selection model.

Some Commonly-Used Strategies

In the past, instructional materials have been produced by publishers and other kinds of media firms. How particular materials and media came to be produced has not typically been decided by professional instructional designers, but by individual authors who may or may not have conferred with teachers as to the material needed. In the usual case, of course, no specific objectives were written as the basis for media selection and materials development. Therefore, the task of the teacher in *selecting* from among available materials has been complex and difficult. Some texts are written primarily to aid teachers in this task (Dale, 1969), and Briggs (1977, Chapter 8) has shown how to integrate materials selection into lesson planning.

While the main course of this book is about how to select and design *new* instructional materials for courses and lessons, we present here some practices which are intermediate between the older publishing conventions and our model for the design of new materials.

In commercial practice, of course, media decisions are primarily dependent on which business one is in. Publishing firms produce textbooks; film makers make films; and programmed instruction companies produce programs. Each industry tends to use its own medium for the widest possible range of marketable materials. This leads to the availability of almost all widely used instructional content in almost all the media. At least there is much overlap in the informational content available in the various media. This growing proliferation of items in catalogs of materials in various media can lead teachers almost to despair of selecting the most suitable items. There simply isn't time to examine or preview all materials on a topic before making a selection.

Furthermore, most materials are not indexed by the learning objectives the materials are designed to foster. Rather, they are indexed by topic. Although indexing does indicate what the materials "are about," it does *not* indicate what performance objectives the materials help to establish. Nor are most available materials pretested so that the producers can state in performance terms what the student learns from the materials. The teacher must try to provide the "instructional events" by which use of the materials can produce desired effects.

Even though much credit is due the originators of the technique of programmed instruction for emphasizing the importance of empirical testing and revision of materials (formative evaluation), surveys have shown that only a small percentage of commercially produced programs has been developed this way. Producers of programmed instruction, more frequently than others, tend to state the performance objectives for which their materials were designed. Without performance data, the buyer has little more reassurance of the value of the materials than he or she has when no objectives are supplied. It may be comforting to know that the programmer *did* have objectives towards which he or she was working, but without test data, there can be little confidence about the way in which the objectives influenced the design of the materials.

In curriculum design projects, there is often considerable improvement over standard commercial practice in deciding on the nature and types of materials to be produced. In the project *Science—A Process Approach* (AAAS Commission on Science Education, 1967), intellectual science-process skills were identified, and a series of exercises was designed for the development of the skills. Mature scientists and classroom teachers, in teams with behavioral scientists, carefully plotted strategies for skill development and selected the various kinds of materials needed for the instruction. While the media selection process used did not parallel the present model, much cross-checking of working assumptions took place among project personnel. And, perhaps most important, extensive tryouts were conducted, first with small experimental groups of learners, and later with the cooperation of a number of schools across the nation. Evaluations included both individual and group testing, reports of observations, and reactions of teachers.

In such projects, the teachers and scientists together select the objectives of the program, and they either develop or prescribe the development of the materials to be used. Commercial suppliers then have the advantage of clear specifications for needed materials, and they can perhaps more confidently estimate the extent of the market demand. Such curriculum projects suggest an ap-proach to a needed overhaul of the procedures by which instructional materials are specified, produced, and marketed.

In the meantime, some course designers may seek simpler means for deciding upon media sequences to be produced by themselves or under their specifications, rather than by the model for media selection presented in Chapter 9.

Many designers may wish to employ a less analytical strategy than the one recommended here. Perhaps one element which some may desire in such an alternate strategy is to make fewer media selections for larger elements or blocks of instruction. Other writers have offered more general guidelines for selecting media; some of these have included cost factors as well as instructional advantages and disadvantages of various media.

Two sets of useful information are presented next for those seeking either a short-cut method for media selection or to apply our model as outlined in Chapter 9. These materials serve to remind the designer of some of the *media characteristics* which he or she can consider when selecting media appropriate for the intended *learner characteristics* and for the *characteristics of the educational objective.*

Some Brief Guidelines for Any Media Selection Model

The two sets of guidelines on the following pages (see Tables 1 and 2) should help you whether you are:

(1) selecting media and material from those available;
(2) selecting media for "large chunks" of instruction; or
(3) selecting media by use of the "small-chunk" model presented in Chapter 9.

The matrix (Table 2) was designed by John G. Wilshusen, Jr., with the assistance of Richard Stowe, and is reproduced here with their permission. Since the matrix presents so much information in a limited space, the authors prepared the following explanations of terms used in the matrix. In the matrix, full shading means "*not applicable*"; partial shading means "partially applicable"; and empty cells means "applicable." Wager has added the "events of instruction" section and the microcomputer row at the bottom of the matrix.

Table 1

Advantages and Limitations of Some Classroom Media*

Medium	Advantages	Limitations	Ways to Overcome Limitations
Lecture	Presents facts and ideas rapidly	Difficult to adjust to individual speed of comprehension	Dynamic, interesting, manner
	Emphasis placed where teacher wishes	Mostly one-way communication	Use audio-visual supports
	Excellent for background information	Little learner participation or activity to maintain interest	Ask questions, even if only rhetorical
	No limit to size of audience	No direct check on learning taking place	Pose questions, and provide answers after a pause
	Can be filmed or taped (VTR)	Difficult to prepare for unknown audience	Use check-up questions with student response devices
	Can be interrupted by requests for more detail	Difficult to maintain attention and interest	Supply printed outline, with space for note-taking
	Can be interesting, lively	Effectiveness depends on skill and personality	Use chart to present outline of objectives
	Teacher controls content and sequencing		Prepare transitions, introductions, and summaries
	Combines readily with other media		Adjust vocabulary to the audience
	Can be broadcast to remote locations		Use short quiz last few minutes; provide answer key
Discussion	Encourages learner activity	Depends on learner capacity and mood for participating	Have a reserve of stimulating questions available
	Maintains interest	Time-consuming	Practice summary, transition, and guidance of learning
	Avoids monotony	Requires preparation of stimulating questions	Good aids, visuals, handouts
	Learner can check his or her ideas with those of others	Requires back-up aids if discussion lags	Permissive communication with learners
	Prepared questions stimulate critical thinking	Requires instructor skilled in human relations, directing and controlling	Start with a viewpoint designed to provoke discussion

*These materials were developed by William Freeman and are reproduced here with his permission.

Medium	Advantages	Limitations	Ways to Overcome Limitations
Discussion (Continued)	Gives learner sense of responsibility for learning	Instructor needs to summarize skillfully, remembering who contributed main points	Be able to predict student response and build upon this
	Exercises skills in democratic cooperation	Instructor must be able to think fast, to shift, adapt, accommodate	Learn the background of students
	Shares experiences of advanced students	Requires permissive guidance	Give advance assignment or briefing
	Mature, cooperative way of learning	Student must read or otherwise prepare in advance	
	Increases student commitment	Size of group limited for active discussion	
	Provides feedback to teacher on progress made	Learners must be homogeneous in background and maturity	
Demonstration/ Performance	Saves time and talk	Requires skilled demonstrator/ assistants to watch learners practice	Encourage student questions/answers between steps of demonstration
	Easier to watch a procedure than to listen to verbal description	During demonstration, no learner participation	Provide immediate learner practice after demonstration
	Helps assure understanding	Requires preparation for effective demonstration	Cue what to watch for during demonstration
	Realistic; adds variety	Outdoor demonstrations affected by weather	Stop action or direct attention at critical points of demonstration
	Demonstration provides model and standards for learner performance	Perform demonstrations at regular speed, then repeat slowly (difficult to do, may confuse learner); opposite approach is piece-meal, then total performance is at normal rate	Repeat parts, then entire demonstration
	Gives learner confidence when he or she performs adequately		If you demonstrate way *not* to do it, follow at once with correct procedure and emphasize latter
	Explanations are more concrete	May require expensive equipment and personnel on standby for long period	Reward correct student performance, employ and space criticism judiciously
	Provides unity for a series of elements	Frequent rehearsal needed to maintain model demonstration	Use relevant units for part-practice, then whole practice
	Can have large class		Alternate small units of demonstration and practice early, then total performance later

(Table 1 Continued)

123

Medium	Advantages	Limitations	Ways to Overcome Limitations
Auto-instruction	Minimizes dangers, errors, waste, damage	Takes many hours to prepare and validate	Be sure teachers, students, and administrators understand purpose and use
Programmed learning;		Requires training and experience to produce	Reward students for timely completion
Teaching machines;	Self-paced rate of presentation	Some learners dislike small steps	Insure mastery by a criterion test
CAI	Designed for performance objectives	Contrary to school periods set for group pacing	Space criterion tests at suitable intervals
	Provides frequent knowledge of results (reinforcement)		
	Learner masters one step before next is presented		
	Active learner participation		
	Low error rate		
	High retention and progressive achievement		
	Program validated (sometimes)		
	Efficient use of time of teacher and learner		
	Content is standard and reproducible; stability of presentation		

(Table 1 Continued)

Table 2

Matrix of Media Utilization

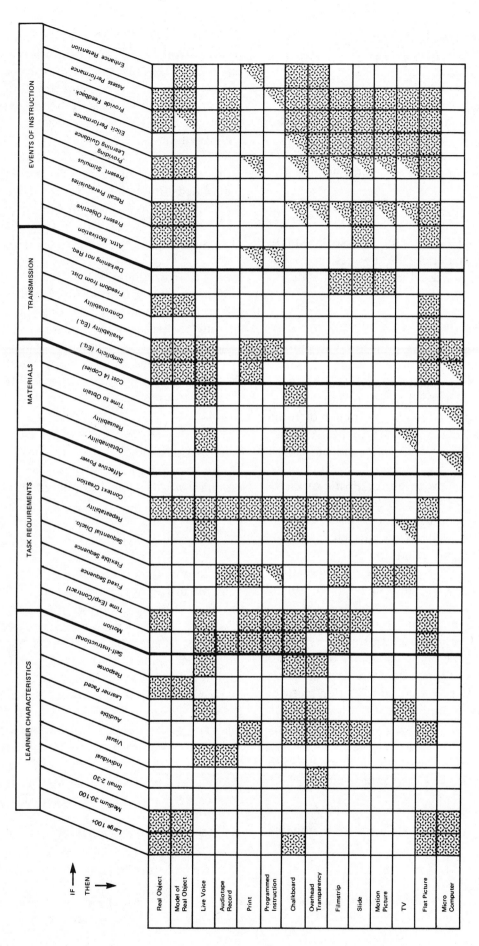

Learner Characteristics (Table 2)

Large, medium, small, individual—Refer to sizes of groups of learners.

Visual—Learner characteristics dictate that the stimulus material be visual.

Audible—Learner characteristics dictate that the stimulus material be audible.

Learner Paced—Learner characteristics dictate that the rate of presentation be controlled by the learner.

Response—The medium contains provision for incorporating demand for learner response.

Self-Instructional—Learner characteristics dictate that stimulus materials be so designed that learner is able to use them with little or no supervision.

Task Requirements (Table 2)

Motion—Task requirements indicate that motion must be depicted.

Time (exp/contract)—Refers to the possibility of expanding or contracting length of presentation as compared with real-time experience of some phenomena: e.g., slow motion or speeded motion pictures, compressed or expanded speech devices.

Fixed Sequence—Refers to characteristic of medium which does not permit change in sequence of presentation beyond forward or reverse.

Flexible Sequence—Medium permits change in order of presentation of stimuli.

Sequential Disclosure—Medium permits revelation of material bit by bit and allows retention of prior bits as further bits are revealed.

Repeatability—Medium allows complete or partial redisplay (replicable instruction).

Context Creation—Refers to capability of media to transport learner from awareness of real world to context artificially contrived. Motion pictures are an obvious example, but it is our contention that all media have this capability to some degree. A book has it, for example.

Affective Power—All media have the power to move people emotionally to some degree.

Materials (Table 2)

We feel that items in this group are reasonably clear.

Transmission (Table 2)

Simplicity—How simple is the equipment to operate?

Availability—How readily available is the equipment required to display the stimulus materials?

Controllability—How much control over the transmission can be exercised by the instructor? (Start/stop, slower/faster, freeze frame, volume change, forward/reverse, repeat, switch to different medium.)

Freedom from Distraction—To what extent does the equipment distract the learners from the intended stimuli?

Darkening Not Required—Medium can be presented without necessity of darkening learner environment.

Events of Instruction (Table 2)

Items in this group are discussed in Chapter 9, and in the recommended readings indicated at the opening of this Chapter.

In the process of choosing media, whether by the recommended model, or by alternate simpler procedures, an important factor is feasibility within the resources available for development and production.

The following section (Types of Visuals) presents various practical factors in the selection, production, and use of various types of visuals. This summary was developed by Merlyn Mitchell.

Types of Visuals*

Flat Pictures—Drawings and Photographs

Many instructional events can be facilitated by the use of a single drawing or photograph. By means of photography and enlargements, an illustration of what is being discussed may be created in a form that is permanent, needs no special equipment to view, and can be edited to eliminate material that is not important or is distracting. A series of photographs may be arranged to illustrate the steps in a sequence. Furthermore, they can be placed in close proximity to the practice area and used as a guide. By preparing suitable captions for the photographs, commentary or instructions that are needed may be made a part of the visual.

Advantages

1. Presentation may be shown one at a time or in groups.
2. Duplication is easy.

*This section of the Chapter was prepared by Merlyn Mitchell especially for use in this handbook.

3. Size may be tailored to fit needs of learning situation.
4. No viewing equipment is needed.
5. Any existing visual can be copied and edited to suit requirements of instruction. An infinite variety of materials can be obtained easily and cheaply from magazines, newspapers, etc.

Limitations
1. Special skills and equipment are required.
2. Color is costly compared to black and white, although color is not needed for some illustrations.
3. They are bulky in mounted, larger sizes—difficult to transport and store compared to other media visuals.

Photographic Slides

Though presenting many of the characteristics of flat, still pictures, slides have the additional characteristic of being presented in a situation that makes them very compelling to the eye. Darkened rooms give the observer little else to view except the screen, and the sudden appearance of the new visual makes inattention difficult.

The same conditions that make slides demand viewer attention are troublesome to create for single-slide viewing, so slides are usually shown in series or groups to justify the preparations.

Though transient in comparison to still photographs, slides may easily add the dimension of color, may be enlarged to much greater physical size, can be shown in rapid sequence, and can be manipulated to give the viewer very exact exposure to the precise visual stimulus prescribed for the instructional event.

Sound, usually music, can be added to the presentation of slides by informal tape recording to fit the general mood of the visuals. Synchronization of sound and slides may be accomplished by interlocked independent sound and projection systems or by recently developed equipment that places sound on a magnetic track surrounding the slide and allows as much as a half minute of sound to be presented during the projection of the particular slide.

This offers flexibility of programming not possible with most tape players that must proceed in a linear format rather than a random one.

Preparation of color slides is constantly being made easier by new developments in equipment and materials. Cameras now exist that can show the exact area being photographed. The camera may be moved to within inches of the subject; the camera can indicate when it should be adjusted for proper exposure; or, it will set itself for taking the picture, either by existing light or with flash, leaving only the adjustment of focus to be done by the operator. The majority of slides produced are double-frame 35mm (24 x 36mm actual picture area). Some 35mm cameras take only a single frame at a time and thus can produce twice as many pictures per roll of film. The cost per slide is thus lowered to about two-thirds that of a regular double-frame slide due to the savings in film and processing charges. These cameras offer the same technical advantages of the larger 35mm format, plus the added ability to produce filmstrips. Some cameras are capable of making either single- or double-frame pictures on the same roll of film by simply turning a lever. The single-frame slide does not give as sharp an image as the double-frame slide when enlarged to equal size, but modern lenses and film emulsions have made the single-frame camera worth serious consideration as a photographic tool.

Other sizes of cameras may be used to produce slides. Roll film sizes 828, 127, 120, and 620 are available in color emulsions that will produce transparencies. The 828 and 127 (12 exposure—4 x 4 cm) sizes can be mounted in the 2 x 2 inch holder of the 35mm projector, but the other sizes (127—8 exposure, 620, 120—8 and 12 exposure) must be cropped to fit the 35mm projector or used in oversized projectors with their accompanying technical and logistical problems.

Advantages
1. Simplicity of preparation processing includes mounting in holders.
2. They are relatively inexpensive.
3. They may be produced and shown with simple, reliable equipment that is relatively available.
4. Copies of existing color visuals from publications may extend subjects available to teacher.
5. There is flexibility in arrangement of slides in teaching sequence; ease of revision.
6. Automatic projection is available.
7. Slides are easily moved and stored.
8. They can be used in individual or group instruction.
9. They may be combined with taped sound.

Limitations
1. Studies require either a good knowledge of

photographic technique or equipment that will be fairly automatic in adjusting for exposures.

2. The image is transient on screen.
3. Slides can be spilled, get out of sequence, or be projected in incorrect positions if not used in an indexed storage system.

Filmstrips

Filmstrips present essentially the same quality and format of visual as the single-frame 35mm slide described previously. The strip itself imposes a sequence of presentation upon the viewer which may or may not be desirable in the instructional program.

The filmstrip does not get out of sequence, is very portable and, once a master strip is created, multiple copies are available at less expense than a comparable slide set.

Preparation by the individual is difficult, though possible. The series must be taken in the order desired for presentation, and exposures must be correct the first time. A more common method of creating a strip is to assemble the slides to be used in order of presentation and send them to a laboratory that can photograph them as a single-frame strip. All visuals must, of course, be in the horizontal format.

Advantages
1. Filmstrips are compact and easily stored.
2. They cannot get out of sequence or position.
3. They may be viewed with a hand- or desk-viewer for individual instruction.
4. Duplicates may be obtained cheaply compared to slides.

Limitations
1. They may not be edited or rearranged as to sequence.
2. They are difficult to produce locally.
3. They are linear rather than random in possible viewing order.
4. Originals are expensive when prepared from slides sent to a laboratory.

Motion Pictures

For many years the standard educational film has been the 16mm size with optical sound. Commercially produced and expensive, these films are usually loaned or rented from a central library rather than owned by a single school.

Recently, the motion picture has been used in less expensive and less sophisticated forms to accomplish specific educational objectives. It is difficult to decide whether the demand for new approaches inspired the improvement in cameras and projectors or if technological improvement has inspired the exploration of new methods of utilization.

In the last decade, the 8mm motion picture has acquired a larger frame area, resulting in a clearer picture. A great many of the features formerly available only in professional equipment have been incorporated into the 8mm amateur camera. Most important of these improvements has been through-lens viewing and focusing, zoom lenses, and automatic exposure control. These improvements allow accurate close-up shots, change of field of view without changing the camera position, and continuous automatic control over the amount of light reaching the film.

Projectors have been improved and their capabilities extended. Film may be shown in loop cartridges that need no rewinding or threading. Newer cartridges will accept roll film and automatically rewind at the end of the showing. Many reel-loading projectors are self-threading. Especially suited to motion study are projectors that can show many or few frames per second for simulated fast or slow action. This is accomplished without the annoying flicker of the image on the screen. In addition to varying the projection rate, these projectors can be stopped to view a single frame, run backward to review frames in fast or slowed rate, advanced or reversed, a frame at a time, for minute examination of a small sequence; or, by punching a hole at the side of the film, they can be programmed to stop after an amount of film has been shown. This flexibility in presentation makes possible the inclusion of student response activities in the motion picture, an activity that has been largely ignored or left to the teacher in most films produced for instruction.

Magnetic sound striping can be added to 8 or 16mm film, and this may be recorded upon or erased as magnetic tape would be. This means of adding sound to the motion visual enhances its use in individual study situations. Needed comments can be made at appropriate points on the film instead of requiring interruption to read an explanation or listen to it on a tape player. Films of this type are possible on a small budget. The cost of 8mm color film, including processing, is less than ten dollars for footage that will run over four minutes on the screen. The cost of adding sound striping to this footage would be about five dollars. A duplicate of the film in color, with sound striping, would cost about ten dollars.

The sum effect to the educator of the technical improvements that have been mentioned above is that he or she now has a new way of using motion pictures. The individual can now produce motion pictures that can accomplish specific teaching objectives. Technical developments in 8mm motion picture cameras have lessened the technical involvement and expertise formerly needed to produce quality footage. With new developments in projection equipment, the motion picture is highly useful in small-group or individualized study. Presentation may include review or detailed study of a sequence; or, if it is needed, sound may be added to question, clarify, or for added special effects. The film may be stopped at will or automatically to include student response to the material presented. In this context, the motion picture is a tool that suits the needs of a teaching situation rather than an entertaining diversion from learning.

Advantages
1. Films can be used to show motion.
2. They can alter time of an event—can speed very slow motion or can slow very rapid motion to an observable tempo.
3. They can show the development of an event or concept.
4. They can combine visual, verbal, and sound effects in a forceful presentation.
5. They can be animated to illustrate abstract concepts or concealed processes.
6. Simple presentations are inexpensive to produce.
7. Equipment is readily available.
8. Many prepared programs are available.

Limitations
1. Linear format—all footage from beginning to end must be shown; there is no provision for random access to material.
2. Films are expensive to produce in more sophisticated forms.
3. Some knowledge of technique must be acquired.
4. Most productions are not compatible with pre-specified objectives. Objectives of most films are not stated in specific terms.

Learner Characteristics

Much research has attempted to match media and learners. This is important in media selection, but in actual practice one must combine consideration of learner variables with consideration of task variables.

In 1968, Briggs studied learner variables concerned specifically with selecting media (Briggs, 1968a). Other studies examined "cognitive styles," or "learner/teaching method interactions." Tallmadge and Shearer (1969) reported that learners possessing one learning style had technological interests, low anxiety, and were introverted. These subjects when given logico-mathematical subject matter (transportation technique) learned best by an *inductive* program, and in a visual discrimination course (aircraft recognition), they learned best using a *deductive* program. People with a different learning style had social/aesthetic interests, high anxiety, and were extroverted. They learned best by programs just the opposite of the ones found to be most effective for the first group described. This was true for both courses. In short, there was a triple interaction among learning style, type of learning (course content), and programming style (inductive vs. deductive). This finding pertains more directly to *how* the content is programmed than to the *media* in which it is programmed, but it does emphasize the importance of learner characteristics.

In general, if the learner is a poor reader, he or she will, of course, do better hearing spoken words than reading written words. Young children will do better by demonstrations using actual objects they can see, feel, and watch being manipulated, while older students may learn just as well by a verbal description. Pictures may be more useful for the young or the poor reader than for the mature adult. In fact, for the well-educated adult, reading is usually as effective as listening or seeing pictures for most subject matter not highly dependent upon pictorial display. Passive, submissive children may do best by teacher-led work, while independent children may do better by programmed instruction or self-directed study or contract teaching from a variety of materials. Books permit backtracking easily to catch a missed point, but this is not readily possible with films, tape recordings, or teaching machines.

In one study, high-anxious girls in grammar school did better when feedback was provided after every response in programmed instruction, while low-anxious girls did better with the same program without the feedback (Campeau, 1968).

Pictures may be better than words for certain students. For low-ability students or for difficult material, programmed instruction is usually superior to regular printed text. Large steps can be taken by bright, mature, independent learners; small steps may be needed for converse learner characteristics. Findings disagree as to whether the learner can select the media and materials best for him or her. Rebellious students, and those motivated to avoid failure, do best by a highly structured, authoritarian mode of instruction; students motivated to achieve success do better by more unstructured, permissive conditions. Dependent students may learn by film; independent students by reading or lecturing.

The above conclusions reported in particular groups of students for particular subject matter prepared in particular media are offered for consideration, not for blind application. Learner characteristics should be considered in conjunction with task characteristics.

The course designer may be aware only of gross characteristics of the students for whom the materials are being prepared, such as age, I.Q., and prior competencies. The classroom teacher using the materials for a particular group of students will, of course, have more knowledge of each child after several weeks of his or her class. Often the teacher will either use the prepared materials somewhat differently for different pupils, or he or she may seek alternate materials for particular portions of the work for some students. The teacher can also modify the *effects* of prepared materials by grouping students. One teacher used programmed instruction in science as a small-group activity for two reasons:

(a) some pupils did not pace themselves well when working alone on the program; and

(b) the pupils shared tasks in laboratory exercises for which the program contained directions. A mature student set the pace for group reading of the material, and assigned some students to do the experiment and others to observe and record the results. Then conclusions were reached in group discussion.

Hershberger (1964) reported that high-ability students benefited from terse texts or self-evaluation test items interspersed with text. Low-ability students benefited from textual brevity only if it was accompanied by the self-evaluation items. Use of self-evaluation test items also helps the students to discriminate core materials from enrichment material, in reference to the objectives the teacher desired, achieved by reading the text. This technique, pioneered by Pressey (1950), is often called "adjunct auto-instruction." This adjunctive use of responding to self-test items after reading textual material may be best for bright students, while linear programmed instruction may be best for slow learners. Adjunct methods can also be used to reinforce learning by other media.

The course designer should have inputs from the intended teacher-user regarding likely pupil characteristics. He or she then uses this, *as one basis among many*, for making his or her media decisions and writing prescriptions as to how each of the media are to be "programmed."

In the present model, media are selected in advance for groups of students having specified assumed characteristics. A teacher should check these assumptions with the characteristics of his or her own students.

Dale's "Cone of Experience"

Dale's (1969) "Cone of Experience" is essentially a listing of media roughly in the order that children of various ages can learn well from them. The various media range from manipulation of real objects (direct, purposeful experiences) for young children, to increasingly simulated experiences, and ending with symbols (reading) for older learners.

Dale's categories are as follows:
12. Verbal symbols
11. Visual symbols—signs, stick figures
10. Radio and recordings
9. Still pictures
8. Motion pictures
7. Educational television
6. Exhibits
5. Study trips
4. Demonstrations
3. Dramatized experiences—plays; puppets; role playing
2. Contrived experiences—models, mock-ups, simulation
1. Direct, purposeful experiences

One can see that the lower numbers refer to media for younger learners, and that the higher numbers refer to older learners.

For cognitive learning (all types of outcomes except attitudes and motor skills), we suggest this "rule of thumb" in using Dale's Cone for media selection: "Go as low on the scale as you need to in order to insure learning by your intended learners, but go as high on the scale as you can for efficient learning." One wishes to make a reasonable compromise between media which tend to result in "slow but sure" learning and media which tend to result in "fast but (possibly) risky" learning. Consider both the learner and the objective in making this choice.

For attitude objectives, Wager (1975) has suggested that the age/media relationship mentioned above for cognitive objectives be "inverted." Thus, a young child may acquire new attitudes by hearing things people say (verbal symbols), especially if the speakers are respected by the child (modeling). But to *change* an established attitude, he suggests, may require real-life experiences.

Transition to Chapter 9

This Chapter has presented material concerning the characteristics of the learner and the characteristics of various media—information you should find useful in making media selections after reading Chapter 9.

We have indicated that this Chapter should be useful in following *any* media selection model. We have alluded to both conventional ways of producing media, and to improvements that could be made by application of the model described in this book.

Chapter 9
Designing Lessons and Materials

Chapter in This Book	Recommended Readings		
	Briggs, L.J. (Ed.) *Instructional Design: Principles and Applications.* Englewood Cliffs, N.J.: Educational Technology Publications, 1977.	Gagné, R.M., and Briggs, L.J. *Principles of Instructional Design*, 2nd ed. New York: Holt, Rinehart, and Winston, 1979.	Gagné, R.M. *The Conditions of Learning*, 3rd ed. New York: Holt, Rinehart, and Winston, 1977.
8	Chapters 8, 9	Chapter 10	Chapter 12
⑨	**Chapters 7, 8, 9**	**Chapters 4, 5, 9, 10, 11, 13, 14**	**Chapters 3, 4, 5, 6, 7, 8, 9, 10, 12**
10	Chapters 6, 10, 11	Chapter 12	

Introduction

In Chapter 7 we dealt with dividing the unit map into a set of lesson maps. The lesson map shows the interrelationships among terminal lesson objectives and enabling objectives. An analogy has been previously made between geographic maps at different levels of scope, e.g., a National map of the U.S., a State map, and a City map. We might think of our lesson maps as a set of trip maps that will lead us to our final destination. Like trip maps, they have a planned sequence, a defined scope, and identifiable milestones.

Within the lesson, there are further subdivisions—the external events of instruction that will cue the internal events within the learner. These external events have to be sequenced also so that the internal events are cued in the right order and so that prerequisite skills are called upon at the proper time in the learning sequence.

Chapter 8 dealt with factors in media selection. It is the media which present the instructional events of the lesson. These events are so prescribed as to use the media to incorporate the relevant conditions of learning into the events.

This Chapter will deal with two instructional design aids for preparing lesson materials: (a) the media analysis worksheet and (b) the time line for sequence of instructional events sheet, in order to specify the format and sequence of the external events of instruction for our lesson materials in the media chosen. These events of instruction will then be operationalized by specifying the stimuli that will impinge upon the learner and the medium or media that will transmit the stimuli. Chapter 8 was written to give you some ideas about how the characteristics of various media may be considered when selecting media to be employed in lessons.

Chapter 9 Information Test

_1._ What previously completed analysis does one begin with when designing a lesson or lesson materials? ....
....

_2._ What major considerations does a designer employ in selecting media? (Recall Chapter 8 also.)
     a. ....
     b. ....
     c. ....
     d. ....
     e. ....

_3._ The function of teachers as well as print and non-print media is to provide the relevant ....
of .... and .... of ....

_4._ The use of largely self-instructional materials changes the role of the teacher from that of an .... to that of ....
....

_5._ What are the advantages of "replicable" instruction?
     a. ....
     b. ....

_6._ Which varies among domains of **outcomes**, **events**, or **conditions** of learning? ....

_7._ Can our model of media selection be used by teachers, or designers of materials, or both? ....

_8._ Name the two key worksheets used in planning the development of media materials.
     a. ....
     b. ....

_9._ The events of instruction correspond quite well to stages in what theory of learning? ....

_10._ In what order are the columns in a media analysis worksheet filled in? (Order from first to last by entering numbers from 1 to 7.)
  ....   a.   instructional event
  ....   b.   stimuli
  ....   c.   media alternatives
  ....   d.   tentative media
  ....   e.   final media
  ....   f.   rationale
  ....   g.   prescription

_11._ After prescriptions are written, name stages of work remaining to be done either by the designer or by others.
     a. ....
     b. ....
     c. ....
     d. ....

Background

Instruction is delivered in any number of ways: books, television, audiotape, computer, and live instructor, to name some of the most common. The choices of media must be made, but these choices may not be as important as how the media presentations are designed—that is, how the "events of instruction" and relevant conditions of learning are incorporated in the lesson by the selected media contents.

In Chapter 8, we characterized our model as a "small-chunk, open" model. By "open," we mean that the design of the lesson includes media consideration only *after* the events of the instruction and the conditions of learning have been selected. Generally this gives the designer considerable latitude for selecting media. Even though the traditional classroom lecture is a viable alternative for most events of instruction, other media should also be considered. In selecting media, characteristics of media that the designer should consider include (a) exportability, (b) convenience, (c) availability, (d) cost, and (e) replicability (assuming that effectiveness factors are similar). The last of

these, "replicability," is to us one of the most important.

Replicability is the requirement that the instruction be *reliable* or *consistent*. This requirement strongly favors "mediated" instruction—that is, instruction that is self-contained and delivered by some medium (or media) that presents the instructional stimulus the same way each time.

This may seem like a very mechanical or unhumanistic requirement—after all, shouldn't the instruction be designed for the individual learner? Actually, instruction is designed for a target group of learners, and it is individualized in the sense that the materials should be effective for a stated proportion of the target group. This may require additional (remedial or supplemental) materials for some students, but such materials are also designed and are in effect a part of the "replicable instruction."

The aim of the designer is to produce a single best set of instructional materials for the target group. These materials should be as effective and efficient as possible and as replicable as possible. We recognize, of course, that in some individualized instruction programs, more than one set of materials may be available for each lesson (Gagné and Briggs, 1979, Chapter 14). In most courses, however, this is not the case, as costs would be prohibitive.

With a "live" instructor and typical classroom instruction, it is difficult to control the stimulus presentation in a replicable way. As a result, a procedure that seems to work with one class does not work with another, although there may be no obvious difference to the teacher in what he or she did. Mediated materials help to prevent this problem, since the stimulus presentation is exactly the same each time it is used. This perhaps is the reason why instructional designers emphasize the "changing role" of the teacher from information disseminator to instructional facilitator. As a facilitator, the teacher takes over a management function with regard to the mediated materials and performs those events of instruction for which mediated materials may not be suitable.

A lesson, as we are defining it, is the formal presentation of instructional stimuli to the learner. This presentation may be made in any of a number of different environments (home, classroom, school bus), or a combination of more than one of these. The lesson may include a "homework" assignment from a book, a TV program, or a newspaper to be used in conjunction with a classroom lecture, simulations, programmed instruction, etc. The point is that all activity is oriented towards attaining new behavior, and the lesson is planned to facilitate the attainment of that behavior.

The Events of Instruction

Gagné and Briggs (1979) describe nine "events of instruction" to be incorporated into lessons. These events are:

1. Provide for motivation/attention.
2. Present the objectives to the learner.
3. Recall prerequisite competencies.
4. Provide the stimulus (problem, topic, concept).
5. Provide learning guidance (how to proceed).
6. Elicit performance.
7. Provide feedback (reinforcement, knowledge of results).
8. Assess performance.
9. Provide for retention and transfer.

Not all lessons will require all nine events of instruction to be designed into the instructional materials. Depending upon the characteristics of the learners, many of them can provide some of the events for themselves. The type of learning also makes a difference; for instance, verbal information objectives often do not require recall of prerequisites. Research also suggests that for some types of learning, when the materials are systematically designed, event 2 (presenting the objectives to the learner) is unnecessary.

Our knowledge is incomplete, however, concerning the necessary and sufficient conditions of learning and the relative importance of events of instruction for different kinds of learners and tasks. This is a fruitful area for future media research, but lacking this information it is suggested that the developer account for all nine events of instruction for *each objective* to be taught. If an event is seen to be unnecessary, the design may omit it or change the order of events, but there should be a clear rationale for doing so. Students learning the process are advised to write the rationale for not including an event for an objective, should they feel the event is unnecessary.

Figure 17 shows the relationships between internal events of learning as yielded by information-processing theory, and external events of instruction as suggested by Gagné (1977b). The

Figure includes teacher comments to illustrate each event. The reader might notice that the external events are in a slightly different order from the list presented above.

In planning for each desired event, think of the stimulus needed to produce it: natural objects; spoken words; printed words; theoretical objects or processes described or represented symbolically or in animation; processes (objects in motion); social stimuli (group interaction); etc. Recall also Dale's Cone of Experience, discussed in Chapter 8. *Then* select a medium which has the right characteristics for presenting the desired kind of stimuli.

How to Do It

The process of designing a lesson for conventional teacher-conducted instruction is similar to the process of designing instructional materials, in selected media, for more self-instructional procedures. The major similarity is that both lessons and materials are organized to implement the instructional events. The major difference is that the teacher *selects materials* and designs learner activities around them. Design teams, on the other hand, *develop materials*, incorporating many events into the materials, but leaving some events and functions to be performed by the teacher.

We present here formats to aid teachers in designing conventional lessons, by incorporating appropriate external events of instruction. Similar formats have been presented elsewhere (Briggs, 1977, Chapter 8).

We also present here examples of the same formats and procedures for designing pre-packaged, replicable, mediated, largely self-instructional materials.

The process of lesson design may be said to have begun in Chapter 7, where we showed how series of lessons are derived from a unit map, with the result of drawing up a lesson map showing the objective(s) for single lessons in the series of lessons for the unit of instruction.

Having thus identified one or more objectives for a lesson in a map which also identifies subordinate competencies of the lesson objective(s), the process of media selection begins. Media are selected for the instructional events planned for a lesson, and *prescriptions* are written, summarizing the *content* to be prepared for each medium chosen.

Learning phases: Internal events of instruction and information processing	Instructional events: External events of instruction	Examples of teacher statements designed to stimulate learning
Motivation phase: Expectancy	1. Gaining attention 2. Informing learners of the objective	Look at this rectangle. Today you will learn how to find the area of rectangles.
Apprehending phase: Attention; selective perception	3. Directing attention	Notice that these two sides are parallel to each other.
Acquisition phase: Coding; storage entry	4. Stimulating recall of prior learning 5. Providing guidance to thinking	Recall the formula for finding the area of a square. How does this differ? What does area mean?
Retention phase: Memory storage	6. Presenting new stimulus	The formula for area of a rectangle is $A = xy$. How do we apply this formula?
Recall phase: Retrieval	7. Enhancing retention	Repeat this formula each day and recall this solution to this sample rectangle, for three days.
Generalization phase: Transfer	8. Promoting transfer and generalization	How could we find the area of this shape: ⟋___⟋ ? Of this one: ⟋___⟍ ?
Performance phase: Responding	9. Eliciting performance	Find the area of all these shapes (shown on a test).
Feedback phase: Reinforcement	10. Providing feedback	Here are the correct answers and an explanation of the procedure.

Figure 17. Relationships between information-processing phases (internal events of instruction) and external events of instruction; and examples of how the external events may be presented.

Then these prescriptions are expanded into complete first-draft scripts for the materials to be developed, produced, tried out, revised, and installed.

The Lesson Design Process

Media analysis worksheets. An aid in doing the media selection is the "Media Analysis Worksheet," as shown in Figure 18. The process of media selection and material design for a lesson begins with the first event of instruction for the first objective to be taught (Column 1 in Figure 18). A media analysis worksheet is started for each objective to be taught in the lesson (Figure 18).

After choosing the type of stimulus and writing it in Column 2, a description of the content to be represented by this type of stimulus is produced (this description of the content is called a prescription, Column 7). Often several media offer equal promise, so you note the possible alternatives (Column 3), and defer the final media selection (Column 5) until you have analyzed the entire lesson. In this way, the number and sequence of various tentative (ideal) choices (Column 4) are reviewed for practicality in presenting the entire lesson. In Column 6 (rationale), you give reasons for your decision.

MEDIA ANALYSIS WORKSHEET

Unit Number _____ ; Specific Objective Number _____ ; Instructional Sequence (Lesson) Number _____ .

Objective:

Column Number: 1	2	3	4	5	6	7
Instructional Event	Stimuli	Media Alternatives	Tentative (Ideal) Media	Final Media Choices	Rationale	Prescription

Figure 18. Blank media analysis worksheet.

At the simplest level, we might have a lesson aimed at teaching a single objective, which may, of course, be a prerequisite for a more complex objective taught later in the series of lessons. A typical example might be a lesson in a consumer economics course with the following objective: "The student will demonstrate the calculation of the arithmetic average of a given set of numbers." It is assumed that a task analysis has been performed and a lesson map produced (Figure 19). The designer realizes that prerequisite entry skills of addition, subtraction, multiplication, and division are needed in the new task. (It is also assumed that the majority of learners possess these entry skills.) At this point, the designer can begin attending to the stimuli that would be necessary in the materials in order to produce instruction, for the objective, that is functionally complete with regard to the information-processing model. This is done on a media analysis worksheet, as shown in Figure 20.

In this example, the event "attention/motivation" is accomplished by the classroom teacher convening the class and giving them the context into which the day's objective fits. This event could also have been accomplished by presenting the learner with a hypothetical problem which would call for application of the new skill for solution. Notice in this example that a formal classroom learning environment was assumed, and that the process of using the media analysis worksheet is as helpful in lesson planning for live instruction as it is in designing mediated instruction. The "ingenuity" of the teacher or instructional designer will be reflected in the interpretation of the events and the prescriptions for the stimulus materials. All the events are listed on the left of the worksheet; and the stimuli, media, and prescriptions are attended to for each event. The designer may omit an event if he or she feels it is not necessary to the task or for a particular audience.

140

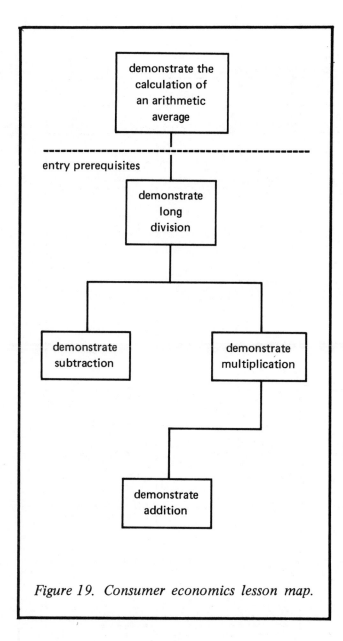

Figure 19. Consumer economics lesson map.

Note that the tentative media choices were all practical for the planned learning environment, so Columns 4 and 5 in Figure 20 are identical. Another example of a media analysis worksheet for a more elaborate media array uses a separate sheet for each instructional event for a lesson (Ackerman, 1977, pp. 493-495).

Time lines. How will these events be presented during the period of instruction? The designer has estimated that it will take between 40 and 50 minutes to teach this lesson. That represents a single class period for the target audience. How will the time be used? A "time line for sequence of instructional events" (Figure 21) will aid in planning the lesson by illustrating graphically how the instructional time will be spent.

The preceding examples in consumer economics (Figures 20 and 21) employed a lesson for a single objective. Often, however, the designer will attend to multiple objectives in a single lesson. In this case it is necessary to think about how the events will be sequenced and integrated for all of the objectives. To do this a "sequence" worksheet similar to that shown in Figure 22 can be used.

This particular worksheet (Figure 22) depicts a 55-minute period in which three objectives are to be attained by the learners (No.'s 6, 7, and 8 listed on the left). The time across the top of the page describes the instructional period, and the boxes in the "objectives/time matrix" show the number of the event and its relationships to other events. In this case, for example, event 1, attention and motivation, is to be taken care of in the first three minutes of instruction. It is also the case that the stimuli presented here are to serve that event for all three objectives at the same time (represented in the diagram by the vertical balloon). The next stimuli are to attend to "presentation of the objective" (event 2), and the next set of stimuli will serve two functions, event 3 for objective No. 6, and event 9 for objective No. 3 (taught in a previous lesson).

These examples show how a single set of stimuli can serve as an event of instruction for more than one objective at a time, and how a single set of stimuli might serve as two different events for two different objectives at the same time. What should be stressed is that the stimuli for each event can be identified. The grouping of events across objectives is a lesson-organization decision, as there are many ways of presenting the events with or without grouping.

Another common practice is to group events within a single objective, e.g., the instructional strategy of drill and practice may be seen as a repeated cycle of eliciting performance and providing feedback. In a problem-solving type objective, the event of "presenting the stimulus" may be grouped with the event "attention/motivation," where the first stimulus encountered by the learner is the problem to be solved. Whenever two or more events are grouped together within a single objective, the prescription should note this fact.

There is probably no way that we could go through all the different ways that events might be sequenced or grouped. Generally, instructional strategies seem to group and sequence events in a consistent manner. The value of the instructional

MEDIA ANALYSIS WORKSHEET

Unit Number _____ ; Specific Objective Number _____ ; Instructional Sequence (Lesson) Number _____ .

Objective: The student will demonstrate the calculation of the arithmetic average of a given set of numbers.

Column Number: 1 Instructional Event	2 Stimuli	3 Media Alternatives	4 Tentative (Ideal) Media	5 Final Media Choices	6 Rationale	7 Prescription
1. attention/ motivation	written word, spoken word	text, live teacher	teacher	teacher	The instruction is to take place in the classroom. A teacher is available and the students expect a live presentation.	Relate the need for being able to find averages as an important step in budgeting. Given an example of a variable expense that must be averaged; e.g., gasoline for the car.
2. present the objective	same	same + chalkboard, handouts, overheads	teacher/ chalkboard	teacher/ chalkboard	The students can copy the objective in their notes—reduces ambiguity that could result from an oral statement.	Write the objective on the chalkboard.
3. recall prerequi-sites	same + written symbols	pretest (oral or written)	written pre-test	written pre-test	Written performance on pre-requisites can be used for diagnostic and remedial pur-poses as well as recalling necessary skills.	Present a small but reliable set of multi-plication and division problems.
4. present stimuli	same	chalkboard, overheads, handouts	teacher, chalkboard	teacher, chalkboard	A problem can be developed from class input; gets the class involved.	Ask class members to estimate their use of some consumable product (coffee, water, gas). List the estimates from each student on the board.
5. provide learning guidance	concrete-visual image, spoken word	chalkboard, teacher, students, illustrated text	teacher, chalkboard, students	teacher, chalkboard, students	This is probably a procedure familiar to most students; they can contribute here. A concrete-visual image will aid encoding.	Ask if anyone knows the first step. Perform example on the board. Do the same with 2nd and 3rd steps. Draw three steps on board; label each from the bottom up; "(1) add quantities" "(2) count quantities" "(3) divide sum by count."
6. elicit performance	written word, spoken word	handouts, teacher, paper/ pencil	teacher, chalkboard, paper/ pencil	teacher, chalkboard, paper/ pencil	The teacher can give oral directions and put a problem on the board. Students can copy problem, and turn in work for teacher review.	The teacher tells the students to figure the average number of hours they spend watching television in a week (Sun. through Sat.).
7. provide feedback	written word, spoken word	teacher, chalkboard	same	same	The teacher can provide a generic model from which the students can judge the accuracy with which they applied the process. Arith-metic can be checked by col-lecting the worksheets.	Teacher solves the problem on the board using hypothetical data, and showing each of the three steps. Students hand in their worksheets.
8. assess performance	written word	worksheets	worksheets	worksheets	Worksheets provide a written record of the student's ability to apply the rules.	Review the worksheets for accuracy. Note any incorrect procedural errors on paper.
9. enhance retention & transfer	written word, spoken word	teacher/ review sheets	same	same	Periodic review with prob-lems the students will en-counter later in the course; will facilitate transfer.	Construct a practice exercise using problems requiring the averaging of variable expenses.

Figure 20. Sample media analysis worksheet.

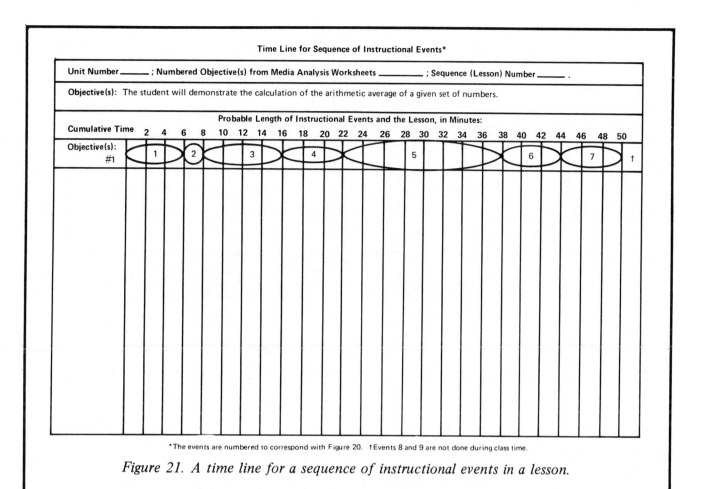

Figure 21. A time line for a sequence of instructional events in a lesson.

design model, when overlaid on a teacher's favorite strategy, is to illuminate the events of instruction that are missing. An analysis of instructional strategies using this technique would make an interesting study but is beyond the scope of this handbook.

The following media analysis worksheet (Figure 23) for objective No. 6, Figure 22, shows how events 5, 6, and 7 can be grouped.

Events 5, 6, and 7 are shown grouped together for objective No. 6, since the student is asked to go through several iterations of the classify/feedback process in the learning guidance event. This is not true in objective No. 7 (see Figure 24), where learning guidance is scripted as an independent event. Combining events across objectives and within objectives changes the nature of the media analysis worksheet. As shown in Figures 23 and 24, a single prescription for event 1 will suffice for all three objectives. Also shown in Figure 23 is how a single prescription may also include more than one event, as in the case of objective No. 6, events 5, 6, and 7.

Unfortunately, it is not possible to make optimum media selections by simply following a chart, table, or "cookbook," which would tell which medium is best for a given competency or instructional event. It is evident, however, that some media can present certain events of instruction better than other media (e.g., computers are much better suited to providing differentiated feedback than is broadcast television). Chapter 8 has provided descriptions of several media so that you can better select media for the events in a lesson.

Summary of Steps in Media Selection

Consider the following steps for media selection when designing instructional materials to attain a lesson objective (or objectives).

1. *Define the boundary conditions.* Note any limiting conditions for both development and implementation in terms of time, costs, skills, and resources available.

2. *Decide between individual and group instruction.* This affects the media choices as well as how the finished instructional materials are used. Two

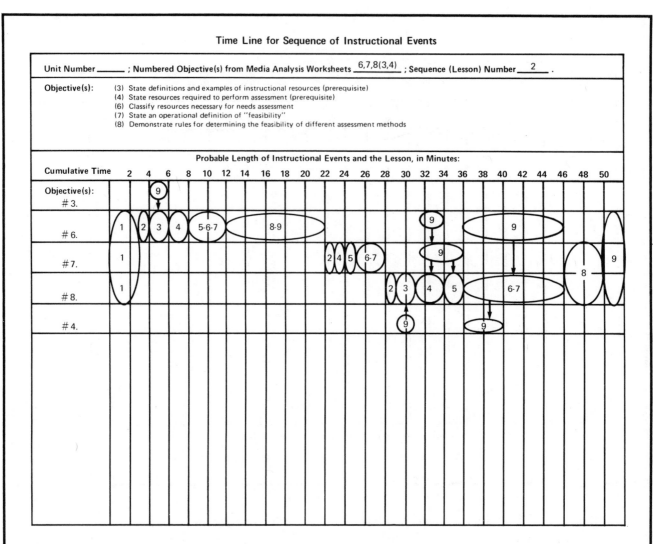

Figure 22. *Time line for a lesson having multiple objectives.*
(Student-prepared example by Nevin Robins.)

analyses of the same objectives and competencies could be made, one for individual instruction and one for group instruction. Or, different lessons could be planned for the two methods, for use with different members of a single group of learners.

3. *Identify the characteristics of the learners.*

4. *Identify a competency to be analyzed.* Note carefully the significant verbs (behaviors) and objects (content reference).

5. *List the nine instructional events.*

6. *Delete those events* that will not be utilized; provide a rationale for not including them.

7. *Arrange the entire list of events in the desired order,* and consider whether more than one application of each event is needed.

8. *List the type of stimuli for each event,* considering learner, task, and media characteristics.

9. *Write a prescription for each event,* or each group of events to be presented.

10. *List the alternate media* from which a choice is to be made for each event.

11. *Make a tentative media selection* for each event from among the alternates recorded. Note a rationale of advantages and disadvantages for group or individual use.

12. *Review an entire series of tentative media choices,* seeking optimum "packaging."

13. *Make final media choices for package units.*

14. *Write a prescription for the teacher* for instructional events not provided by the other media.

144

MEDIA ANALYSIS WORKSHEET

Unit Number _____ ; Specific Objective Number ___6___ ; Instructional Sequence (Lesson) Number _____ .

Objective: . . . Classify resources necessary for needs assessment.

Column Number: 1 Instructional Event	2 Stimuli	3 Media Alternatives	4 Tentative (Ideal) Media	5 Final Media Choices	6 Rationale	7 Prescription
1. attention/ motivation	wrtn. wrd. spkn. wrd.	text, chalkboard, overheads, instructor, VTR, audiotape	instructor, transparencies	instructor and overhead transparencies	Entire group of participants will begin instruction at the same time. A live instructor will facilitate group order. Projected transparencies will focus attention on the lesson.	Briefly introduce the entire lesson as the development of one of several basic skills for selecting assessment methods. Develop cartoon-like graphics illustrating feasible and non-feasible assessments. Preview each of the three objectives to be accomplished in this lesson.
2. present the objective	same as above	same as above	text	text in form of a handout	Available for future reference.	Write the objective in clear, concise terms. State that this behavior will be used in performing a needs assessment.
3. recall prerequisites	same	same	text	text in form of worksheets	Provides an opportunity to perform exercises without external judgment.	Present a list of types of resources from obj. #3. Ask participant to recall and write one or two examples of each type.
4. present stimuli	same	same	text		Continuity of media.	Present a comprehensive list of resources frequently required for needs assessment.
5. provide learning guidance 6. elicit performance 7. provide feedback	same as above	text, worksheets, overheads, slides, instructor, VTR, audiotape, student-recitation	worksheets	worksheets	Continuity of written medium, self-paced, immediate, neutral feedback.	Present list of resource types and list of common resources. Ask the participant to match the resources and types and to indicate appropriate units of measurement. Provide answer key; have participant check accuracy and reconsider answers found to be in error.

Figure 23. Media analysis worksheet, events grouped.
(Student-prepared example by Nevin Robins.)

Coordinating the Two Worksheets for Multiple Objectives

When designing instruction to teach two or more related objectives, the process of using the "time-line events sequence sheet" and the media analysis worksheets becomes a little more complex. It is suggested that the designer work on both simultaneously. The first step is to list the objectives to be taught on the left side of the sequence sheet. Then the first event for the first objective to be taught should be considered. The designer would consider if this event should be expanded to include the same event for the other objectives or other events for the same objective.

The stimulus(i) necessary for accomplishing this event is (are) specified next, and a tentative medium selection is made. At this point the prescription for the event should be written, and a time estimate for accomplishing the prescription can be made. The next step is to graphically represent that prescription on the instructional events sequence sheet by enclosing the time spaces with a box and putting the event number in the box.

For example, in starting to do a media analysis for the lesson, the objectives to be taught in the lesson would be put into the spaces on the left of the "sequence" worksheet (Figure 25).

145

MEDIA ANALYSIS WORKSHEET

Unit Number _____ ; Specific Objective Number __7__ ; Instructional Sequence (Lesson) Number _____ .

Objective: . . . . State operational definition of "feasibility."

Column Number: 1 Instructional Event	2 Stimuli	3 Media Alternatives	4 Tentative (Ideal) Media	5 Final Media Choices	6 Rationale	7 Prescription
1. attention/ motivation						Conducted simultaneously with objective # 6.
2. present the objective	wrtn. wrd. spkn. wrd.	text, overhead, slides, instructor VTR, tape	text	text	Appropriate for the participant's level of education; congruous with media used to this point.	State the objective as a question: "Can you operationally define *feasibility*?" Use a cartoon character pointing finger—balloon caption.
3. recall prerequisites					None needed for this type of objective or this audience.	
4. present stimuli	wrtn. wrd.	text, pictures	text, drawings		Cartoons to hold interest— text to present the verbal information.	Present two tasks . . . one that is feasible and one that is obviously not feasible. Relate verbally the definition of feasibility to availability and sufficiency of resources.
5. provide learning guidance	wrtn. wrd.				None needed with this audience.	
6. elicit performance	wrtn. wrd. spkn. wrd.	test, worksheet, paper/ pencil	paper/ pencil	paper/pencil	Sufficient for this task.	Ask the participants to write down their definition of feasibility.

*Figure 24. Media analysis worksheet showing how event 1
is coordinated with a prescription on another worksheet (Figure 23).*
(Student-prepared example by Nevin Robins.)

Time Line for Sequence of Instructional Events

Unit Number __20__ ; Numbered Objective(s) from Media Analysis Worksheets __1 & 2__ ; Sequence (Lesson) Number __1__ .

Objective(s):

Probable Length of Instructional Events and the Lesson, in Minutes:

Cumulative Time	2	4	6	8	10	12	14	16	18	20	22	24	26	28	30	32	34	36	38	40	42	44	46	48	50
Objective(s): (objective # 1 for this lesson)																									
(objective # 2 for this lesson)																									

Figure 25. Time-line sequence sheet, starting a new lesson.

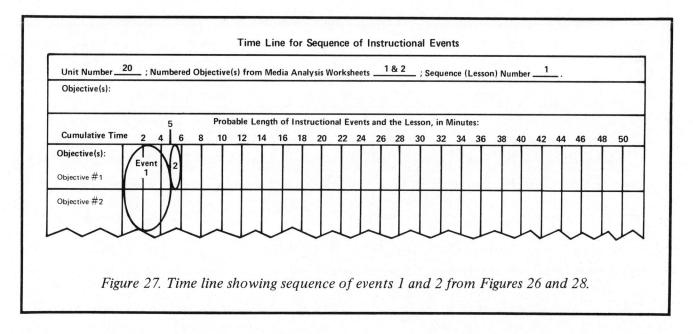

MEDIA ANALYSIS WORKSHEET

Unit Number __20__ ; Specific Objective Number __1__ ; Instructional Sequence (Lesson) Number __1__ .

Objective:

Column Number 1	2	3	4	5	6	7
Instructional Event	Stimuli	Media Alternatives	Tentative (Ideal) Media	Final Media Choices	Rationale	Prescription
1. attention/ motivation	wrtn. wrd. spkn. wrd.	text instructor	text	text	Replicable instruction, self-paced and suitable for learner.	Present the learner with a question that pertains to objective.

Figure 26. Media analysis worksheet for objective No. 1.

Time Line for Sequence of Instructional Events

Unit Number __20__ ; Numbered Objective(s) from Media Analysis Worksheets __1 & 2__ ; Sequence (Lesson) Number __1__ .

Objective(s):

Probable Length of Instructional Events and the Lesson, in Minutes:

Cumulative Time 2 4 5 6 8 10 12 14 16 18 20 22 24 26 28 30 32 34 36 38 40 42 44 46 48 50

Objective(s):

Objective #1 — Event 1 — 2

Objective #2

Figure 27. Time line showing sequence of events 1 and 2 from Figures 26 and 28.

We would then go to the media analysis worksheet for objective No. 1 for this lesson (Figure 26). The first event is motivation, so the columns for event 1 are filled in. If further analysis indicates that the original motivational event will carry the other objective, a single prescription may be written that will serve as event 1 for both objectives; it will be the first instructional stimuli the learner encounters with regard to this lesson. This prescription is thus for two objectives.

Now the designer would go back to the time-line sequence worksheet and block in event 1 for both objectives (Figure 27). (In this case, the motivational material is scheduled to be five minutes.)

The process now goes back to the media analysis worksheet (Figure 28) for objective No. 1, event 2, "present the objective." Let's hypothesize that this is easily done in writing and follows naturally from event 1. At this point we need only to present the first objective; we will present the second later in the lesson when it is time for it. The reading time should only be a few seconds, and it is entered in a very small space in Figure 27.

The process continues from media analysis sheet to sequence sheet for each event in objective No. 1 until design work on objective No. 2 is about to start. At that point the media analysis worksheet for objective No. 2 is started (Figure 29). Since the first event for objective No. 1 served for both objec-

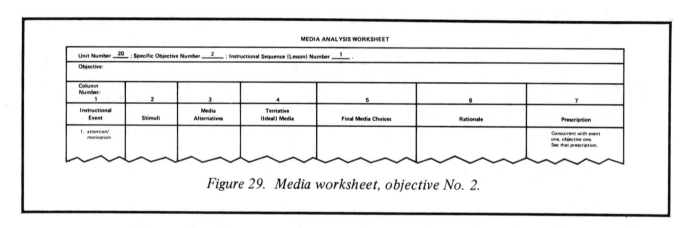

MEDIA ANALYSIS WORKSHEET

Unit Number __20__ ; Specific Objective Number __1__ ; Instructional Sequence (Lesson) Number __1__ .

Objective:

Column Number: 1	2	3	4	5	6	7
Instructional Event	Stimuli	Media Aleternatives	Tentative (Ideal) Media	Final Media Choices	Rationale	Prescription
1. attention/ motivation	wrtn. wrd. spkn. wrd.	text instructor	text	text	Replicable instruction, self-paced and suitable for learner.	Present the learner with a question that pertains to objective.
2. present the objective	written word	text	text		A written statement of the objective can be used as a later reference by the learner.	After the introduction (event one), present the first objective of the lesson. Highlight the objective by using bold print.

Figure 28. Media analysis worksheet.

MEDIA ANALYSIS WORKSHEET

Unit Number __20__ ; Specific Objective Number __2__ ; Instructional Sequence (Lesson) Number __1__ .

Objective:

Column Number: 1	2	3	4	5	6	7
Instructional Event	Stimuli	Media Alternatives	Tentative (Ideal) Media	Final Media Choices	Rationale	Prescription
1. attention/ motivation						Concurrent with event one, objective one. See that prescription.

Figure 29. Media worksheet, objective No. 2.

tives, the media analysis worksheet for objective No. 2 simply records this fact (Figure 29).

The process continues until all the events for both objectives are accounted for, or a reason why they were deleted is given.

In summary, the time line and media analysis worksheets are thus used together and prepared together. It is probably not possible to do one completely and then fill in the other, since a change in sequence decisions would call for an entire rewriting of prescriptions or confusing amendments. The purpose of the time line and media prescriptions is to lay the foundation for the next step in the materials production process. There, the media specialist takes the prescriptions and scripts, and creates prototype materials. On pages 156 and 157 are a time line and a media analysis worksheet that you may duplicate and use in your lesson planning, or modify to fit your needs.

Writing the Final Set of Prescriptions

Once the final media choices have been made, write a final set of prescriptions for how the materials are to be developed for each continuous use of the media chosen.

Such prescriptions may include directions to the film maker or other specialist who is to prepare the first-draft materials. The prescriptions specify the content as well as the "programming techniques" to be employed and the way the content is to be presented.

Depending upon the knowledge that you have of the various media, elements of your prescriptions may contain some of the technical terminology of the specialist with whom you are communicating. For example, you may prescribe "dissolves" for a film, or you may simply instruct the film maker to "show that time has elapsed," leaving him or her the choice of how to show this.

Your prescriptions may indicate not only "variety of examples," but also what the examples are to be, how they are to be interspersed with explanations, and how the learner should respond.

Keep the direction of S-R the same for the learning situation as for the real-life performance situation (symptom, then cause, as in electronic troubleshooting, not the reverse). Also,

(1) alternate "small steps" and "leaps forward";
(2) consider whole vs. part approach;
(3) build in review techniques;
(4) use selective stimulation of recall as a means of guiding thinking; or
(5) check likelihood of one-trial learning.

For content, you may specify pairs of pictures or words to be presented, the type of question about each to be posed to the learner, the form of the response, and the feedback form desired.

The course designer should have inputs from teachers concerning likely pupil characteristics, so matters such as the following can be specified:

inductive or deductive approach;
large or small steps defined;
frequency of student response defined;
type of feedback to be provided;
amount of repetition or redundancy;
vocabulary level desired;
sentence length and complexity;
use of self-test questions;
how to direct attention for discriminations;
when to use motion or still pictures;
pacing of the materials; and/or
kinds of generalizations to be tested.

Sample Prescription No. 1

The following four paragraphs are excerpted from course design materials prepared by Judith Garrett. In her original material, verbatim scripts were given for first-draft materials for some instructional events. Those scripts were interspersed with the following prescriptions for items to be prepared by other persons.

Globe is to be 24" in diameter and made of a plastic-like material such that it can be written on with a "grease" pencil and erased easily. The globe is to be air-filled so it can be manipulated by the students themselves with-out fear of its being damaged by dropping or any other treatment fourth graders would be likely to subject it to. The water areas are to be colored a very light blue, with each country's boundary and name lightly printed. The predominant feature of the globe is to be its lines of latitude and longitude, which are NOT numbered as to degrees. The directional lines are to be placed so there will be 17 lines of latitude and 12 lines of longitude. (Note: the above materials can be used for stimulus in several instructional events.)

The pictures should be at least 8" x 10" in size, and there should be only one vertical object in each picture. The background should be white so the vertical line suggested by the tree in the first picture is in sharp contrast to the white background of the picture. The next picture used should be one with the same format, but a different vertical object.

The booklet should be spiral bound with pages encased in a plastic covering. Each page should be 5½ x 8½ inches. The pages should be constructed in a manner similar to the examples to be provided, with a place for a new card to be inserted in each page each time the booklet is to be used by a different student. The answers are to be written in the window of each page and thus on the card, and not on the page of the booklet itself, so that the booklets are reusable. The booklet should have ten examples of objects in vertical positions and ten objects in horizontal positions, so that the booklet can be used for assessing attainment of either competency.

A poster presents ten objects, five of which are in a vertical position and five in a horizontal position. The objects are to be arranged in a numbered column on the left side of the poster, with a column on the right side of the poster stating whether each object is vertical or horizontal. A cardboard strip is to be provided to cover the answers. If the test is administered in an individualized instructional situation, the answer will be revealed to the student after he or she responds and the teacher makes note of his or her situation. If the entire group is ready for this instructional event at the same time, this device can be used to administer a group test. In this case, the students are told to number their papers from one to ten. All the objects are displayed; then after all responses have been made, the responses can be checked immediately by removing the cardboard cover and revealing the answers all at once.

Sample Prescription No. 2

The following set of prescriptions is taken from course design materials prepared by Nancy Benda.

COMPETENCY: Principle: Humans Exert Influence on Groups of People

Event	Stimuli	Prescription
Motivate.	Process	*Film:* Edit the student film provided to show that a change brought about by an individual for a specific purpose has a wider influence than planned . . . the influence was felt by whole groups of people.
Present objective and show value.	Spoken word	*Teacher:* Points out that man has the capacity to bring about change and that the change is often extensive enough to influence the lives of whole groups of people. No reference is made to "good" or "bad" changes, simply that man makes use of human and natural resources to bring about changes, which can influence the lives of people.
Provide model.	Printed word	*Handout:* Produced as follows: During the period of the westward movement of the United States, laws were made to govern the mass movement of people. In the western territories, the land was owned by the federal government. In order to encourage the development of the land, the government enacted the HOMESTEAD ACT, which allowed individuals to claim a limited amount of land for their own use. There was another act called the SWAMP LAND ACT, which gave every state all swamp and overflowed land within its borders. What influence would the HOMESTEAD ACT have? Would people move to new land if they could make it their own? Would you buy swamp land, when you could get high, dry land free?
Stimulate recall.	Spoken word	*Teacher:* Guides students to recall geography of Florida; the amount of swamp land within the state and the amount of land covered by high water part of the time. What was the main source of livelihood in this country at that time?
Induce transfer.	Spoken word	*Discussion:* Teacher leads students to see differences in HOMESTEAD ACT and the SWAMP LAND ACT.

Writing Scripts for the Prescriptions

The earlier sections of this Chapter showed how lessons may be *designed;* it now remains to be seen how they may be *developed.* After materials for learning are designed and developed, they must next be *produced*, and finally *tried out and improved.*

The writing of the prescriptions for the lesson events has been presented as a result of the development of *Media Analysis Worksheets,* and worksheets called *Time Line for Sequence of Instructional Events.* The writing of the *prescriptions* is a brief guide for *scripts* to be developed.

A recap of these design steps may assist the reader at this point:

1. Prepare a lesson map (Chapter 7).

2. Prepare a *Media Analysis Worksheet,* and a *Time Line for Sequence of Instructional Events* worksheet for the lesson (earlier parts of this Chapter). Select media having appropriate features (Chapter 8); write the prescriptions.

3. Write a first-draft *script,* which is a word-by-word and picture-by-picture summary of the content to be presented to the learner in the media chosen for each instructional event of the lesson (this section of Chapter 9).

4. Produce the instructional materials, as scripted, for the media selected.

5. Conduct tryouts and revision of the produced instructional materials (*formative evaluation,* Chapter 11), using the tests and assessment instruments (Chapter 10) to measure the attainment of the lesson objective(s).

The *design* phase may be thought to end with the writing of first-draft *scripts,* which implement the intent conveyed by the *prescriptions.* This book concentrates on *design* in order to write appropriate scripts based on all previous design steps accomplished. It thus does not cover further *development* of the scripts to take full advantage of the capabilities of the various media, nor does it include *production techniques* for each medium. However, the book does include formative evaluation of the materials (in Chapter 11), and a brief discussion of summative evaluation (Chapter 12).

If printed media are employed, either in self-instructional form (as in programmed booklets), or as a part of conventional instruction, the sophisticated techniques known to editors and publishers may not be needed to assess the adequacy of the content of the materials. If media such as motion pictures or TV are prescribed, the novice designer would need assistance in the production phase.

Even so, crude production in videotape or slide tape may be sufficient for early tryouts of materials. For more polished productions, the reader would either need to learn production techniques or work as a member of a team. However, teachers can use much of the material in this book in their own lesson designs, while teams usually produce the materials for the lessons. (See Chapters 8 and 9, respectively, in Briggs, 1977, for further details for the teacher and for teams.)

In summary, this handbook is devoted to the "design" phase; it does not contain information on how to "program" each of the media. This can be found in books on "programming." Special skills are needed for writing or preparing first-draft materials in various media, and there is also a need for special "production" techniques, such as those used to convert a film "script" into a "film." This handbook does not deal with techniques either for "scripting" (programming, writing, graphic art), or for "producing" (using a camera, developing film, or printing processes) materials in various media.

You may, perhaps, plan to end your work at this point, leaving to the specialists the job of preparing and revising the materials. If so, keep in close touch with the specialists who are completing your design.

If you plan to prepare your own "scripts" and/or participate in the production of the materials, a few general suggestions and comments are in order. You may want to consult references in special fields, or you may take courses in script writing or production for the separate media, as well as courses in speech, art, and graphics.

If you are using this book in a formal course, you may be encouraged to learn that many students produced simple but effective materials in specific media with no prior experience or training. With careful attention to the prescriptions, many have completed media new to them, and, after tryouts of scripts with individuals or classroom groups, found their materials were successful.

If you plan to prepare first-draft materials as contemplated in the performance objectives for this Chapter, the following suggestions may be helpful:

1. Develop the prescriptions into draft materials, using as much creativity and ingenuity as possible in developing the content for each instructional event.

2. Pay attention to presenting content, posing questions and problems, evoking responses, and providing feedback.

3. Build in evaluation frequently enough to be able to detect *where* a student has trouble and *what* the trouble is.

4. Have a plan for how much repetition, review, prompting, and vanishing to use.

5. Try to "weave a web" of learning by having the student respond in many ways to a variety of presentations of key concepts and principles.

6. Try to strike a good balance for problem-solving exercises between too little guidance to thinking and too much. Or, start with more guidance and gradually reduce it.

7. Provide opportunities for students to discover certain principles, when the preceding materials have helped prepare them for this. But don't take the time for them to "discover" everything they need to know.

8. Make some use of "rule-example" programming. Vary sequences of rule-example-example, with example-rule-example, etc. Have the learner supply some missing parts, then reconstruct the whole.

9. Vary the parts of the problem that are the "givens" as well as the parts the learner is to supply.

10. "Reverse" the elements "given" and "supplied."

11. When maps, pictures, drawings, tables or figures, or bar graphs are used, be sure to require the student *to do* something about them so you will know he or she won't skip over them. Be sure it makes a difference when he or she does skip over them. Don't use pictures just to decorate the page. Use them, as in using words, to evoke a definite response, as in programmed instruction. Use such phrases as " 'After studying the above graph, finish this sentence: 'These data show that the effect of increasing pressure is to _____ ,' or 'The principle illustrated in the picture on the right is _____ ,' or 'This drawing illustrates gravity _____ or pressure _____ (check one).' "

12. Plan a sequence of "information items," "test items," and "review items," to increase learning and retention.

13. Design "transfer" test items as well as "recall" items to increase the learner's ability to use the skills he or she is developing.

14. Use the "conditions of learning" discussed later in this Chapter.

Further research and experience will be needed to show the extent to which programming skills learned for one medium are generalizable to other media. However, it is our impression that with some training, such as in programmed instruction, "programming" skills transfer well to work in "scripting" for other media. Although specialized courses do add to one's capability, someone who can apply the above suggestions probably has acquired a rather generalizable skill already.

Sample Script for a Motivational Film

The following is taken from materials prepared by Nancy Benda.

COMPETENCY: Concept, "Natural Resources"
EVENT: Motivate
MEDIA: Film

	NATURAL RESOURCES
No audio.	Cartoon character pops through one line in credit.
Drum beat begins as character pops in. Beat becomes jazz.	Character listens to beat. Begins to snap fingers and clap to the beat (credit out). Character starts "swinging" down country path (no evidence of human life in sight).
Jazz combo joins beat and music becomes very "now."	Character looks for origin of sound, finds none, so decides to simply enjoy it and dances on down the path. As he or she passes, eyes of various shapes and sizes pop into picture from behind shrubs, branches, and holes in the ground.
Music goes out as action stops and comes back as action returns. Music builds to loud pitch and then *sudden quiet*.	Character "feels" eyes, turns quickly to try to see them but they close and are gone. He or she tries again, and again they are gone. Tries a third time; each time the movement is a little faster but always the same. Character shrugs off feeling of being watched and dances on down the path. Turns sharp corner and slams into large sign and falls back into sitting position. Camera follows character's gaze to the sign which reads:
No audio.	ENJOY OUR NATURAL RESOURCES
(Slow change of color from loud psychedelic shades to soft pastels.) Character voice:	Character turns to kneeling position. Turns full face to camera and asks: "What's a natural resource?"
	As camera pulls back, it is discovered that character is alone; the background is simply a pastel screen. Character scrambles to feet, "Hey! Where is everything? Everything has disappeared!" Sign pops back in.
Character voice:	"Oh, why, it's like the sign is trying to tell me something. OK, Sign, I'll go along; show me."
Music sneaks back and builds.	Scene builds again to the beat of the music. As various natural resources come

	on the screen, the character's face pops in and asks:
Character voice:	"That's a natural resource?" or says: "Now that's a natural resource!" Picture builds beautiful land of rich soil, lush forests, rocks, waterfalls and streams, fish, birds, animals .... All join character and dance to music.
	Letters dance in from all sides and form:
	NATURAL RESOURCES
Music fades.	Go to black.

Comment on the Above Script

The reader should note carefully that the above script was designed for only one instructional event: *motivate*. The main purpose, therefore, is to draw attention to the objective of the lesson, which is to learn the concept, "natural resources." Otherwise, one might criticize the script as having "no content," only a mood. If this script were designed for any other of the nine instructional events, it would be deemed to be faulty and inadequate. This script is actually a good example of the use of a film for motivation.

It is clear that an entirely different kind of film would be required were the purpose of the film to provide any event other than "motivate."

Perhaps most often, a film presents the stimulus after the teacher provides "attention" and "informing of the objective." Following the film, the teacher evokes "responding."

Sample Script for a Teacher Conducted Activity

The following script is taken from materials prepared by Judith Garrett.

Competency: The concept "vertical."
Stimuli: Real objects, pictures, and teacher actions and teacher comments. Teacher actions are shown to the left; comments in the middle column.

TEACHER ACTIONS	TEACHER COMMENTS	INSTRUCTIONAL EVENTS
Point to longitudinal lines on a globe.	The lines you see going from top to bottom of the globe are called vertical lines. Any line going from top to bottom or up and down is a vertical line, not just a line on a globe. All lines that go up and down or from top to bottom on a	Gain attention and present stimulus.

page, a globe, or anywhere are *vertical*.

Hold a pencil upright.	When I hold a pencil this way, the pencil is in a vertical position.	Present stimulus and guidance to thinking by use of a variety of examples.
Go to closet, get a broom, hold it upright.	I am holding this broom so that it is vertical.	
Place stick of chalk in upright position.	This chalk is vertical when I hold it in this position.	
	Now, I am going to show you some pictures of objects that are in vertical positions.	Enhance generalization.
Show a picture of a redwood tree.	This is a picture of a redwood tree. It is in a vertical position. Most trees grow in vertical positions.	
Show picture of telephone pole.	This telephone pole is in a vertical position.	
Show a picture of the edge of a cliff.	The edge of this cliff is vertical.	
Show picture of car, point to radio aerial.	This aerial is in a vertical position.	
Show "Peanuts" cartoon: Snoopy with ears erect.	In this cartoon, Snoopy's ears are vertical.	
Show booklet according to prescription.	Now let's find out how well you can recognize vertical lines. I'm going to give you some booklets.	Assess attainments and provide feedback.

(End of quotation from script)

Comment on the Above Script

At this point in the lesson, the teacher changes media to accomplish another event, "assess attainment." The booklet was prescribed on page 149. It is designed to enable the teacher to conduct either individualized or group testing, with feedback. This illustrates the use of two media to provide four instructional events for a lesson having a single objective.

Alternate Formats for Media Analysis

On page 139 we gave a very condensed summary of the purpose of each of the seven columns in the Media Analysis Worksheet. If you would like more detail, see the expanded discussion given elsewhere (Briggs, 1977, pp. 265-273).

Note also that simpler Media Analysis Worksheets can be used. These simpler sheets have been called "Lesson Plans," and examples are given elsewhere (Briggs, 1977, Chapter 8).

Still a third way to do lesson design is to combine a simple worksheet with a condensed script. This is especially appropriate when a teacher is both the designer and the presenter of the instruction. The *Sample Script for a Teacher Conducted Activity*, just presented, is an example of this. Note, in this example, that there is a single lesson objective (competency), and that the stimuli for the whole lesson are listed once. Then the instructional events and the corresponding teacher actions and comments are presented.

Still a further alternative is shown in *Sample Prescription No. 2*, on p. 150. There, only three columns were used, for event, stimuli, and prescription.

These simplifications omit the explicit listing of media alternatives and ideal media and rationales, giving only the final media choices. Thus, the *Media Analysis Worksheets* shown earlier in this Chapter could be reduced from seven columns to three or four. A suggestion is to use the full sheet when first learning the process, then simplify it as experienced is gained in its use.

Using Conditions of Learning When Writing Prescriptions and Scripts

Having completed our brief glimpse of writing prescriptions and scripts, and our recap of the final procedures in production of instructional materials, we now devote special attention to one set of guidelines for scripting which has been mentioned frequently but not dealt with systematically up to this point in this book. This omission is planned rather than accidental. One reason for the omission is simply that Gagné (1977b) has devoted an entire book to this subject, and it is one of the three books recommended as essential reading at the opening of this Chapter, along with the other two books which cover the subject more briefly.

While "conditions of learning" broadly refer to all the principles of lesson design, they are used more specifically as an analytical tool in writing scripts to enhance their instructional effect. Stated another way, use of these "conditions" helps insure that the instructional events are scripted with due regard for the *variety of outcomes* represented in lesson objective(s). A convenient table has been prepared to summarize how these *conditions* may be used as one guide to scripting for *each instructional* event for *each domain of outcome* (Briggs, 1977, pp. 275-277). A similar, briefer summary table is also presented by Gagné and Briggs (1979, p. 166).

It may be further noted that whereas the *instructional events*, discussed earlier, represent what is *common* to effective lessons *among* all domains of outcomes, the *conditions of learning* portray what is *special* for events in a specific domain or sub-domain. For example, *guiding thinking* is done by giving direct prompts to the learner for an *information objective,* while for an intellectual skills objective, *indirect* cues are given. For cognitive strategies, providing *opportunity* for thinking and a *challenging* problem are appropriate conditions. Thus, the instructional event of *guiding thinking* is to be handled very differently for objectives in different domains of learning.

Other instructional events, like *gaining attention*, may not vary much among domains; it may vary more according to the age of the learner. *Stating the objective* also may not vary much among domains.

In summary, the events of *presenting the stimulus* and *guiding thinking* are the two events deserving of special attention with reference to employing appropriate conditions of learning when writing scripts for a lesson.

The reader is strongly urged to refer to the recommended readings on this subject. However, a very brief recap is given here for *conditions of learning* to be designed into appropriate instructional events when writing prescriptions and scripts.

Memorized Verbatim Learning
1. Provide mnemonic devices or memory "bridges" which are meaningful. Example: "Spring forward; fall back," to remember which way the clock is to be reset twice per year.
2. For memorizing poems, call attention to the meaning. Then rehearse a stanza at a time if the poem is lengthy, adding a stanza with each repetition.
3. Frequent practice and spaced reviews.

Learning of Facts
1. Make meaningful associations to provide a rich context.
2. Rehearsal and review.

Substance Learning
1. Present questions to be answered after reading or

hearing the material.
2. Teach learners to "read; recite; review."
3. Provide a set to look for the major ideas rather than details.
4. Encourage students to paraphrase ideas, section by section.
5. Provide an "Information Test" like those in this book.

Discriminations
1. Point out the distinctive features of the shapes or other features of objects or symbols to be discriminated.
2. Use a variety of examples.

Concrete Concepts
1. Point out the relevant and irrelevant attributes so that the relevant ones will be encoded.
2. Use a variety of examples of non-relevant features in objects which also have the relevant features.

Defined Concepts
1. Give a definition.
2. Show relevant and irrelevant (correct and incorrect) instances of the definition, emphasizing their differences.
3. Provide a variety of instances to be classified as relevant, *using* the definition.
4. Make clear the difference between a definition and *use* of the definition to classify examples.

Rule Using
1. Demonstrate the application of the rule.
2. Have the learner demonstrate the rule for a variety of applicable instances.
3. State the rule.

Problem Solving
1. Make clear the features of a successful solution.
2. Use only indirect guidance, when needed.
3. Provide feedback.

Cognitive Strategies
1. Make clear the meaning of a "novel" solution.
2. Provide a stimulating environment.
3. Provide feedback.

Motor Skills
1. Provide a verbal "executive subroutine."
2. Demonstrate and explain each part.
3. Provide whole and part practice, if lengthy.
4. Use verbal prompts.

Attitudes
1. Provide a respected model displaying the attitude and receiving reinforcement.

2. If persuasive communications are used, begin them close to the learner's current attitude, then widen the gap.

3. Conditioning and shaping methods.

Summary of Steps in Media Selection

In the present model, media are selected for each instructional event for each competency of each objective. While making media selections for each instructional event may occasionally lead to the use of a single medium for all the events of an entire competency or even an entire objective, this is not usually the outcome of the analysis. In making final decisions, one seeks when possible to employ each medium for some optimum length of time—that is, to change media often enough to avoid boredom, but not often enough to make the change awkward or too time-consuming. Final decisions should be made by scanning tentative choices for some fairly lengthy series of events to decide upon the "packages of units" to be prepared. Then a prescription is written for each package, i.e., for one continuous period of use for each medium.

In preparing both prescriptions and scripts, incorporate the appropriate *conditions of learning* for the type of outcome represented by the objective.

Production of the scripts may be accomplished by the designer who wrote the prescriptions, or by media production specialists. The two persons should work closely together to retain the *intent* of the prescriptions, while modifying scripts in accordance with the full capabilities of the media to be employed.

Blank Worksheets for Your Use

On the following pages, we have provided a blank *Time Line for Sequence of Instructional Events* and a blank *Media Analysis Worksheet*. You may reproduce a supply of each at will for your lesson designs.

TIME LINE FOR SEQUENCE OF INSTRUCTIONAL EVENTS

Unit Number _____ ; Numbered Objective(s) from Media Analysis Worksheets _____ ; Sequence (Lesson) Number _____ .

Objective(s):

Probable Length of Instructional Events and the Lesson, in Minutes:

Cumulative Time	2	4	6	8	10	12	14	16	18	20	22	24	26	28	30	32	34	36	38	40	42	44	46	48	50

Objective(s):

MEDIA ANALYSIS WORKSHEET

Unit Number _____ ; Specific Objective Number _____ ; Instructional Sequence (Lesson) Number _____ .

Objective:

Column Number: 1	2	3	4	5	6	7
Instructional Event	Stimuli	Media Alternatives	Tentative (Ideal) Media	Final Media Choices	Rationale	Prescription

157

Chapter 10
Student Assessment

Chapter in This Book	Recommended Readings		
	Briggs, L.J. (Ed.) *Instructional Design: Principles and Applications.* Englewood Cliffs, N.J.: Educational Technology Publications, 1977.	Gagné, R.M., and Briggs, L.J. *Principles of Instructional Design*, 2nd ed. New York: Holt, Rinehart, and Winston, 1979.	Gagné, R.M. *The Conditions of Learning*, 3rd ed. New York: Holt, Rinehart, and Winston, 1977.
9	Chapters 7, 8, 9	Chapters 4, 5, 9, 10, 11, 13, 14	Chapters 3-10 Chapter 12
⑩	**Chapters 6, 10, 11**	**Chapter 12**	
11	Chapter 10	Chapter 15	

Introduction

The purpose of instructional design is to produce effective instructional materials or instructional environments. How do we know when these have been accomplished? The only way is to observe, measure, and evaluate the student's behavior after the instruction has taken place. This calls for evaluation instruments that are valid, reliable, and efficient in assessing what the student knows or can do. In Chapter 4, we dealt with writing valid test items; in this Chapter, we deal with other aspects of performance test development. Good evaluation instruments are not easy to construct, and designers typically underestimate the task. This Chapter discusses the problems and considerations of designing instruments and the related issue of student grading. Some of the major issues are:

(1) selecting valid tests for identified objectives;
(2) distinguishing among the several meanings of reliability;
(3) recognizing factors in efficiency and practicality of tests;
(4) distinguishing norm-referenced grading from criterion-referenced grading; and
(5) defining ways of adjusting to inadequate time or resources for conducting the preferred evaluations of student performance.

Chapter 10 Information Test

1. For reasons of time and economy, you can't afford to directly measure an objective. Give three alternative test strategies.

    a. ....

    b. ....

    c. ....

2. You give a test of 20 arithmetic problems. Tell how it would be graded under norm-referenced and criterion-referenced grading systems.

    a. norm-referenced ....

    ....

    ....

    b. criterion-referenced ....

    ....

    ....

    ....

3. What would be the major purpose of giving these tests?

    a. end-of-course ....

    b. end-of-unit ....

    c. single objective ....

    d. subordinate competency ....

    ....

4. State the difference between productive and reproductive learning. ....

....

....

5. When is it acceptable to "teach for the test"? ....

....

....

6. What are the arguments against grading on the curve?

    a. ....

    ....

    b. ....

    ....

    c. ....

    ....

7. What is meant by setting standards in terms of prediction?

....

....

....

8. What two kinds of items might be included in a test for a rule-using objective? ....

....

....

_9_. Multiple-choice tests are convenient and widely used. When should they not be used? ....
....
....

 _10_. A test is valid if it measures what it ....
....

 _11_. Often a test can be made by merely changing a few words in the corresponding ....

 _12_. The validity of a criterion-referenced test can be judged by comparing the .... with the ....

 _13_. Correlation coefficients are used only when the test is an .... measure of the objective.

 _14_. Tests requiring complex judgments are often scored by comparing the student's answers with those of ....

 _15_. Give some synonyms for reliability of a test. ....
....

Chapter 10 Performance Objectives

26. Generate an evaluation instrument for assessing student performance on stated objectives.

27. Generate a criterion-referenced grading system that includes the importance of the objectives and transfer of learning when setting criterion-performance levels. (See the answer key on page 257 for criteria for evaluating performance on these objectives.)

The Units for Testing

Once the course objectives, unit objectives, and lesson objectives have been defined and arranged in the three levels of ICMs, it is desirable to prepare evaluative tests for two general uses:

(a) for use in tryouts and revisions of first-draft materials *to evaluate the materials*; (formative evaluation, Chapter 11); and

(b) for normal classroom use, *to evaluate student performance*. That is, the performance of *tryout learners* is used as a guide to evaluate and improve the materials; and when course revisions are completed, and the course is in normal operation, *regular student performances* are evaluated to see if the objectives of the instruction have been met (student assessment).

Since tests are needed for both the above purposes, the course-development phase *could* include preparation of tests for all of the following levels of objectives in the course:

(a) end-of-course objectives;
(b) end-of-unit objectives;
(c) lesson objectives; and
(d) subordinate competencies of specific lesson objectives.

(And in programmed instruction, a "criterion (test) frame" follows every few teaching frames.)

Tests at all four levels of objectives are useful for evaluation of performance of the student population after the course is in normal operation. Tests over competencies of an objective are useful for remedial purposes, to find the source of trouble when a student fails a test over a specific behavioral objective. Tests at the level of specific objectives can assure the teacher that the student is ready to go on to the next objective. Tests over units can reveal the learner's mastery over more complex objectives. End-of-course tests can measure the student's ability to use all of his or her prior learning to solve still more complex problems or to apply his or her knowledge to a wider range of situations.

Preparing Suitable Tests

Fortunately, the basic principles are the same whether one is preparing an evaluative test over a course objective, a unit objective, a specific behavioral objective (lesson objectives), or a subordinate competency. Incidentally, tests at all these levels are actually tests over four different levels of *behavioral* objectives. The terminology often used in this book, associating behavioral with specific objectives, is employed only to follow a common convention in defining behavioral objectives at the level here called *specific*, e.g., somewhere between unit objectives and subordinate competencies in complexity. Thus, a lesson objective may consist of a single behavioral objective or several of them, or of a subordinate competency of an objective.

It is therefore not necessary to treat separately the procedures for preparing these different levels of tests, nor to provide separate exercises at each of these levels. Accordingly, in the examples and exercises in this Chapter, objectives at all levels are chosen to provide practice in evaluating the congruence of objectives and tests.

Validity of Tests

It is conventional in textbooks on test construction to speak of four characteristics of tests:

(a) validity,
(b) reliability,
(c) efficiency, and
(d) practicality.

These are covered briefly; standard texts may be consulted for more detail.

A test is valid if it measures what it is *supposed to measure*—in the present context, if it measures the *objective* for which it is intended. It is particularly important to examine the *verbs* in an objective to see if the *kind of capability* and the kind of test behavior (action verb) are actually measured by the test. If the objective says, "Without references, the student will correctly summarize in writing two of the three standard processes for the commercial production of steel," then it is clear that the only relevant kind of test would be a *written essay* test requiring him or her to correctly *summarize* two of the three processes taught. No true-false nor multiple-choice test would measure the performance, "summarize." Nor would it be valid to have the learner check which of six printed descriptions of processes are the correct ones, nor to have him or her set up a laboratory demonstration of the process. It would also be an invalid test to ask the learner to summarize by writing how to manufacture *brass* or *silver nitrate*. Both the *verbs* and the *object* (steel) must be correctly used in the test for it to be valid. This illustrates the importance of stating the objective to reflect what the designer really means. If the designer really means "recognize the processes" or "demonstrate the processes," he or she should state it in the objective. If he or she meant silver nitrate, not steel, he or she should say so in the objective. It is not only *invalid testing* to state one thing in an objective but ask for something else on the test, it is also self-deceiving and unfair to the student.

Reproductive and Productive Learning

You have undoubtedly noticed that some objectives are more complex than others. Some require recall of specific facts and information, and others require the application of concepts, rules, or problem-solving strategies. For the sake of discussing types of tests and test items, we need to distinguish between two major categories: productive learning and reproductive learning.

Productive learning (and associated objectives) requires use of previously learned concepts and principles often needed to solve problems.

Reproductive learning involves rote memorization and recall (verbal information) as well as motor skills learned through repetition or practice.

For reproductive learning objectives, the teacher usually tells the student the exact content that will be used for the test, and he or she also has the student practice the content. Diagrammed below are some ways to achieve suitable compatibility among the *objective*, the *test*, and the *learning situation* (practice condition) for *reproductive tasks*. For brevity, not all the objectives are expressed in the five-component format.

Examples of Reproductive Learning

Objective	Test	Practice Condition
1. Given a printed checklist to follow, the student will adjust the power supply, making no procedural errors, and achieving a setting within two volts of normal.	1. "Perform the power supply adjustment using this checklist as a guide. Observe the procedure printed here; your final setting must be accurate within two volts."	1. Give student practice in doing the procedure, with a checklist to be followed. Correct errors as he or she practices.
2. Upon request, the student can orally recite "Old Ironsides," without error or noticeable hesitation.	2. "Recite 'Old Ironsides' exactly as it is printed in the book; do not hesitate, or change any words."	2. Give student practice, with feedback, in reciting orally to a listener; earlier give him or her the poem to study and practice alone, using the poem in the book to prompt himself or herself.
3. Student will be able to state the probability of either a head or a tail on the flip of a fair coin.	3. "State the probability of a head on the flip of a fair coin."	3. Tell the student the probability, and give examples. Ask him or her practice questions, and provide correction.
4. Student will be able to type 40 words per minute from a text not seen before, using standard scoring for time and accuracy.	4. Administer text B (not seen before by student) under standard test conditions.	4. Give student practice on texts A, C, and D. Give practice tests under standard conditions for texts E, F, G.
5. Student will be able to write the chemical symbols for all the elements.	5. Administer list of names of elements; student is to write in the chemical symbols.	5. Give list of paired names and symbols for study and drill, with feedback. Use "prompts" when necessary; then withdraw them when they are no longer needed.

Examples of Productive Learning

Objective	Test	Practice Condition
1. Student will demonstrate solution of any set of linear equations with one unknown in writing, arriving at correct answers for at least eight out of ten.	1. Give a test of ten problems not encountered during learning.	1. Teach each subordinate competency. 2. Give practice in solving problems with feedback. If student fails practice tests, give test over each competency, and provide necessary remedial instruction.
2. Student will learn principles of social science, and apply them to ex-	2. Give a written "case study test," describing a novel social situation. Ask	3. Teach the principles. Demonstrate applications to practice case study prob-

plain novel situations, in writing.	student to explain the situation.	lems. Give student practice, with feedback, on other case study problems.
3. Using principles about human and natural resources, student can predict which new industries might succeed in Florida.*	3. Describe several proposed new industries for Florida, and ask student to tell which would be most likely to succeed, and why.	4. Teach principles relating to human and natural resources. Teach Florida resources. Give practice on problems with industries other than those to be used on the test.
4. Given mass and velocity, student will solve for force.	4. Give student problems to solve for value of force.	5. Teach relevant concepts, principles, and formulas. Give practice at problem solution, with feedback.

*The writers have paraphrased this example from a course planning document by Nancy Benda.

We may now examine the circumstances in which it is proper to "teach for the test." We will see that this has a different meaning for different kinds of learning.

To summarize the gist of the above examples: for *reproductive* learning, the objective, the test, and the practice condition for each involve clearly identified actions or words to be acquired and used; the student *directly practices* the *identical* verbal content to be tested in memorizing the poem and the chemical notations; he or she practices with *similar* verbal content in the example on typing; and he or she practices the *exact procedures* with the aid of a *standard checklist* in adjusting the power supply. In the case of the toss of a coin, only the specification of "heads" on the test differs from the statement of the objective.

In the examples of *productive* learning, the student is taught the principles he or she is to learn to apply, and he or she is given practice in solving problems of the *same nature but different specific content* compared to those used for the test. In problem-solving, the student must learn:

(a) the principles;
(b) how to apply them in a relevant situation; and
(c) how to decide *which* principles are *relevant* to a given problem situation. These three things must be taught before the test is administered, and the specific test problems should always be different from those used for teaching. Because

productive learning requires that *transferable* skills be learned and applied in a selective manner to *relevant* problems, it may be appropriate to describe the *reproductive* learning situation as "stimulus bound," while *productive* learning is not limited to stimuli encountered during practice (learning).

Valid tests may often contain words much different from those used in the statements of objectives or for instruction for *productive* learning, while for *reproductive* learning the words in the objective and the test may be almost the same, and the *practice words* are often identical to the responses to the test.

For the benefit of those readers who have studied test validity in other contexts, it might be useful to note that the above examples of tests are *direct measures of the desired criterion performance described in the behavioral objectives.* Only an exercise in precise thinking is required to determine that the tests are indeed valid. No "correlation coefficients" are needed in justifying the tests in terms of the objectives, because we have set out to measure the desired performance as stated in the objectives as *directly* as possible. Whether the tests are over problem solving or rote memory, the learner's performance is "scored" in terms of a "correct answer key" prepared by the test designer, who should record the "correct" answers in the scoring key.

There are some situations in which the "correct" answers may be in doubt because experts disagree. For example, a student in psychology may be given a written case history describing the behavior and psychological test records of a hypothetical child. The student may be asked to interpret the data and to "diagnose" the behavior deviation described. Experts who take the test may give differing diagnoses. Therefore, the student may be "scored" in terms of the degree to which his or her answers agree with the combined (or averaged) judgments of the experts. The student's score represents a correlation of his or her answers with those of the experts. On a diagnosis for which there is close agreement among experts, a matching diagnosis by the student would represent a "valid high score." But on a case in which the experts widely disagree, the validity of the student's answer (score) is indeterminate. Validity may then be lacking because of uncertainty as to what the "scoring key" should contain.

Another source of lack of validity in a test arises when the learner performance measured differs from the performance described in the objective. Suppose the objective is as follows: "The student will generate in writing at least six behavioral objectives for the course he or she is designing." But due to class size and the lack of assistants, the instructor is unable to read and score six objectives written by each member of the class. So he or she gives a multiple-choice test, asking students to select which of several phrases is appropriate for one of the criteria for objectives. This test could contain items such as the following:

1. Which phrase expresses the action verb?
    a. given ten algebra problems
    b. within 30 minutes
    c. solves for value of "x" in writing
    d. without errors in procedure
    e. demonstrates the solution of equations
2. Which of the criteria for objectives is met in this phrase: "without deviating from the checklist provided?"
    a. tools and constraints
    b. object
    c. action verb
    d. capability verb

The hypothetical instructor may or may not have designed a valid test. It appears *invalid* because the behavior of *selecting* the correct answers is not the behavior described in the objective—"generate in writing at least six behavioral objectives." So, the test items appear to lack congruence with the objective. We may conclude then that it appears that the test is not valid. To be consistent, the instructor should either change the nature of the test, or change the objective to describe the multiple-choice behavior measured in this test.

But suppose our hypothetical instructor has fewer students in his or her class (or more assistants) the next semester; so he or she tests the students *both ways*. That is, he or she asks the students to take the same multiple-choice test used last semester, and then asks each student to write six behavioral objectives. He or she scores both tests, and finds that the correlation coefficient between the two sets of sources is .60. His or her written test of six objectives is valid because it is the *criterion performance* he or she wants to measure. Does the multiple-choice test score *predict* the desired criterion performance? If it predicted completely, the correlation would be perfect (1.0). If the prediction were completely useless (invalid), the correlation would be zero. So the multiple-choice test has some validity; but how much? If we square the value of the correlation (.60) we get .36. This is commonly interpreted to mean that the multiple-choice score predicts the desired criterion performance about 36 percent better than mere guessing (or random assignment of scores) would predict criterion performance.

If the correlation between the two tests had been .90 instead of .60, the predictive value would have been .81 instead of .36. The instructor then might have preferred the ease of scoring of the multiple-choice test to the added validity of grading all the written behavioral objectives.

But the reason for writing the behavioral objectives was that students could go on to other steps in a model for the design of instruction. It would appear better to grade three rather than six objectives written by the students than to use the (only somewhat valid) multiple-choice test.

Why did the correlation of .60 occur? Possibly because the recognition responses (matching examples to the criteria) required in the multiple-choice test is a subordinate competency for generating behavioral objectives, or at least for judging one's own objectives before deciding they are ready for evaluation. However, the correlation also suggests that matching behavior is not all that is required to write good objectives; there are other needed subordinate competencies which the multiple-choice test does not measure. Thus, the lack of validity is due to *incomplete* testing more than to *irrelevant* testing.

It is thus possible to evaluate the validity of a test by starting with one which lacks *face* (apparent) validity (however convenient it is to construct, administer, and score), and correlating it with criterion performance. Such an indirect approach to test validation is to be avoided when possible.

However, for practical reasons, sometimes it is too costly or inconvenient (or impossible) to measure performance. Then, this correlational approach, using *indirect* rather than *direct* measures, can be employed.

But, in most cases, the desired objectives *can* be measured *directly*, thus simplifying validation and avoiding the need for calculating correlation coefficients.

Is the evaluation of three (rather than six) behavioral objectives from each student in the above example better than resorting to the multiple-choice test? In the writers' opinion, yes it is, because writing objectives is a valid test; it is a direct measure of the criterion performance described in the course objectives. But multiple-choice tests can measure some relevant subordinate competencies, and are often used for this purpose in this book. The scoring of three rather than six objectives leads to the next topic.

Reliability of Tests

A reliable test gives a stable, adequate measure of whatever it measures. While professional test designers treat reliability as a complex matter, for present purposes, reliability is simplified.

When constructing a test that will be valid for a given objective it is designed to measure, it is also important to test the student thoroughly enough to be satisfied that resulting scores accurately reflect his or her true ability to perform on the objective. Within limits, longer tests generally result in more reliable scores. A teacher's judgments about this appear realistic. For example, a test of ten problems in algebra may be enough to give a fairly accurate indication of how well a student might have done on a longer test. If scores on a test of ten problems would correlate .80 with a test of 50 problems, the teacher would probably prefer to keep the ten-problem test, and use the extra time to teach the next objective.

There are several reasons to expect less than a perfect correlation between the tests of ten and 50 problems, respectively. The ten problems might be preferred because the student could do his or her best on them before getting tired or impatient. If he or she did not get tired or impatient, however, the 50-problem test might be better, because

(a) it samples more of the entire range of possible problems;

(b) getting early problems right might contain practice value for later problems (strengthen subordinate competencies); and

(c) if momentary distractions of attention or variations in well-being or alertness occur, the longer test may permit these effects to "average out" better (e.g., there may be more distractions during certain portions of the total test period).

Thus, *moderately long* tests might serve better in avoiding effects from the "accident" by which particular problems were selected for the test, and might be a more accurate measure of the student's best possible performance, as compared to longer or shorter tests. Such moderate-length tests might also be best in view of warm-up effects, distraction, energy, and practice effects.

Reliability of tests is estimated in several ways, such as:

(a) correlating scores on one half of the test with scores on the other half, such as by totaling scores on odd-numbered items separately from scores on the even-numbered items; or

(b) correlating scores on two halves of the test (or the whole test) taken a day apart. These and other techniques are designed to evaluate the internal consistency of the test itself, the consistency of the student's performance from time to time, and the effects of the length of the test.

Such measures are often used not only to estimate the reliability of a test, but also to change the test in ways designed to increase its reliability. But, unfortunately, some changes intended to increase reliability may also decrease the validity of the test, although this is not always so.

In design and evaluation of instructional materials and procedures, if one must choose between validity and reliability, the writers strongly advocate seeking the highest validity consistent with acceptable reliability.

Using the example in the previous section of this Chapter, the writers would prefer to evaluate only three written behavioral objectives, with the degree of reliability likely to be possible using specific criteria for scoring, than to use the multiple-choice test with the validity coefficient cited in this example. The writers found close agreement among five evaluators using criterion sheets to evaluate the same assignment.

Thus, ten problems may be enough for a certain algebra test, and one composition may be enough for some English tests.

Reliability of test scores may be improved for essays and other less objective evaluations by

(a) making the scoring system explicit for students and evaluators, such as by using the criterion sheets mentioned in evaluating "assignments" in this volume;

(b) scoring one essay question for each student first, then scoring the next question for each student, rather than scoring the entire test before going on to the next student's paper; and

(c) reshuffling the papers when starting to score another question (especially if the class is small). These procedures improve the *objectivity* of scoring, considered to represent one aspect of reliability. There may be greater ease of scoring in focusing on one judgment at a time for each student, rather than trying to judge an entire test for each student (which requires keeping all criteria in mind at all times).

Efficiency of Tests

Efficient use of evaluation time is important in obtaining the most valid and reliable evaluation data per student per unit of time for test administration and scoring. One aspect of efficiency is to design as short a test as possible, which yields validity and reliability. An objective (multiple-choice, true-false, matching) test usually rates high on efficiency, because it raises many issues for student responses in a short time. But such tests should be carefully scrutinized for validity, as mentioned earlier.

Efficient use of time in scoring is also important. While evaluation of essay tests and student products (term papers, art products, research reports) may be more time-consuming than objective-type test scoring, it may also yield the most information about the student and prove to be the most valid test for a given objective.

Practicality of Tests

Practicality is determined by considering all factors relating to time, effort, space, or equipment needed to administer, score, and interpret tests.

For example, a chemistry teacher might wish to evaluate the laboratory technique of his or her students, but he or she is probably more likely to evaluate reports written by the students than to observe each student's technique for each experiment. The records of procedures each student keeps may be used for practicality, although this is not a very valid measure of many aspects of laboratory technique. However, a cumulative record of student performance may be very reliable

and valid, without need for the physical presence of an evaluator, e.g., a batting average for the season. An art teacher may judge the finished product of a student without having observed him or her make each brush stroke. A music teacher may listen to a concert performance and judge how well scales have been practiced. A speaker's knowledge of his or her subject may be determined by a qualified observer without using a detailed record of the speaker's study and work history. These are examples of evaluation of rather large units of study and performance; whereas tests of subordinate competencies are often needed to

(a) improve the course,
(b) attempt to prevent failures, and
(c) remedy failures already made.

Converting Raw Test Scores to "Grades"

Earlier, this Chapter implied that some appropriate form of evaluation can be designed to measure student attainment on any stated behavioral objective. It was mentioned, however, that such evaluations may often be made not by pencil and paper tests, but by evaluating the *process* a student follows in meeting an objective, or by evaluating a *product*, such as a completed project, whether it involves baking a cake, writing a research paper, or following accepted rules of social behavior.

Usually when a student knows he or she is working on something (an assignment, a test, or a product) to be evaluated in terms of grades or some other desired reward of value to the student, such evaluation is called a measure of the "maximum performance" of the student. This assumes the student will try to do his or her best on the activities on which he or she expects to be evaluated.

In contrast, measures of "typical performance" are frequently taken without the student's knowledge, using a "time-sampling" technique, within the total period during which the evaluator *can observe* the student. Most educational tests and evaluation of a formal, scheduled nature are considered as tests of *maximum performance*. But in elementary school especially, a teacher often makes rather continuous observations of both the general behavior and the "work behavior" of a child, yielding evaluations of *typical performance*.

Raw data from tests or other evaluations in the form of numbers representing raw scores on tests, or numbers representing ratings recorded by the teacher require still another step—converting raw scores into some kind of standard score that has a common meaning for all school subjects. Letter grades (A, B, C, etc.) or their numerical equivalents (1, 2, 3, etc.) are common ways to designate level of performance: superior, above average, average, poor, or unsatisfactory. Other reporting systems may require unstructured verbal descriptions of the quality of work done by each pupil.

Regardless of the method of recording (letter grades or satisfactory/unsatisfactory), there must be either an *objective* or *subjective* way of converting the raw scores, ratings, or observations to these common indicators of performance expressed in some form of "grade."

There are several methods of making this conversion. Features of each are discussed below.

Grading "on the Curve": Norm-Referenced Grading

Suppose a very good test (reliable and valid) is available for measuring a major objective of a course on which the highest possible raw score is 150. Suppose further that letter grades for each group of students are to be assigned on the basis of the following (commonly used) rule:

A = 10% (students with highest scores)
B = 20% (students ranking next in scores)
C = 40% (students in middle range of scores)
D = 20% (next lower scores)
F = 10% (students having the lowest scores)
100%-e.g., all the students in this class

This method of grading does describe *performance differences among the individuals in this class.* The grades are arrived at *objectively* because the same scoring key was used to score all tests, and letter grades were assigned on the basis of raw scores on the test, not on the subjective judgment of the teacher. Thus, personal *bias* against certain persons was avoided, as well as "halo effects"—impressions of each student based on behavior unrelated to the test. This method of grading is *objective, unbiased,* and *uninfluenced* by irrelevant considerations. In these respects, grading on a curve is fair and impartial in the treatment of *each student in the group, compared to treatment of others in the group.*

But, apart from philosophical questions of whether and why 30 percent of *any* group should receive D or F, or whether any "failure" grade

recording is desirable, there are two definite weaknesses in this method:

(a) there is no reference back to the statements of objectives (in fact, this method is a favorite when there are no predetermined objectives and standards); and

(b) a given student's grade depends upon how well *other* students did on the test; hence, his or her grade depends upon *which group* he or she happens to fall into.

Regarding point (a) above, it would be better to state, in advance, the test score equivalent to the minimal acceptable standard and to consider the meeting of this minimum standard as "passing," "acceptable," or a *B* or *C,* depending on the general interpretation these letter grades have to the users of the grades (future teachers, registrars, or employers). Then performance above or below this standard could be described as *A, D,* or other relevant grades.

Regarding point (b) above, suppose that the poorer students happen, for some reason, to take the course in the first semester, and the better ones take it in the second semester. Exaggerating the *probable* difference between two such groups, given usual enrollment and assignment procedures, here is what *could* happen:

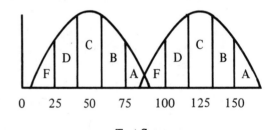

Test Scores

First Semester Class   Second Semester Class

Since the distributions and ranges shown above for the two classes are not recorded by the registrar, another person judging a student's achievement in this course by merely inspecting the records would tend to be grossly misled by these grades based on "the curve."

Thus, it appears that grading on the curve, if ever justified, is sound practice *only when*

(a) a clear standard of acceptable performance is established and the grades issued are referenced to this standard; and when

(b) a given letter grade has a stable meaning over a period of time, regardless of the group to which the student is assigned.

It may be further observed that in this type of *norm-referenced grading* (comparing one student's performance with the performance of others rather than in terms of a predetermined standard), the tests employed are often deliberately designed to *exaggerate* the size of the differences among students. When no instructional objectives have been stated, and there is no way to judge the *validity* of the test, and no way to set a score for "passing," test makers often "go for the highest possible reliability and discriminating power" by the way they make and remake the test. They may do this by "sampling the content of the materials" rather than sampling performance relevant to a stated objective. Then, if the first distributions of scores are not "normal" (bell-shaped), they may introduce a different mixture of "difficult," "easy," or "medium" items to "smooth out the curve." (Make it look more like curves measuring intelligence, based on a similar test strategy.)

Popham and Husek (1969) have shown that the concepts of "item difficulty" and "discriminating power" are irrelevant to *criterion-referenced testing procedures*, discussed next.

Pass-Fail Grading: Objective-Referenced (or Criterion-Referenced) Grading

This method has much merit, especially when the objectives and the standards are reasonable (can be attained feasibly by most well-motivated students of the ability of those likely to take the course, given the available teaching methods and materials).

It is preferable that the standard set for passing (receiving "satisfactory" credit) be logically or mathematically related to some meaningful future performance, of which the grade in the present course is a predictor. Thus, suppose that the above test (of 150 possible points) is a final examination over Algebra I, and that *raw scores* earned in Algebra I are recorded for each student. Suppose further that *all students* in the two previously shown distributions are allowed to enroll in Algebra II. Now, suppose that past records indicate that most students who scored over 110 pass Algebra II; and most students scoring under 110 on Algebra I fail Algebra II. Then it would be *reasonable, useful,* and *predictive* to admit to Algebra II those scoring over 110 in Algebra I, and to advise the rest to repeat Algebra I, or to select an alternate curricu-

lum (assuming that standards for passing Algebra II have important implications). But, in the two classes whose distributions appear earlier, *all* students in the first semester of Algebra I would *fail* Algebra II, *regardless* of the letter grade, because no one in that entire class had a raw score of at *least* 110 (the lower limit of those who tend to succeed in passing Algebra II).

Setting "satisfactory" at 110 for Algebra I would obviously be a more realistic way of setting standards than using the letter grades assigned separately under the "curve" for these two classes.

Actually, prediction of performance on a second course from scores on a first course is seldom perfect. Using the results from the two hypothetical algebra courses, a more typical expectation might be: Of the students scoring *over* 110 in Algebra I, 75% passed Algebra II and 25% failed; of students scoring *under* 110 in Algebra I, 88% failed Algebra II, and 12% passed Algebra II.

Of course, somewhat better predictions, in terms of the *probability* of failing Algebra II, could be made from the above data if scores were kept separately for various narrow ranges on the Algebra I test, such as 0-25, 25-50, etc.

But, whether or not predetermined minimum performance standards for "passing" can be based on prediction of some future success, as in Algebra II or on a job, it is better to specify a definite, arbitrary standard than to accept the serious shortcomings of norm-referenced procedures, as illustrated for the two classes in Algebra I.

When objectives are well defined, and when clear, reasonable performance standards are set for appropriate minimum test performance, it is then possible to realize many benefits.

First, if all the students are capable and hardworking, all can meet the standards, so all can pass. This fact can then be recognized, avoiding the arbitrary (false) failures that occur under the "curve."

Second, if some students fail, it is due to their own performance level, not to the performance of other students in the class, as in norm-referenced grading.

Third, with definite objectives and standards, it is possible to define standards for both groups and individuals in a meaningful way. That is, when the minimum performance standard is set, the course designer can proceed to design a test for a given objective which will enable "90 percent of the class to identify (the standard of) 80 percent of 20 animal pictures with *no student* identifying less than 60 percent." Thus, the standards can be clearly set for the class as a whole, as well as in terms of the poorest acceptable individual performance. Note also that the tests are over the specified objectives, so they are *valid*. The tests are not random samplings of the "materials covered," as in many achievement tests.

Fourth, the overworked "normal curve" of achievement can be ignored in relation to achievement standards. Only two points on a score distribution need be of interest:

(a) the minimum standard to be reached by 90 percent (or any other designated percentage) of the class; and

(b) the lowest score expected of any one person in the class (or any designated number of persons). Such standards give the course designer a means of knowing when he or she has met *his or her objectives*. This way there is no need for a test having precision in discriminating between pairs of scores of all persons above the standard. The test need not yield a normal distribution. Hopefully, practically all scores will fall at or above the standard set for the class, and none, or only a few, below that point. In pass-fail grading, more precise discriminations are not needed, so tests can be simpler and less expensive to design appropriately. Objective-referenced tests can also be valuable for diagnosis and remedial instruction (Gagné and Briggs, 1979, Chapter 12).

What *can* happen under a self-paced individualized program is that *all* students may equal or surpass the minimum standard for a given objective, even though *time to meet the standard* may happen to be distributed in accordance with the normal curve.

Arbitrary Percentage Scores

Another method of criterion-referenced grading is to call 90 percent on the test an "A," 80 percent a "B," etc. This may or may not be better than grading on the curve. It does not refer to any standard required that is related to specific objectives; but it would not be subject to the group-to-group inequities of the curve, as long as the same test (or an equivalent test) is used, and *provided* the same evaluator did the grading.

But such percentage grades mean little from one teacher to another, or from one test to another, since tests not designed for specified objectives and standards vary in "difficulty." One teacher may tend to make tests on which the average score is 60 percent of the possible score; another teacher may make "easy" tests, on which the average would be 90 percent for the same class. This is due in part to differences among teachers, but also largely to an absence of objectives and standards. Percentage scores based on the importance of various objectives are possible when objectives are used as the basis for tests.

Setting Standards Referenced to Practical Outcomes

When one wishes to set standards to define the minimum performance required in terms of a test, it is desirable to show meaningful standards by statements such as:

"In the past, a person who scored less than 110 on this objective was not able to pass the next unit of this course; so, he or she needs either to repeat this unit so he or she can pass the next one, or he or she should drop the course."

"A score of less than 110 would suggest that this student could not pass the college entrance test at 'X' college because they require . . ."

"A student who scores less than 110 on this objective cannot (do something needed, such as):

... keep his or her check stub accurately."
... write an acceptable business letter."
... become a successful engineer."
... finish an A.B. degree in social science."
... expect to pass a test for job X."
... do well in course X because . . ."

In most of the above discussion, it is assumed that failure to meet standards on *this course* or *this objective* is predictive of failure to succeed on some needed everyday skill, or is predictive of failure in passing some other course, or entering some job or school. Setting standards under these conditions has *guidance value*, or suggests needed *remedial instruction*.

In other circumstances, perhaps *anything* the student learns is valuable to him or her because it makes him or her happier; he or she enjoys life more; or he or she now feels himself or herself to be a more enlightened citizen. Or, perhaps the student wants to develop a hobby to enjoy, not to enter a college or a job on the basis of this course. Or, it may be a "familiarization" course, not a "competency-developing course"; so, any familiarization that is achieved is better than none. If any of these apply, perhaps the "certificate of completion" is more relevant than tests and standards. The same may hold for "enrichment" objectives, in contrast to "core" objectives, even in an overall job-oriented curriculum or course. Perhaps tests should then cover only the core objectives.

For present purposes, we assume the presence of core objectives, and hence some reason for converting test scores to grades. If you are preparing tests to measure accomplishment of objectives, then, you should not only write the test, and tell how it is to be administered and scored, but also give a key for grading and your rationale for the assignment of grades.

Alternate Strategies: Constructing Tests

It has been shown that most behavioral objectives lend themselves to being measured *directly*; that is, by a test which requires exactly the kind of learner performance described in the objective.

When behavioral objectives are very difficult to measure within the time and other resources available, one may measure the subordinate competencies of the objective separately, or may measure some performance which is known to be correlated with (predict) the criterion performance specified in the objective.

For example, a lifelong objective may be that the learner will be a wise purchaser; that is, in his or her adult life he or she will weigh quantity and quality of products per dollar when making purchases. This behavior cannot be measured directly for children, at least if purchase of large items is intended. So, one might either evaluate the child's wisdom in purchase of small items; or, more likely, perhaps, measure his or her "simulated purchasing performance," as by a "case study test," in which the "real-life" information is presented in a "school context." Solutions to such problems may or may not be predictive of later adult buying behavior (what he or she *will do then*), but they could indicate present ability to make good decisions, when "money" is replaced by "points" in a game.

Such evaluations may be the closest that one can come to feasible measurement of some objectives. So measurement of a *simulated* problem may replace measurement of a real-life problem.

In other instances, the component parts can be taught and measured separately, supplemented by evaluation of the entire simulated objective.

Objectives, Tests, and Scoring Keys

Scoring keys are simple to prepare for objective-type tests, such as multiple-choice, matching, true-false, etc., so no examples are needed here. However, we do present an example (Figure 30) of a criterion-sheet type of scoring key such as is applicable for evaluating essay tests, "products," or "performances."

The Concepts of Mastery and Standards

It would appear that the most perfect indicator of a student's ability would be a direct observation of his or her performance on a task. But one must remember that the observable performance (action verb and object) called for in an objective is simply the "indicator" of the learned capability. For instance, when asked to "generate a 1000-calorie diet for a diabetic," a student could put his or her response on paper, but the observer wouldn't know if the student had actually generated the diet (the product of a problem-solving ability) or memorized one and recalled it (reproductive learning). Indeed, one of the most common criticisms of giving objectives to students is that they tell the learner what he or she is to be able to do after instruction, and thereby give the student the questions to be encountered on the test. The legitimacy of "teaching for the test" was discussed earlier. This matter was seen in terms of what is appropriate for objectives representing productive learning on one hand, and reproductive learning on the other hand.

Due to the inferential nature of evaluation, any examination is likely to be less than perfect. The best we could hope for would be direct observation of the behavior called for in the objective under the conditions specified. However, due to other constraints, this is sometimes unlikely, if not impossible. For instance, we might train a soldier

*Objective**: Given details regarding an instructional situation (to include types of students, subject content, objectives, student background, and class size and time for presentation), the student will generate a decision whether or not to use the discussion method, and will justify his or her decision in writing by indicating the advantages and/or limitations of that method which influenced the decision.

Test: "Your class will consist of 15 inexperienced adults. The classroom is a meeting room with lounge chairs. Coffee will be available and served. Presentation time is 0900 Tuesday. You have been told to take as long as two hours, if needed. The objective is that the learners will be able to administer artificial respiration.

a. Will you use the discussion method?
b. Justify your decision by indicating what advantages or limitations affected it.
c. If you selected discussion, how will you overcome any limitations?

Scoring Key: (Note: Factors such as informality, coffee, lounge chairs, etc., were deliberately inserted in the test to suggest discussion.)

a. Student answers "no" .... 2 points
b. If student provides *at least* two of the following reasons he or she earns a maximum of .. 6 points
   1. Performing artificial respiration does not lend itself to discussion, but requires demonstration, performance, and critique of performance.
   2. Inexperienced persons can't usefully discuss an unfamiliar objective.
   3. Discussion requires active student participation, and these students aren't prepared for this.
   4. The performance objective is not very debatable or "discussable"; there are approved, set procedures for doing it.
   5. Purpose of discussion is to develop critical thinking or to share viewpoints—not applicable here.
c. If student chooses discussion, but includes at least some demonstration, maximum permitted is .... 4 points
d. If student overcomes a limitation of discussion adequately, allow an additional .... 2 points

Possible: 8 points
Minimum standard: 6 points

*This sample objective and related test material were provided by William Freeman.

Figure 30. Sample objective, criterion-test, and scoring key.

to engage in a particular maneuver in the event of war, but we could not test performance in an actual war. Therefore, we have to create a simulated environment for the testing, and this reduces, somewhat, the validity of our observation.

Less obvious are faults with the typical classroom test in which very often the student is to demonstrate a rule-using behavior or even problem-solving behavior in a multiple-choice test. The first problem here, of course, is that the student is already confronted with a set of alternatives. Had he or she been asked to construct a response, he or she would have to *recall* rather than *recognize* the answer, and the recalled responses may have contained none of the multiple choices presented on an objective test. Furthermore, in a four-item multiple-choice test, he or she can employ "strategies" for determining the answers that have little or nothing to do with demonstrating the desired rule behavior. For example, when uncertain of the answer, the student may eliminate as many foils as possible before guessing. This may or may not result in a good score, but it certainly does little for assessing performance on the desired behavior. Does this mean that multiple-choice tests are inappropriate for assessing rule-using and problem-solving behavior? No, just that they require a greater degree of inference back to the learned capability of the original objective than some other type of test might require. The validity of the item suffers; that is, it is less likely to measure the desired capability.

One of the most common mistakes of designers is to think that they can directly test *everything*. This is very often beyond the capability of the available resources. Most tests contain items that are selected from a domain of items that could have been included. They "sample," therefore, the behaviors that the student should be able to exhibit. It is generally agreed that the test should contain, at the least, a number of items representing the terminal behavior, in as valid a format as possible. Other items from the prerequisite or supporting objectives are also included to test for the students' level of achievement, should they not attain the terminal skills. These behaviors, by definition, are less complex than the terminal behavior, and we should find students passing them if they can perform the terminal behavior.

The converse, however, is not the case. That is, we can not assume that because the students can perform well on the enabling skills, they can also perform the terminal skill. Herein lies one of the difficulties with criterion-referenced testing and grading. How do we specify mastery; and how do we grade student performance?

Mastery is a concept that relates to a student's ability to demonstrate competence on learning objectives. Since we know that tests are not perfect, we are generally advised to set levels of mastery at 80 percent or 90 percent of the items. Realizing that the instruction will not be effective for everyone in the target audience, we generally specify the proportion that we would find acceptable; again, this is generally set at 80 or 90 percent.

What does 80 percent of the items mean? This is a problem of interpretation. The 80 percent level was chosen as a balance between what would be desirable (100 percent) and what is realistic, taking into account teaching and testing error. We would suggest that there is nothing magic about these numbers, and that a criterion of 100 percent might be called for in some cases (where performance is critical; e.g., in a life-and-death type situation), and perhaps 60 percent in other instances (where there is little threat to safety or further learning). The first criterion (100 percent) might be envisioned if we were considering a medical student's performance in tying a surgeon's knot. It would be unacceptable if he or she tied every fourth knot or so incorrectly. Here the criterion is appropriately set at 100 percent. On the other hand, a child playing a game such as checkers might make a wrong move 40 percent of the time and still do well, especially if he or she were playing against other children with approximately the same skill level. The nature of the subject matter is also a consideration. Whereas mathematics skills are clear-cut, skills in the social sciences are not (where experts can't reach consensus), and mastery levels should be set accordingly.

While it would be desirable to test students on each objective, most often tests are constructed to include items that represent a number of objectives. Each objective may have a representative number of items, but generally the criterion is stated as a function of the total test score (rather than as a proportion of the items for each objective). So, a test that has items representing ten objectives may contain 30 or more items. Eighty percent mastery would imply that the student scores 24 items correctly, but does this really represent mastery? Does one master a test or an objective?

As an illustration of the problem, let's say the objectives are related as shown on the hypothetical map shown in Figure 31. Here we might generate three items for each objective, which would give us a 30-item test. If we considered every item equal in weight, the student could miss all three items associated with the terminal objective (No. 10) and still be evaluated as having "mastered" the test.

Obviously, while behavior on the subordinate objectives is important, items for them are not of the same value in determining mastery as are items for the terminal objectives. Therefore, the designer should weight terminal items more heavily than items for subordinate objectives. In terms of test points, the terminal objective might be considered as "worth" one-quarter of the total points rather than simply ten percent (as would be the case if every item were weighted equally). This 25 percent rating would mean essentially that the student would have to correctly answer at least one of the items relating to objective No. 10 in order to "master" the test.

This was determined as follows. The total test is worth 30 points (an arbitrary number based on the total number of items). Mastery is 80 percent, which means that the learner must score 24 points. We would not want the students to score "mastery" if they could not perform the terminal skills; however, we want to recognize progress towards mastery, so we make mastery dependent upon a "reliable" performance on the terminal objective. If we weight the final objective as worth 25 percent of the total points, it makes each of the terminal items worth 2.5 points. Therefore, if the student misses two terminal skill items out of three, the highest possible score would be 25, two points above failure. It is likely that if the student misses two or three terminal skill items, he or she will also miss one of the subordinate skill items, and would not have been considered to have mastered the material. If he or she misses all three terminal items, the total score would also be below mastery.

The point of this illustration is that the designer should not arbitrarily set a criterion score without considering what it means in terms of student performance. This may seem obvious, but it is easy to overlook the relationship of performance to criterion scores and mastery levels.

Hopefully, the illustration just given will be helpful when establishing a criterion and weighting scheme for a criterion-referenced test. With regard

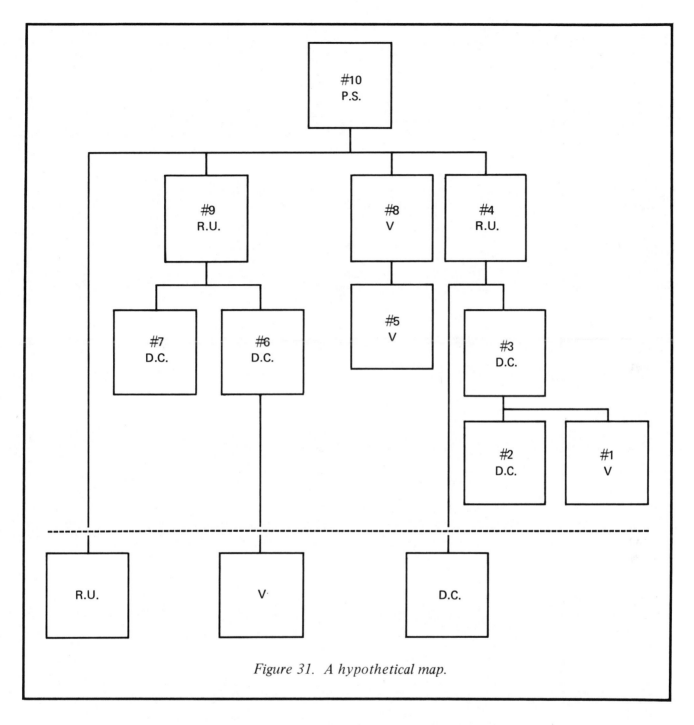

Figure 31. A hypothetical map.

to grading, the designer must analyze the purpose for grades. In most cases, grades serve to inform the student how well he or she is doing with regard to stated standards. Simply indicating mastery or non-mastery gives very little information to the student who doesn't reach mastery. For this reason, it is desirable to indicate to the student which elements of the total performance are correct or incorrect, as well as to indicate how close to mastery the student has come.

There are also motivational reasons for giving

grades. In public schools and college, course grades are important motivators of student study behavior. In some situations, it might be possible to specify multiple criterion levels; e.g., 70 percent passing (C), 80 percent good (B), 90 percent excellent (A). These multiple criterion levels allow for consideration of fluctuation in test quality and student performance. However, again, the designer must analyze what it means to score 70 percent, and still be considered as exhibiting "satisfactory" performance.

Exercise No. 8: Validity, Reliability, Practicality, and Efficiency of Tests

1. Place a *V* or an *R* to indicate validity or reliability; use *-V* or *-R* to indicate the lack of either.

   .... a. a test measures accurately whatever it does measure.

   .... b. a test measures the performance specified in the objective.

   .... c. a test measures the objective only indirectly.

   .... d. a test is too short to measure all aspects of the objective.

   .... e. a test is too short to measure accurately the learner's ability to perform the objective.

   .... f. performance on a test differs for the same learner on two successive days.

   .... g. for each learner, scores on one-half of the test are about the same as his or her scores on the other half of the test.

   .... h. the objective says "construct a correct example of Rule A," but the test requires "identification of a correct example."

   .... i. the objective says "distinguish between nouns and verbs," and the test requires marking "N" for noun and "V" for verb.

   .... j. the objective says "adjust the TV," and the test says "describe how to adjust the TV."

2. Use *E* or *P* to indicate efficiency or practicality; use *-E* or *-P* to show lack of either.

   .... a. only one decision is measured per hour of testing.

   .... b. the test requires expensive equipment.

   .... c. the test takes too much time to score.

   .... d. the learner marks a question every two minutes.

   .... e. the test can be scored by machine.

   .... f. it takes half an hour to give the directions for the test.

Exercise No. 9: Congruence of
Tests and Objectives (Validity of Tests)

Directions: For each numbered objective, select the most congruent or valid measure.

1. The student can demonstrate the application of Ohm's law to compute any one of the three values which may be missing in a circuit diagram.
   a. Write Ohm's law.
   b. Explain Ohm's law.
   c. Talk about Ohm's law in a really understanding manner.
   d. Solve circuit problems, using Ohm's law.

2. The student can identify hexagons and rectangles.
   a. Draw a hexagon and a rectangle.
   b. Define hexagon and rectangle.
   c. Point to the hexagon; then to the rectangle.
   d. Solve area problems for hexagons and rectangles.

3. Generate a dialog in French.
   a. Translate English to French in writing.
   b. Translate French to English in writing.
   c. Conjugate French verbs.
   d. Speak French to the teacher.

4. Demonstrate calculation of the area of a rectangle.
   a. Trace the history of the discovery of the formula for area of rectangles.
   b. Recognize the formula $A = xy$, whether stated verbally or in symbols.
   c. Given a drawing of a rectangle, showing the two dimensions in feet, the student supplies the correct area in number of square feet.
   d. Be able to define, as well as apply, the formula by which the area of circles may be computed.

5. Given a malfunctioning TV set in which the *symptom* of trouble is wavy lines across the viewing tube, the student can demonstrate troubleshooting and remedy the problem by replacing the defective part or by making an adjustment. Successful performance is indicated when the symptom clears up.
   a. Give student a defective TV set. Ask him or her to correct it; then check to see if the symptom disappears.
   b. Give student a defective TV set. Ask him or her to identify the symptom.
   c. Give student a written test (to save time), telling him or her the faulty part and asking him to write the symptom.
   d. Give student a defective TV set. Tell him or her what part is faulty, and ask him or her to name the symptom.

6. The student will use principles of weather, geology, and geography to generate hypotheses about where, on a hypothetical continent, wheat will grow well. (Wind directions, rainfall, and other necessary data are supplied on a map of the continent.)
   a. Ask student to name the principles of weather, geology, and geography.
   b. Ask student to mark on the map where wheat will grow.
   c. Tell student where wheat grows, and ask him or her to explain why.
   d. Ask student to explain the data marked on the map.

7. The student at all times will habitually choose to observe the conventional rules of courtesy, fair play, and tact.
   a. Watch the student in the classroom and on the playground, making notes of his or her behavior at systematic intervals during which he or she does not know he or she is being observed and evaluated. Use the notes to make your evaluation.
   b. Given a three-page description of a difficult social situation which students of this age typically encounter, the student will correctly indicate the course of action he or she should take, identifying the rules he or she is following at each behavioral step.
   c. Stage a test situation in the classroom, in the form of a simulated social situation. Have one student coached to give the other student a social problem situation to respond to; and evaluate his or her reaction on a ten-point scale.
   d. During a baseball game, have the umpire deliberately call an obvious "ball" a "strike," and observe what the student does.
   e. Give a true-false test on rules of social conduct.

8. The student will be able to recite the alphabet orally.
   a. Have the student recite the alphabet orally, but backwards, from Z to A.
   b. Have the student recite the alphabet orally from A to Z.
   c. Give a written test on letter discrimination.
   d. Have the student write the alphabet.

9. "The purpose of this course is to learn to use knowledge of past history to understand events of today and originate predictions of the near future."
   a. Ask student to name the dates on which past historical events occurred.
   b. Give case study tests, describing developing situations, and asking student to name parallel situations in the past and show how he or she uses that knowledge in arriving at a prediction.
   c. Ask the student to name three periods of thought in the methods of teaching history and to show the advantages and disadvantages of each.
   d. Give a matching test, calling for association of events in history with the leading personalities associated with the events, and the dates and other associated facts.

Chapter 11
Formative Evaluation

Chapter in This Book	Recommended Readings		
	Briggs, L.J. (Ed.) *Instructional Design: Principles and Applications*. Englewood Cliffs, N.J.: Educational Technology Publications, 1977.	Gagné, R.M., and Briggs, L.J. *Principles of Instructional Design*, 2nd ed. New York: Holt, Rinehart, and Winston, 1979.	Gagné, R.M. *The Conditions of Learning*, 3rd ed. New York: Holt, Rinehart, and Winston, 1977.
10	Chapters 6, 10, 11	Chapter 12	
(11)	**Chapter 10**	**Chapter 15**	
12	Chapter 15	Chapter 15	

Background

The purpose of instruction is, of course, to bring about learning. In order for the designer to know how effective the design effort has been, careful testing of learner performance is necessary. It is necessary to ascertain the extent to which groups of learners have achieved the instructional objectives. For this reason, Chapter 4 dealt with construction of test items which are *valid* measures of learner performance with respect to the objectives, and Chapter 10 dealt with achieving *reliable* tests by attending to the adequacy of testing. This latter issue is related to the thoroughness of testing, which in turn relates to the length of the test. It was emphasized in Chapter 10 that when designing a test, one attends to all five components in the objectives—situation, capability verb, action verb, object, and tools and constraints. One also decides when all the test items should measure only the terminal performance, and when items measuring the subordinate competencies should be used.

The above testing refers, of course, to the actual classroom situation in which the final draft of instructional materials is being used. According to our instructional design model, however, much testing has been done of the materials *before* this point. It is the *improvement* of the original draft of the instructional materials or the lesson plans with which we are concerned in this Chapter—improvement in instruction that has been accomplished *before* use of materials in the regular classroom setting. This is called *formative evaluation*.

While the process of formative evaluation includes the use of tests administered to learners after they study an early draft of the instructional materials, other kinds of data are also gathered. All types of data gathered are analyzed for the purpose of deciding where improvements can be made. While improving the materials or lesson plans is the goal of formative evaluation, the data also often reveal defects in the planning that took place *before* the materials were written. These defects may lie anywhere—in needs analysis, analysis of objectives, the tests themselves, or in faulty sequencing or instructional strategies. The purpose of formative evaluation is to find and remedy these errors, wherever they may lie.

Recall, then, that formative evaluation of instruction takes place while the instruction is being *formed*. Therefore, first-draft or second-draft materials are used for formative evaluation, when the course is heavily materials dependent. The same holds true for courses or lessons that are heavily teacher dependent. In the teacher-dependent case, lessons would be evaluated the first or second time they are tried out in the classroom. Formative evaluation, then, can be accomplished for a lesson in which a teacher provides the information (stimulus) and the other instructional events, as well as for a lesson in which the materials provide the instructional events.

In both cases, it is well to first design "bare bones" instruction—the minimal instruction that the designer believes may be adequate. Such "lean" design is important because, as Dick (1977) points out, formative evaluation and revision procedures are most effective for identifying gaps in instruction and for pinpointing needed additional material. It is not always as easy for formative evaluations to reveal excess instruction. By using the "bare bones" approach to begin with, the designer can add instructional elements if many students, during formative evaluation, do not pass relevant test items. This approach has been used successfully for a training program in first aid consisting of a combination of films, programmed instruction booklets, and practice with feedback from an instructor (Markle, 1977). It has also been employed in carefully-controlled classroom instruction conducted by the teacher (informal personal communication from David Felder).

Not all stages of formative evaluation, however, employ tests as the sole, or even the principal, method of gathering data. Techniques of data gathering for the purpose of formative evaluation include:

1. Obtaining background information from participants.
2. Watching learners to see if they can follow the directions for the study of materials.
3. Answering questions the students ask and recording the questions.
4. Documenting any cues, remarks, or prompts made to students to supplement the tryout materials.
5. Interviewing students as to what they found interesting, dull, easy, or difficult.
6. Recording student comments about any of the directions, materials, or tests.
7. Noting the length of time taken on individual lesson components.

8. Doing item analysis to determine how many students passed or missed each test item.

9. Placing item analysis data into learning hierarchies and instructional maps to study the validity of assumptions about sequencing, subordinate relationships, domain interactions, and transfer implied in the hierarchies and maps.

10. Administering and interpreting attitude questionnaires and debriefing interviews.

Data from all the above procedures are used to improve the objectives, the tests, and the instructional materials or lesson plans.

Chapter 11 Information Test

*Enter a "1," "2," or "3" to show which stage of formative evaluation is **most** suitable for each of the following instruments, practices, or procedures.*

"1" = one-on-one tryouts
"2" = small-group tryouts
"3" = field tryouts

.... __1.__ Make notes of classroom and administrative problems.

.... __2.__ Use "moderately polished" materials.

.... __3.__ Detect major errors in directions and materials.

.... __4.__ Use informal conversations about the materials.

.... __5.__ Begin to interpret test scores to change the materials.

.... __6.__ Begin to interpret test scores as showing the value of materials.

.... __7.__ Write observations in your copy of the materials.

.... __8.__ Tape-recording may be useful.

.... __9.__ Use rough 8mm films.

.... __10.__ Detecting faults in directions and tests.

.... __11.__ Prompt the learner when necessary to help him or her respond correctly.

.... __12.__ Answer questions only to clarify directions.

.... __13.__ Begin to estimate time needed for study.

.... __14.__ Consider school class schedules in arranging units of study.

.... __15.__ Use final format of materials.

How to Do It

Dick (1977) has presented a succinct set of guidelines for conducting the three stages of formative evaluation:

(1) one-on-one evaluation;
(2) small-group evaluation; and
(3) field-trial evaluation.

He has also described how to prepare instruments for use, and he has presented illustrative data and interpretations of the data. An example by one of his students, Neuza Lindahl, summarizes procedures and results for an actual formative evaluation. His chapter should be consulted for further details by readers planning to conduct such an evaluation. However, a brief summary of the above three phases is presented next.

One-on-One Evaluation

This phase of formative evaluation is often called the "clinical" phase. A very rough draft of the instructional materials is prepared in some readable form, if print materials are used. If visual presentation is employed, the pictures may not be artistically complete, but the essentials are there. Crude 8mm film may be used, later to be produced in 16mm after the instructional faults in the film are detected.

The designer sits with an individual learner in a quiet place. The learner reads or views the materials, asks questions, volunteers comments, points out difficult or confusing passages, asks for clarification of directions, etc. In an informal manner, the designer "fills in" gaps in the instruction, and notes them. A posttest is then given to the learner mainly for the purpose of detecting faults in the directions or in the items of the test. If a test question is confusing, or if no instruction is related to it, this is also noted. The learner may even suggest ways to present some of the material more effectively. A tape recording may be made of the entire conversation relating to the lesson—difficulties encountered, material left out or confusing, etc. As a result of these tryouts, gross problems are detected and noted for further analysis and correction. Whatever revisions are indicated are made in the directions, the materials, the tests, or the sequencing of the instruction. One may even find that the print is not legible to the learner, or that he or she needed an introduction to what the lesson was all about, or a statement of why it was important to learn it. Scores on the posttest are not taken too seriously because of the informal prompting the designer offered, when needed.

Small-Group Evaluation

Using the second draft of all materials, tryouts are conducted next with small groups, ranging perhaps from five to 20 learners. The materials have been revised both in content and in format. They are now "semi-polished." The designer answers questions only to clarify directions, not to supplement the instruction in the materials. No prompting is given on the posttest, except to clarify directions. The resulting posttest data are taken more seriously as clues to faults needing correction. An item analysis is prepared showing how many learners missed each test item. Still these data are interpreted cautiously because the test as well as the material may be faulty. These data are placed, however, in the learning hierarchy or map, to begin to check on the analysis and sequencing of the lesson objective(s). Reactions are solicited from the learners after the study and testing are completed. Data are kept on study time and testing time, and any clues as to possible later classroom procedural problems are noted. Written attitude questionnaires partly take the place of individual interviews with students. The total procedure is a group procedure, partly simulating the classroom situation. These tryouts may be conducted by the designer, a teacher, or other project personnel.

Field-Trial Evaluation

Materials and tests have again been revised. Material may have been added, deleted, resequenced, or rewritten. Faulty test items have been revised. Media of presentation have been changed, improved, or placed in a more attractive format. Materials are now arranged to fit class schedules, and storage problems have been considered.

The tryouts are conducted by teachers in a normal classroom situation. The teachers continue to note any problems arising, but they do not conduct either group or individualized supplemental instruction. Both learning and administrative problems are noted for further correction. Posttest scores are now taken as an indicator of the effectiveness of the materials, considering also the results of tests over assumed entry skills and a pretest over component parts of the lesson objectives.

Often field-testing merges into summative evaluation. A later section of this Chapter discusses how to decide when to stop field-testing for formative purposes.

So far, we have spoken as though only a single lesson is being designed and tried out. In practice, entire courses or curricula have undergone the process of both formative and summative evaluations.

During the formative stage, many tryouts of single lessons and entire groups of lessons (units) have been conducted, first by the curriculum design team, then by individual teachers or entire schools. It is beyond the scope of this book to describe the complicated schedule by which entire curricula undergo formative evaluation, but in Chapter 12 we summarize such procedures for summative evaluation.

We have also, in this section, dealt largely with materials-centered instruction. Teachers can formatively evaluate lessons, but it takes careful planning and record-keeping to be sure the instructional content and procedure are recorded well enough so that the instruction is "replicable." This concept of repeatability and reliability was discussed in an earlier chapter. Essentially, the instruction must be "reviewable" as in playing back a videotape of the lesson for later analysis and correction.

Does It Pay Off?

Considering all the effort it takes to conduct the three stages of formative evaluation just described,

a relevant question arises: "Is it worth the trouble?"

Rosen (1968) was perhaps the first to investigate this question experimentally. He prepared a draft lesson (in a replicable format) whose degree of effectiveness was known through empirical tryout and resulting test data. He provided some teachers with the test data as one basis for revising the lesson. Another group of teachers revised the lesson without benefit of the test (item analysis) data. The first group made revisions resulting in significant learning gains, while the revisions made only on an intuitive (subjective) basis by the second group of teachers resulted in little or no gain in lesson effectiveness. The results of this controlled experiment are in agreement with the experience of instructional designers who work with a development/evaluation research paradigm rather than a formal-experiment paradigm.

Numbers of doctoral students have experienced first-hand the benefits of tryouts and revisions of learning materials they develop for their dissertations. In fact, one such student, Reese Parker, prepared two versions of a lesson, differing intentionally in "quality of instruction," in order to ascertain the interaction of quality of instruction with amount of study time upon criterion-test performance. He found that, within limits, increased study time can compensate for some lack of quality of instruction (unpublished doctoral dissertation, Florida State University, 1974). This finding is related to the cost-effectiveness question referred to later in this Chapter: "When is it economical (or necessary) to stop conducting formative evaluation?"

The above experimental and developmental experience provides objective data to be considered along with the theoretical argument that, since our theory base is not strong enough to permit us to predict with certainty that first-draft material will be effective, we need some amount of formative evaluation. Doing these tryouts, then, can be supported on both theoretical and empirical grounds. The degree of tryout justified relates to the importance and criticality of the objectives. If mastery of some lessons is a matter of great importance, then more money and time would be justified as compared to the case of objectives of lesser importance.

With this brief commentary on the importance of conducting formative evaluation, we turn next to details of procedures.

An Outline of Formative Evaluation Procedures

The following outline of formative evaluation procedures, commentary upon the outline, sample instruments, and exercises were prepared by Carol Marlin and are included here with her permission.

The outline which follows lists some of the major considerations in developing a formative evaluation plan, conducting the tryouts with participants, and revising the instruction. Placed after the outline, some selected topics are discussed in greater detail. The topic headings and numbers referenced in the discussion correspond to those in the outline. You should consider each element in the outline to determine which of the three stages of formative evaluation, previously discussed, are most relevant for each part of the outline.

I. *Developing the Formative Evaluation Plan*
   A. Generate or select data-collection instruments
      1. Background information
      2. Entry skills test (both general study skills and specific skills which are assumed to transfer to the new skills to be taught in the new lesson materials)
      3. Pretest (over the objectives and competencies of the new lesson)
      4. Within-course test items or responses (such as responses to questions posed in the lesson text)
      5. Evaluator's comments to students
      6. Students' questions and remarks
      7. Length of time required
      8. Posttest (over the objectives and competencies taught in the materials)
      9. Attitude questionnaire
      10. Debriefing interview
      11. Questionnaire for subject-matter experts
   B. Schedule a time for tryouts
      1. Based on the size of the instructional component
      2. Two-to-one factor is a rough guideline (allow twice the tryout time compared to expected time for operational use)
   C. Select a place to conduct evaluations
      1. Lighting
      2. Electrical outlets
      3. Work space
      4. Seating
      5. Some environmental factors will change from one-on-one to small-group and field-trial evaluations
   D. Arrange for participants
      1. Factors to consider: Are they members of the target population? Do they represent various subgroups within the population? Do they possess entry skills but not the terminal behaviors?
      2. Why representativeness is important
   E. Arrange for materials and equipment
      1. Manuals, paper, pencils, etc.
      2. Sufficient copies of all tests, questionnaires, and other forms
      3. Recording equipment, if desired
      4. Set up materials and equipment
      5. Try out equipment and double check materials
   F. Arrange for required support personnel
      1. Train additional observers or interviewers in advance
      2. Train any teachers/evaluators who will conduct the evaluations
      3. Thoroughly review the procedures for conducting evaluations with all observers, interviewers, and teachers

II. *Conducting the Formative Evaluations*
   A. Explain the participant's role
   B. Snags in the plan
      1. What if the participant does not possess the entry skills?
      2. What if the participant successfully passes the pretest?

III. *Revising the Instruction*
   A. Data summary and display (see Dick, 1977)
   B. Decide in advance the priority of data sources
      1. Pretest-posttest achievement
      2. Within-course test items or responses
      3. Attitude questionnaire
   C. Examine summarized data in relation to:
      1. Learning hierarchies/instructional maps
      2. Objectives and test items
      3. Events of instruction and conditions of learning

D.   When do revisions end?
  1.   Design decisions
  2.   Time constraints
  3.   Cost-effectiveness

I. Developing the Formative Evaluation Plan

I.A. Generate or select data-collection instruments. Some of the instruments needed for formative evaluations will have already been designed and developed as part of the instructional package. These instruments include the entry skills test, pretest, within-course test items or responses, and the posttest. Because these tests are integral components of the instruction, they should be administered to participants in all three stages of formative evaluation.

Other data-collection instruments will have to be generated or selected especially for the formative evaluation process. The exact kind and number of instruments will depend on the stage of evaluation being conducted and the particular needs of the designer. In each stage, however, it is important to collect only data that will be applicable to revising the instruction.

During the design and development process, many assumptions have been made about the skills and characteristics of the target population. While an entry test can measure the actual skill level of participants, it is sometimes helpful to collect additional data to verify target population characteristics. This can be accomplished with a background information questionnaire. The questionnaire may ask for the age, educational level, and prior experience of participants as well as other information that will assist the designer in validating his or her assumptions. Background data can also be used to ascertain and document the representativeness of the sample selected to participate in evaluations.

A sample background information questionnaire is presented at the end of this Chapter. It was designed for a module on computing fringe benefits for grant proposals. As can be seen from this example, a background information questionnaire must be tailored to the specific instruction being tested and to the designer's assumptions about critical target population characteristics.

Two other data collection instruments are frequently used in formative evaluations, an attitude questionnaire and a debriefing interview. If an attitude questionnaire is to be administered during the small-group evaluation and field trial, it is

worthwhile to try it out during the one-on-one evaluation. Student feedback at this first stage can help to pinpoint ambiguous items and items which do not yield useful data. Open-ended debriefing interviews are often conducted with individual participants. The designer may wish to ask questions not included on the attitude questionnaire, or he or she may follow up on specific responses made by the student. Interviews may also be conducted with teachers during the small-group and field-trial evaluations. Examples of an attitude questionnaire and debriefing interview are provided at the end of the Chapter. As with all formative evaluation data-collection instruments, the designer must ensure that questions will lead to specific revision decisions.

Students' questions and remarks may be documented in several ways. During the one-on-one stage, the designer may record this information on a separate form or on a copy of the instructional materials. Students may also be requested to write their comments directly on the materials. This latter option is commonly selected for the last two formative evaluation stages, where the interaction between students and the designer is minimal.

The designer's comments to students should be documented in a systematic manner too. During the one-on-one evaluation, this is particularly important if the designer provides cues or prompts to aid student performance and understanding. Again, the designer's comments may be recorded on a separate form or on the materials themselves. A specific form for this purpose is not required during the second and third stages, since the designer does not usually interact with students while they complete the instruction.

Data on the length of time required to complete materials can help in determining the administrative feasibility of the instruction. Dick (1977) notes that time is most reliably estimated from small-group and field-trial evaluations when the designer is not actively involved with students. Designer/student interaction during the one-on-one evaluation results in artificially inflated time estimates and posttest scores. While such warnings are well heeded, it is sometimes desirable to obtain *rough* time estimates for the administration of data-collection instruments during the one-on-one trials. This information can furnish input into scheduling the subsequent small-group evaluation. Although such "guess-timates" may be too high, they can provide rough guidelines and may prevent the designer from reserving too little time for the small-group evaluation.

Questionnaires for subject-matter experts are especially recommended for the one-on-one stage (Dick, 1977), but they may be employed whenever substantial content revisions have been made and the designer perceives a need to verify content accuracy.

I.B. Schedule a time for tryouts. Setting a time to conduct formative evaluations is an essential step in the planning process. The length of time required is based in part on the size of the instructional lesson under consideration. Clearly, it will take longer to evaluate a 60-minute lesson than it will to evaluate a 30-minute lesson. Unfortunately, there is no empirically proven formula to compute required evaluation time given the size of the lesson to be tested. However, a useful rule of thumb for one-on-one trials is to double the estimated time of the lesson. For example, if the lesson is approximately 45 minutes long, plan for at least an hour and a half to conduct each one-on-one evaluation. This amount of time will be necessary for the designer to administer all data-collection instruments and to interact with the student as he or she studies the materials.

The time required for small-group and field-trial evaluations may be somewhat less, since the designer does not sit with each student and go over the materials page by page. The final decision should be based on the estimated time needed for the lesson plus the estimated time required to administer data collection instruments. Rough time estimates for data-collection instruments may be obtained during the one-on-one stage; however, as mentioned previously, time estimates for the lesson itself should not be generalized from the one-on-one data.

If formative evaluations must be conducted within specified limits, as in a school setting, it is advisable to collect background information and administer the entry skills test and pretest on a separate day. It may even be necessary to arrange for an extended time period in order to debrief participants and have them complete the attitude questionnaire.

I.C. Select a place to conduct evaluations. After a time frame has been determined, an appropriate place must be selected and, if necessary, reserved. The actual testing site will depend largely upon available facilities and the type of trial being conducted. However, regardless of the type of trial,

there must be adequate lighting, work space, electrical outlets, and seating for the participants and the designer/teacher. For the one-on-one evaluations, it is not essential to duplicate the actual instructional setting. A quiet, private location is desirable so that the designer and student can interact without disrupting others. For field-trial evaluations, every effort must be made to use the materials in their intended environment.

I.D. Arrange for participants. One of the most difficult aspects of formative evaluation is obtaining an appropriate student sample. In order for the evaluations to be most useful, the following three criteria should be applied when selecting students to participate:

1. Students must be members of the target population.
2. They should represent several segments of the population in terms of their characteristics.
3. Students should possess the entry skills but not the terminal skills for the lesson being tested.

The representativeness of participants is critical in order for the designer to be able to generalize his or her findings to the entire population. Sub-groups within the target population must be clearly identified and then representatives chosen from each sub-group. Why go to all this trouble? The reason is because participants directly impact the kind and extent of revisions made to the instruction.

For example, suppose that a lesson on interpreting bar graphs has been developed for fourth-grade students. Also, suppose that for the formative evaluations an available sample of neighborhood children ranging from fifth to sixth grades has been selected. If all the revisions to the lesson were based on this sample, the instruction might very well be effective—for fifth-grade and sixth-grade students, that is. The designer would not have collected data on the effectiveness of the instruction for the intended audience. Since the purpose of formative evaluation is to improve instructional materials, the designer is cautioned to use only those students who are representative members of the target population.

I.E. Arrange for materials and equipment. In addition to having sufficient copies of all materials, it is sometimes necessary to obtain equipment for formative evaluations. The designer may wish to tape record one-on-one sessions, or perhaps use a slide-tape to present the material for a field-trial evaluation. It is always a good idea to set up the required equipment and try it out prior to use with participants.

II. Conducting the Formative Evaluations

II.A. Explain the participant's role. One of the first steps in conducting formative evaluations is to explain the role of the participant. Most students are unaccustomed to critiquing instructional materials, and this will be a new experience for them. It is important for them to understand their part in the evaluation process and to feel at ease. For one-on-one and small-group trials, general instructions may be provided to participants to explain their role. With field-trial evaluations, pertinent directions would be given to the teacher responsible for administering the instruction. An example of general instructions is presented at the end of this Chapter.

II.B. Snags in the plan. It is not unusual to arrange for participants and then discover that they do *not* possess the requisite entry skills or that they *do* possess some of the terminal behaviors. In these situations, the designer must use his or her best judgment, keeping in mind the stage of the formative evaluation and the number of untested assumptions which have been made.

If a one-on-one participant does not possess the entry skills, for example, the designer might decide to proceed with the evaluation. This decision would be justified if assumptions regarding entry skills had not yet been tested. The designer could capitalize on such an opportunity to verify his or her assumptions about entering competencies. On the other hand, if the necessity of certain skills had been verified at an earlier stage, the designer would probably want to select a different participant. In this latter case, continuing the evaluation would be frustrating for the student and unfruitful for the designer.

When a participant possesses some or all of the terminal behaviors, the designer faces a different problem. Time and cost constraints may require the evaluation to proceed as scheduled. However, the results of the evaluation would have very limited value. Already knowledgeable students could detect obvious errors in visuals and in the text; but they would not be valid sources of information for sequencing, pacing, or adequacy of practice and feedback exercises. Since it is important to collect as much useful data as possible from

each evaluation, the designer should obtain a participant who does not possess any of the terminal skills.

III. Revising the Instruction

After formative evaluation data have been collected and summarized, the designer must translate the findings into decisions for revising the instruction. To date little research has been done on inferring the types of revisions to be made from various data sources. To assist in the revision process, however, the designer can make decisions regarding the priority of data sources and examine the results in relation to various components of the instructional design.

III.B. Decide in advance the priority of data sources. The designer can facilitate the revision process by deciding in advance the priorities to be assigned to various sources of data (Baker, 1974). Pretest and posttest achievement scores are usually assigned the highest priority. This is because the intended learning outcomes are reflected in behavioral objectives and their associated test items. If the instructional materials do not promote intended learning outcomes, revisions are definitely in order. Within-course test items or responses on practice and feedback exercises are informative in terms of student progress through the materials, but are probably less essential than posttest performance. Attitude questionnaire data would be given high priority for courses which depend on voluntary enrollment or in cases where student motivation is known to be low. Establishing the relative importance of data sources in this manner helps the designer focus attention on critical indicators of needed revisions.

III.C. Examine summarized data in relation to components of the instructional design. The reader is encouraged to review the examples presented by Dick (1977) for examining formative evaluation data in relation to learning hierarchies for intellectual skills. This same procedure may be employed with instructional maps. By placing item analysis data into instructional maps, the designer can study the validity of assumptions about sequencing, subordinate relationships, domain interactions, and implied transfer effects.

After reviewing data in terms of learning hierarchies, instructional maps, objectives, and test items, the next step is to check the events of instruction and conditions of learning incorporated into the design. Perhaps insufficient learning guidance was provided or relevant prerequisite skills were not recalled. It may be that additional spaced reviews and a broader range of rule applications are necessary. Only after checking these components of the design process should the designer revise the actual materials.

III.D. When do revisions end? The decision to end the revision cycle may be based on several factors: design decision, time constraints, or cost-effectiveness.

One question the designer must ask is, "How important is the objective?" In some instances, the consequences of non-performance may be serious, particularly in military or industrial settings where physical danger may be a consideration. If a design decision has been made such that 90 percent of the learners must attain 90 percent of the objectives, then revisions will end when this criterion has been reached.

Time constraints may also bring an end to revisions. This is an unfortunate, but frequently encountered, circumstance. If deadlines slip during the design and development stage, the time allotted for revisions may be shortened. When little time is left for revisions, the designer is forced to establish priorities for the different data sources; and it is best to have planned this in advance.

Even when adequate time is available, cost-effectiveness may be a factor in terminating revisions. The largest gains in improvement generally come from the one-on-one evaluation, with smaller improvements being gained in the later stages of formative evaluation. At some point, the improvements will be so small that they do not result in important gains in student achievement. Such would be the case when a second field trial increased posttest performance from 93 to 94 percent. When revisions cease to make substantial differences, their costs outweigh any added benefits.

The Importance of Formative Evaluation

Instructional design principles, while considerably advanced as compared to the status 20 years ago, are still in an early stage relative to the more established disciplines. Therefore, even experienced designers need to use formative evaluation to improve the instructional strategies as incorporated into instructional materials and lesson plans.

The importance of the above observation can be appreciated by teachers who felt that they made excellent "presentations" to their students, but who found afterwards that the students' performance on tests was greatly disappointing. This same experience has been found by designers of first-draft self-instructional materials or "modules," which were deemed to incorporate appropriate instructional events and conditions of learning. So, all too often, what was "taught" was not "learned."

Formative evaluation data can often reveal many kinds of weaknesses in the instruction:

1. Inadequate analysis of objectives in terms of the proper sequencing of teaching the subordinate competencies or enabling objectives.

2. Inadequate provisions for needed interaction among categories of objectives and domains of learning.

3. Failure to incorporate the conditions of learning into the instructional events for the lesson.

4. Omission of needed instructional events, such as guidance to thinking, student responding and feedback, and generalizing experiences.

5. Unclear writing style and faulty preparation of pictures, graphs, and other illustrative material.

6. Failure to monitor student progress sufficiently to assure that subordinate competencies were mastered.

7. Too much emphasis upon presenting information and too little emphasis upon how well it is learned, recalled, and used.

8. Inadequate schedules of review and rehearsal.

9. Too little use of introductions, transitions, and advance organizers.

10. Use of unfamiliar vocabulary.

11. Complex sentence structure.

12. Lack of use of "readability" indexing.

13. Faulty projection of visual aids.

14. Failure to provide more than one set of materials or methods for learning.

15. Too rapid or too slow pacing.

16. Lack of remedial instruction in case of absence of assumed entering skills or prerequisite skills.

17. Failure to arouse interest and motivation.

18. Faulty test items.

19. Failure to achieve congruence among objectives, instruction, and tests.

20. Trying to rush the design work.

It is perhaps ironical that while research suggests that motivation is a greater source of variance in achievement among students than are methods effects, designers pay so little attention to motivation. This research finding might be modified, of course, if all instruction were well designed, in both structural and motivational aspects.

One of the research areas that is not far enough advanced to be of much help to the designer is research in trait-treatment interactions. Even if that research provided more specific guidelines for how to adjust instruction to individual differences in learning style, the economy of providing alternate materials and methods would pose a problem. However, such individualized instruction programs as PLAN and IPI (Talmage, 1975) do provide practical provisions for self-pacing, if not adjustment of objectives and methods to suit students' interests and learning styles. Such individualized

programs may represent one of the greatest areas of impact of instructional systems design theory.

Examples of Instruments Used in Formative Evaluation

While we do not suggest that you adopt instruments for evaluation in any routine or "cookbook" fashion, we do present on the pages that follow examples of the types of instruments that may be useful to consider. We recommend that you use these only as a source of ideas, and proceed to develop your own instruments to suit your objectives and circumstances. (See Figures 32, 33, 34, and 35.)

NAME .... Age ....

Present Occupation or Course of Study ....

....

Have you completed at least one year of college? ....

Have you had any prior experience in preparing proposal budgets? If so, what kind of experience?

....

....

Have you had any prior experience in computing fringe benefits for a university-related proposal? If so, what kind of experience?

....

....

Do you feel that a knowledge of fringe benefits would be useful? If so, in what way?

....

....

Figure 32. Background information form.

Please mark your response to each statement with an "X" at the appropriate point on the scale.

1a. How difficult was the instruction?

    (Too Easy)   (Average)   (Too Difficult)

b. Where was it too easy or too difficult? ....

....

2a. How was the length of the instruction?

    (Too Short)   (OK)   (Too Long)

b. Where was it too short or too long? ....

....

3. How was the information presentation?

    (Too little at one time)   (OK)   (Too much at one time)

4a. Was the information clear or confusing?

    (Clear)   (Neutral)   (Confusing)

b. Where was it confusing? ....

....

5. How was the vocabulary in the lesson?

    (Too Simple)   (OK)   (Too Complicated)

6a. How were the directions?

    (Clear)   (Average)   (Confusing)

b. Where were the directions confusing? ....

....

Figure 33. Attitude questionnaire.

7. How were the practice exercises?

(Too Few)   (About Right)   (Too Many)

8. Did the practice exercises hold your interest?

(Yes, interesting)   (OK)   (No, boring)

9. How was the lesson's pace?

(Too Slow)   (OK)   (Too Fast)

10. How was the content structured?

(Logically)   (OK)   (Randomly)

11. After learning the content, how did you find the review at the end of the lesson?

(Helpful)   (OK)   (Unnecessary)

12a. How were the test questions?

(Clear)   (OK)   (Confusing)

   b. Where were the test questions confusing? ....

   ....

13. How were the statements of the objectives?

(Helpful)   (OK)   (Unnecessary)

14. How confident are you of your performance?

(Very)   (OK)   (Not at all)

15. Any other general comments? Write them below. Thanks.

(Figure 33 Continued)

The individual participants will be asked the following questions. Their responses should be indicated in the spaces provided.

1. How difficult was the instruction?

2. How was the length of the instruction?

3. Was the information clear or confusing?

4. How was the vocabulary in the lesson?

5. Were the directions clear or confusing?

6. How were the practice exercises? Were they necessary?

7. How was the lesson's pace?

8. How was the visual art?

9. How was the narration?

10. Did you feel any pressure?

11. How confident are you of your performance?

Figure 34. Debriefing interview for evaluating a slide/tape lesson.

The individual participants will be asked the following questions. Their responses should be indicated in the spaces provided.

1. How difficult was the instruction?

2. How was the length of the instruction?

3. Was the information clear or confusing?

4. How was the vocabulary in the lesson?

5. Were the directions clear or confusing?

6. How were the practice exercises? Were they helpful?

7. How was the lesson's pace?

8. How were the graphic illustrations?

9. How were the test questions?

10. How confident are you of your performance?

11. Any other general comments?

Figure 35. Debriefing interview for evaluating a written lesson.

General Instructions

The following instructions were provided to participants in a small-group evaluation. Since the lesson was self-paced and intended for home use, the instructions were written and attached to the materials. This type of general introduction could be adapted to other stages of formative evaluation and to other instructional settings as well.

The attached instructional materials are presently in the process of revision. Your help in making them more effective and more interesting is both needed and appreciated!

There are five parts to complete: a background information sheet, a pretest, the lesson, a posttest, and an attitude questionnaire. The total time to complete these parts is approximately one hour. First, you will receive the background information sheet, the pretest, and the lesson. When you have completed these materials, we will pick them up and give you the posttest and the attitude questionnaire. At this time, we will have a chance to discuss your reactions to any or all of the materials.

As you go through the materials, please:

1. Mark on the materials the time it takes you to complete the pretest, the lesson, and the posttest. Please note *separate* times for each component. This is by no means a "timed" activity. These data will simply help to verify some assumptions that have been made about the materials.

2. Circle any words that are unclear.

3. Note in the margins any comments you may have about the directions, tests, content, examples, etc.

These materials have not been tried out before with students; so, many errors are anticipated. Don't hesitate to point them out. Again, thanks for your time in evaluating these materials. Your comments and suggestions will be most helpful in revising the instruction.

Exercise No. 10: Planning Formative Evaluations

1. Describe the differences in one-on-one, small-group, and field-trial formative evaluations in terms of their stated purposes.

2. Describe the inputs into each stage of the formative evaluation process.

3. State three criteria to apply in selecting formative evaluation participants.

4. How many students should participate in each stage of formative evaluation?

5. Describe the role of a subject-matter expert in formative evaluation.

6. State the rule of thumb for scheduling time to conduct one-on-one evaluations.

7. List at least six types of data-collection instruments that may be useful during formative evaluation.

8. Name at least four kinds of weaknesses in the instruction that formative evaluation data can reveal.

9. During the revision cycle, formative evaluation data must be compared to several elements of the instructional design process. Describe a procedure for comparing formative evaluation results to the steps taken in the design and development of materials.

10. Why is the formative evaluation of instructional materials considered important?

Exercise No. 11: Deciding Upon Revisions, Using Test Data

1. Suppose the following distribution of posttest scores was obtained from formative evaluation data. What components of the instructional design should be examined first and why?

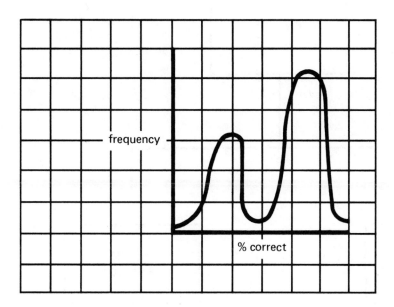

2. Suppose that the following distribution of posttest scores was obtained from formative evaluation data. What component of the instructional design should be revised based on this information?

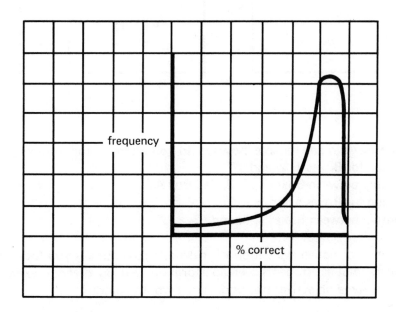

3. Suppose you have conducted a formative evaluation on a module designed to teach "computing standard deviation." In the design process, you constructed a learning hierarchy. The results of a pretest and posttest administered in a field trial were placed into the hierarchy. The teaching sequence is indicated by numbers beside each box.

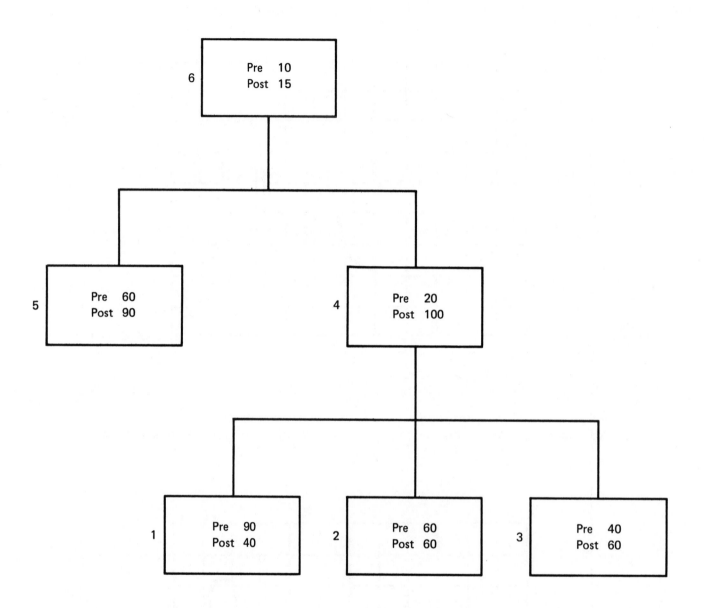

Assuming all tests were valid and reliable, how would you interpret the following?
  (a) The instruction for Boxes 1, 2, and 3?
  (b) The relationship between Boxes 1, 2, 3, and Box 4?
  (c) The instruction for Boxes 4 and 5?
  (d) The relationship between Boxes 4, 5, and 6?
  (e) The instruction for Box 6?
4. Suppose that during a formative evaluation of instructional materials you found that within-course responses were high (that is, students were performing well on practice exercises), but posttest performance over the *same* objectives was poor. What would you do?

Chapter 12
Teacher Training; Summative Evaluation; Diffusion

Chapter in This Book	Recommended Readings		
	Briggs, L.J. (Ed.) *Instructional Design: Principles and Applications.* Englewood Cliffs, N.J.: Educational Technology Publications, 1977.	Gagné, R.M., and Briggs, L.J. *Principles of Instructional Design*, 2nd ed. New York: Holt, Rinehart, and Winston, 1979.	Gagné, R.M. *The Conditions of Learning*, 3rd ed. New York: Holt, Rinehart, and Winston, 1977.
11	Chapter 10	Chapter 15	
(12)	**Chapter 15**	**Chapter 15**	

Background

It is not always the instructional designer's function to have responsibility for three aspects of a complete instructional system: teacher training, summative evaluation, and diffusion. However, in some cases, the person who directs the design effort also conducts these three activities. Sometimes the design director would serve only a coordinating role to others who direct these three functions.

Due to the variations in arrangements, just mentioned, this book does not provide a "how to do it" section for this Chapter. Instead, we merely describe the purpose of these three functions to complete our account of the total instructional design process; we refer the reader to other sources for more detail. Therefore, we do not provide objectives for this Chapter, as we have done for most other chapters.

Teacher Training

When teachers serve as both the designers and the implementors of instruction, there may be no need for special training for the teachers, because they design only the kinds of instruction they already know how to conduct. Thus, when teachers accept the concept of "instructional events" as the central building blocks for lesson planning (Briggs, 1977, Chapter 8), they choose media, materials, and learning activities which they feel competent to utilize in the classroom. Even when textbooks and other materials have already been selected for the course by somebody else, teachers can still utilize the concept that their lesson plans must bring congruence among their objectives, their teaching, and their ways of evaluating pupil achievement. When the materials have not already been selected by somebody else, teachers proceed to *choose* (rather than design and develop) those materials which contain the appropriate content for helping teachers implement the instructional events in such a way as to enable the learners to achieve the objective of each lesson. As a consequence, teachers tend to design lessons so as to employ procedures with which they feel comfortable, given their prior training and experience. Teaching methods, under these conventional arrangements, tend not to change rapidly or to depart markedly from these prior experiences.

In contrast to the above situation, when a school adopts a new delivery system, such as one of the nationally known systems of individualized instruction (Talmage, 1975), teachers usually need additional training on how to manage aspects of the system which are new to them. The same often holds true when a new curriculum in a subject area is adopted by the school. Sometimes the needed special training relates to a change in role for the teacher—a change from an information-presenting role to that of a manager of a self-paced learning system, in which each pupil progresses at his or her own rate. In other instances, teachers may need to learn a new content orientation for a new curriculum.

Whatever the nature of the new training needed for teachers, several methods are employed. These include orientation sessions, workshops, demonstrations, and observations of classroom procedures.

In an ideal situation, when a new instructional system or curriculum is being designed with the intent of later widespread adoption by schools, teachers and administrators are invited to participate in the design process. For example, if a new system of teaching science is to be designed, advisory groups would be formed to include a sample of school personnel like those who are to become intended adopters. Other people included in advisory groups would be scientists, instructional designers, evaluators, students, parents, and perhaps others. Some members of such groups would serve only a needs-verification and approval function; others would assist in the detailed design of the new system.

There are two important reasons for including teachers and school administrators in both advisory and working groups. One reason is to utilize their prior knowledge and experience about the pupil population and the school environment. A second reason is to include them in the decision-making process so that they help design the procedures they will later be asked to adopt and implement in the schools. Even an ideal new system is likely to be rejected by school personnel if members of their group were not included in the design process.

Given the advance participation of samples of the potential user groups so that other teachers and administrators feel they were represented in the planning process, there are a number of options for the training of teachers who may become adopters and implementors of the new system.

Orientation Sessions

Often, while the new system is still in the design stage, members of the design team meet with groups of teachers to describe philosophy, content, methods, and classroom management plans. If this is done early, teachers may make suggestions to improve the effectiveness as well as the acceptability of the new system. Even if the design is essentially completed, such meetings can help potential adopters understand the requirements for operating the new system so that they can make a realistic decision about adopting the system in the future. The implications of such meetings for administrators and school board members as well have been discussed elsewhere for systems of individualized instruction (Briggs and Aronson, 1975). Often a year or more is devoted to such orientation and feedback sessions before teachers are asked to make a decision to adopt the new system.

Workshops

After the details of system design are known, teachers are often invited to more intensive sessions to learn more about the separate components of the system: the underlying rationale; the strategies of teaching; the materials to be employed; and the intended classroom organization and management. The practical details of operating the system may be viewed in the form of teachers' guides, filmed demonstration, etc. Discussions are then conducted both for continued orientation of teachers and for identifying possible problems.

Demonstrations

Still later in the design process, teacher members of the project team serve as demonstration leaders to enable other teachers to view the process in a simulated or real classroom setting. Sometimes teachers are scheduled as visitors for a few days each while the new system is carried on during an actual school year. The visitors may gradually assist the demonstration teachers, after which they return to their own schools to be resource persons for still other teachers. In some cases, a visitor may implement the system in his or her own classroom as a local demonstration for other teachers in the school, before the entire school adopts the system. Continuous contacts are often maintained by "networks" of early adopters, who also keep contacts with the design center.

First Implementation

Often teachers participate in some or all of the above teacher-training methods before their first regular use of the new system. During their first year of classroom utilization, they work out their own modifications in procedures and report the results to the design center. These data can be a part of the continued formative evaluation of the system (Chapter 11), although modifications may be discouraged while a classroom or school is a "pilot" school during evaluations undertaken under presumed uniform conditions.

The first year of experience with a new system is often a difficult one for teachers. No matter how enthusiastically they may support the intent of the system, they find many unexpected problems to be solved and new roles to perform. In systems of individualized instruction, teachers must learn new ways to: monitor pupil progress; determine the "starting point" for each pupil; make prescriptions for individual needs; monitor materials storage and acquisition; teach pupils to operate simple audio-visual equipment; conduct small-group activities while monitoring pupils working alone or in pairs; and report pupil progress. While some teachers who volunteered to try the new system may choose to go back to their earlier methods, those who can get through the first year often would be strongly opposed to dropping the new system (Briggs and Aronson, 1975). Other teachers may not be entirely comfortable with their new roles until after more than one year of utilization.

Summative Evaluation

There is no standard point at which formative evaluations and revisions end and summative evaluation begins. This may be influenced by the size of the project (e.g., a single course or an entire curriculum) and by the original intent (e.g., to try a new program as an experiment for research purposes or to plan for widespread adoption). Sometimes extensive field tryouts will be conducted in a large number of schools before summative evaluation is undertaken. On the other hand, methods and materials for a limited portion of a single course (often called a "module" of instruction) may undergo summative evaluation immediately after the three initial stages of formative evaluation described in Chapter 11.

Whatever the intent of the new instruction as to size of unit or marketing goal, the purpose of a summative evaluation is broader and different from the case of formative evaluation. While the purpose of formative evaluation is to *improve* the instruction by comparing goals and objectives to actual outcomes of the instruction, as defined by the goals and objectives, and making needed improvements, the purpose of summative evaluation is to answer such questions as these:

1. Was the instruction effective in terms of achievement of *stated* goals and objectives?

2. Did the instruction result in *unexpected* outcomes, good or bad?

3. Were the objectives *worth* the cost of achieving them?

4. Would *other* objectives have been more desirable?

5. Is the instruction better than available alternate forms of instruction?

6. What were the attitudes of pupils, parents, teachers, administrators, and the school board towards the instruction?

7. Were new problems or values created by the instruction?

It is evident that the purposes of summative evaluation include, but are not restricted to, the question of whether the system met its intended goals and objectives. It is not surprising, then, that the methods and instruments used also differ for the two forms of evaluation, although both include measures of learner performance. It is sometimes said that the purpose of formative evaluation is to *improve* the instruction in efficiency and effectiveness, while the purpose of summative evaluation is to *prove* the value of the system, both in pedagogical and economic terms. Therefore, *measurements* of a rather objective sort are the mainstay of formative evaluation, whereas *value judgments* take a prominent place in summative evaluation.

It is beyond the scope of this book to present an account of the methods of summative evaluation; brief accounts are given in the books referred to at the opening of this Chapter. More comprehensive treatments are found elsewhere (Cooley, 1971; Scriven, 1967; Stufflebeam, 1974).

Diffusion

Some new instructional systems are designed from the outset to be adopted as widely as possible by schools or training agencies. The designers in this case will give careful attention to further diffusion of the system while it is being designed. One implication of this intent concerning diffusion and adoption is that the designer will either (a) avoid radical innovations which, being foreign to potential adopters, will result in resistance or opposition, and hence few adoptions, or (b) he or she will seek acceptance of the radical innovations by bringing in potential adopters as members of the design team. Perhaps, in practice, some of both strategies are used in new systems which do actually receive wide adoption.

Because of the above, a designer may face the choice of designing the very best system he or she knows how to design, with the result of few adoptions and hence little impact; or he or she may settle for less radical change from conventional instruction and achieve wide adoption. The value of experimental programs is to *demonstrate* what can be done when acceptance is achieved in advance in a selected, small number of schools. The value of a widely adopted program is to achieve *some impact* and improvement in many schools. The former tends to be preferred by the researcher; the latter is preferred by the entrepreneur. One approach achieves *maximum* improvement in a few schools, and the other achieves *some* improvement in many schools. Is such a choice real, and if so, why is it necessary?

We believe the choice *is* real. While we do not claim that the most radical changes are always best, we also object to labelling existing conventional instruction as "tried and true" or "best." In science, new research findings usually lead eventually to improved technology, although it has been increasingly recognized of late that new technology can create new problems. But an analysis of potential consequences of new technology, can, in turn, lead to improved design to avoid new problems. At least it is not clear that such new educational technology as the systems of individualized instruction mentioned earlier (Talmage, 1975) have created an educational pollution problem. While the long-term value of such systems remains to be evaluated, the designers of those systems attended to and planned for the classroom delivery system needed to implement the theories on which the systems were based.

Reasons for the present necessary choice between degree of change and extent of adoptions have been discussed, in the case of higher education, by Wager (1977). More general issues and problems in diffusion have been discussed by Havelock *et al.* (1969).

The overall history of educational technology and its acceptance appear to indicate that many instructional innovations arose in military training and industry, and were only much later, if at all, adopted for use in education. To be sure, the objectives are sometimes easier to identify for special training than for education, but as we saw in Chapters 2 and 3, objectives *can* be identified down to the level of objectives for single lessons or parts of lessons. The difference in goal complexity has often led to the argument that instructional design principles can be applied to training but not to education. Our reply is that the purpose of both is to promote *learning*, and that avoidance of careful analysis of objectives is the real reason for some of the opposition to systematic instructional design.

There are, however, some fundamental differences between education and military and industrial training. Some important aspects of the latter are listed next.

1. Teachers in military and industrial situations would rather be in the field than in the classroom. They therefore welcome automated learning and self-instructional techniques which result in less time for them as instructors in the classroom.

2. Instructors are often not trained as instructors but as experts for some job in the field. They do not wish to protect their tenure as instructors but, rather, to shorten it.

3. Profit-making organizations are willing to pay well for effective instructional systems, and they will support design and development activities which reduce training time.

4. Military and industrial personnel are accustomed to machines in their jobs, and hence will accept effective machines used for training.

5. The military and industry will pay costs of evaluating effectiveness and efficiency.

6. Budgets allow for costs of materials design and production (in whatever media are deemed effective), when relatively high "preparation costs" are amortized over years for thousands of trainees, resulting in relatively low classroom costs. That is, a higher ratio of costs for materials and equipment to salaries of instructors will be tolerated. Thus, the ratio of "preparation" to "teaching" costs is far different than in education.

7. The degree and closeness of supervision that will be accepted is higher than in education.

The above is not to say that radical changes in instruction are as easily accepted in any organization as are changes in other areas of life, such as clothing styles. We are products of how *we* were taught, and that influence is not easy to overcome.

In any event, changes do not generally take place rapidly in instruction, and the reasons are quite complex. Mechanisms for inducing change have been reviewed by Havelock *et al.* (1969).

A Closing Comment

It would be interesting, 20 years from now, to evaluate the design model presented in this book and in the recommended readings. Changes now unforeseen will no doubt influence how this book is viewed from that future vantage point. Probably the changes in educational technology will be greater during the next 20 years than during the past 20 years, partly because instructional design as a graduate degree program is so new.

Without any effort to forecast the future, we, in closing, offer our own views of the strengths and weaknesses of instructional design, as presented in this book. The judgments of others, of course, will be more objective.

Strengths

1. An intellectually consistent set of theories and practices has been presented.

2. Both theory and practice draw as heavily as possible upon research, but many gaps have been filled by ordinary common-sense thinking.

3. Several novel formats for recording and reviewing design decisions have been offered.

4. Specific techniques have been suggested, with no intent to design a "cookbook" approach to decision-making.

5. While we have utilized learning theory when we could, we have relied more heavily upon such concepts as learning taxonomies, task analysis, instructional maps, learning hierarchies, media analysis worksheets, instructional events, and conditions of learning. We acknowledge a large debt to Dr. Robert M. Gagné for the origin of many of these key concepts.

6. The overall procedures presented here can well utilize the resources of experienced designers and can serve as a training source for novices.

7. The overall model is a complex one, but it can be simplified for use by less trained designers or for projects of limited time and budget.

8. Using this complex model as a base, one could expand from it or simplify, as needed.

Weaknesses

1. We apparently know more about task variables than learner variables. We have shown how instruction may vary according to domain of outcome intended, but we have not the knowledge to apply known or suspected trait-treatment interactions or "learning styles."

2. Due to our emphasis upon instructional materials and media to implement many of the instructional events, we have not delved into the teacher's role in any detail. This was not done to downgrade the importance of the teacher, but to imply that the role changes from "presenter of information" to "manager of learning" when pre-designed materials "carry" much of the instruction. (Our intent was not to train teachers, except in their design role, and to provide information to train designers of instructional materials.)

3. While we know that some research suggests that ability and motivation of students account for more variance in achievement than do "methods effects," we don't know much about ability and motivation. Also, much of the research deals with moderately or poorly designed "methods." We suggest that the reader consult sources we have not referred to here for research in ability and motivation.

4. In spite of our failure to say much about trait-treatment interactions, we have tried to show relationships between learner characteristics and media for instruction.

5. We have not dealt directly with the capabilities of computers for instruction, and we have presented only brief comments about effective utilization of other media. However, media selection as a component in lesson design has been emphasized.

6. We have not taken the space for acknowledging that the kind of design model we present here has many vocal critics. Other sources present competing design models, whose advantages and shortcomings are of interest to us. We realize that the kind of model espoused here is not followed by the majority of teachers and curriculum designers. Our use of the word "system" does not imply that other kinds of models fail to use systematic planning.

7. Finally, we have been careful to list here more strengths than weaknesses.

References

AAAS Commission on Science Education. *Science—A Process Approach*. Washington, D.C.: American Association for the Advancement of Science, 1967.

Ackerman, A.S. Income Tax Preparation. In L.J. Briggs (Ed.), *Instructional Design: Principles and Applications*. Englewood Cliffs, N.J.: Educational Technology Publications, 1977, Chapter 16, pp. 475-500.

Ausubel, D.P. *The Psychology of Meaningful Verbal Learning*. New York: Grune and Stratton, 1963.

Ausubel, D.P. *Educational Psychology: A Cognitive View*. New York: Holt, Rinehart, and Winston, 1968.

Baker, E.L. *Evaluating Instructional Programs, Version E*. Los Angeles: University of California, April, 1974.

Bem, D.L. *Beliefs, Attitudes, and Human Affairs*. Monterey, Calif.: Brooks/Cole, 1970.

Bloom, B.S. (Ed.) *Taxonomy of Educational Objectives. Handbook I: Cognitive Domain*. New York: Longman, 1956.

Bradshaw, J. The Concept of Social Need. *New Society*, March 30, 1972, pp. 640-643.

Branson, R.K. Military and Industrial Training. In L.J. Briggs (Ed.), *Instructional Design: Principles and Applications*. Englewood Cliffs, N.J.: Educational Technology Publications, 1977, Chapter 12, pp. 353-391.

Briggs, L.J. Learner Variables and Educational Media. *Review of Educational Research*, April, 1968a, *38*, pp. 160-176.

Briggs, L.J. *Sequencing of Instruction in Relation to Hierarchies of Competence*. Pittsburgh, Pa.: American Institutes for Research, 1968b (Monograph No. 3).

Briggs, L.J. *Handbook of Procedures for the Design of Instruction* (First Edition). Pittsburgh, Pa.: American Institutes for Research, 1970 (Monograph No. 4).

Briggs, L.J. (Ed.) *Instructional Design: Principles and Applications*. Englewood Cliffs, N.J.: Educational Technology Publications, 1977.

Briggs, L.J., and Aronson, D. *An Interpretive Study of Individualized Instruction in the Schools: Procedures, Problems, and Prospects*. (Final Report, National Institute of Education, Grant No. NIE-G-740065.) Tallahassee, Fla.: Florida State University, 1975.

Bruner, J.S., Goodnow, J.J., and Austin, G.A. *A Study of Thinking*. New York: Science Editions, Inc., 1962.

Burton, J.K., and Merrill, P.F. Needs Assessment: Goals, Needs, and Priorities. In L.J. Briggs (Ed.), *Instructional Design: Principles and Applications*. Englewood Cliffs, N.J.: Educational Technology Publications, 1977, Chapter 2, pp. 21-45.

Campeau, P.L. Test Anxiety and Feedback in Programmed Instruction. *Journal of Educational Psychology*, 1968, *59*, pp. 159-163.

Carey, J., and Briggs, L.J. Teams as Designers. In L.J. Briggs (Ed.), *Instructional Design: Principles and Applications*. Englewood Cliffs, N.J.: Educational Technology Publications, 1977, Chapter 9, pp. 261-307.

Cooley, W.W. *Methods of Evaluating School Innovations*. Pittsburgh, Pa.: Learning Research and Development Center, University of Pittsburgh, 1971 (26).

Dale, E.A. *Audiovisual Methods in Teaching (Third Edition)*. New York: Holt, Rinehart, and Winston, 1969.

Dick, W. Formative Evaluation. In L.J. Briggs (Ed.), *Instructional Design: Principles and Applications*. Englewood Cliffs, N.J.: Educational Technology Publications, 1977, Chapter 10, pp. 311-333.

Estes, W.K. Reinforcement in Human Behavior. *American Scientist*, Vol. 60, Nov., Dec., 1972.

Gagné, R.M. Analysis of Objectives. In L.J. Briggs (Ed.), *Instructional Design: Principles and Applications*. Englewood Cliffs, N.J.: Educational Technology Publications, 1977a, Chapter 5, pp. 115-148.

Gagné, R.M. *The Conditions of Learning* (Third Edition). New York: Holt, Rinehart, and Winston, Inc., 1977b.

Gagné, R.M., and Briggs, L.J. *Principles of Instructional Design* (Second Edition). New York: Holt, Rinehart, and Winston, 1979.

Gropper, G.L. Why Is a Picture Worth a Thousand

Words? *AV Communication Review,* 1963, pp. 75-95.

Havelock, R.G. *et al. Planning for Innovation Through Dissemination and Utilization of Knowledge.* Ann Arbor: Institute for Social Research, University of Michigan, 1969.

Hershberger, W. Self-Evaluation Responding and Typographical Cueing: Techniques for Programming Self-Instructional Reading Materials. *Journal of Educational Psychology,* 1964, *55,* pp. 288-296.

Hovland, C.I., Janis, I.J., and Kelley, H.H. *Communications and Persuasion.* New Haven: Yale University Press, 1953.

Joyce, B., and Weil, M. *Models of Teaching.* Englewood Cliffs, N.J.: Prentice-Hall, 1972.

Kaufman, R., and English, F.W. *Needs Assessment: Concept and Application.* Englewood Cliffs, N.J.: Educational Technology Publications, 1979.

Kibler, R.J., and Bassett, R.E. Writing Performance Objectives. In L.J. Briggs (Ed.), *Instructional Design: Principles and Applications.* Englewood Cliffs, N.J.: Educational Technology Publications, 1977, Chapter 3, pp. 49-112.

Klausmeier, H.J., and Davis, J.K. Transfer of Learning. Preprint to appear in *Encyclopedia of Educational Research,* Edition No. 5, University of Wisconsin, 1980.

Krathwohl, D.R., Bloom, B.S., and Masia, B.B. *Taxonomy of Educational Objectives. Handbook II: Affective Domain.* New York: Longman, 1964.

Mager, R.F. *Preparing Instructional Objectives.* Palo Alto, Calif.: Fearon Publishers, 1962.

Markle, D.G. First Aid Training. In L.J. Briggs (Ed.), *Instructional Design: Principles and Applications.* Englewood Cliffs, N.J.: Educational Technology Publications, 1977, Chapter 15, pp. 439-459.

Melton, A.W. Summing Up. Comments Toward the Future. In G. Finch (Ed.), *Educational and Training Media: A Symposium.* Washington, D.C.: National Academy of Sciences–National Research Council, 1960, Publication 789, pp. 196-206.

Parker, R. The Effects of Amount of Study Time, Quality of Instruction, and Degree of Initial Learning upon Retention of an Intellectual Skill. Unpublished doctoral dissertation, F.S.U., 1974.

Popham, W.J., and Husek, T.R. Implications of Criterion-Referenced Measurement. *Journal of*

Educational Measurement, 1969, *6,* pp. 1-9.

Pressey, S.L. A Simple Apparatus Which Gives Tests and Scores—and Teaches. *School and Society,* 1926, *13,* pp. 373-376.

Pressey, S.L. Development and Appraisal of Devices Providing Immediate Automatic Scoring of Objective Tests and Concomitant Self-Instruction. *Journal of Psychology,* 1950, *29,* pp. 417-447.

Rohwer, W.D. Elaboration and Learning in Childhood and Adolescence. In H.W. Reese (Ed.), *Advances in Child Development and Behavior.* New York: Academic Press, 1975.

Rosen, M.J. An Experimental Design for Comparing the Effects of Instructional Media Programming Procedures: Subjective Versus Objective Procedures. Final Report. Palo Alto, Calif.: American Institutes for Research, 1968.

Scriven, M. The Methodology of Evaluation. In R. Tyler, R.M. Gagné, and M. Scriven, *Perspectives of Curriculum Evaluation.* AERA Monograph Series on Curriculum Evaluation, No. 1. Chicago: Rand McNally, 1967.

Stufflebeam, D.L. Alternative Approaches to Educational Evaluation. A Self-Study Guide for Educators. In W.J. Popham (Ed.), *Evaluation in Education.* Berkeley, Calif.: McCutchan, 1974.

Tallmadge, G.K., and Shearer, J.W. Relationships Among Learning Styles, Instructional Methods, and the Nature of Learning Experiences. *Journal of Educational Psychology,* 1969, *60,* pp. 222-230.

Talmage, H. (Ed.) *Systems of Individualized Education.* Berkeley, Calif.: McCutchan, 1975.

The Futurist. Washington, D.C.: World Future Society, Volume XIII, No. 3, June, 1979.

Tyler, R.W. *Basic Principles of Curriculum and Instruction.* Chicago: University of Chicago Press, 1949.

Wager, W. Media Selection in the Affective Domain: A Further Interpretation of Dale's Cone of Experience for Cognitive and Affective Learning. *Educational Technology,* July, 1975, *15*(7), pp. 9-13.

Wager, W. Instructional Technology and Higher Education. In L.J. Briggs (Ed.), *Instructional Design: Principles and Applications.* Englewood Cliffs, N.J.: Educational Technology Publications, 1977, Chapter 13, pp. 395-419.

Wilson, R.M., and Geyer, T. *Readings for Diagnostic and Remedial Reading.* Columbus, Ohio: Charles E. Merrill, 1972.

Answer Key: Chapter 1 Information Test

_1._ non-instructional solutions to problems include:
   a. changes in laws or regulations
   b. changes in incentives
   c. changes in budgets
   d. changes in operating procedures

_2._ the objectives in terms of what learners must **do** with the content may never be identified

_3._
   a. components are analyzed in a systematic order
   b. the process is orderly but flexible
   c. the procedures are based on research and theory
   d. empirical data are gathered to test the program
   e. a delivery system considers the environment and the characteristics of teachers and learners
   f. the model is consistent with openness and accountability

_4._ to facilitate learning by the reader

_5._ "recycling," to permit revisions of earlier work and changes in plans for future work

_6._
   a. to measure achievement for an information course
   b. to serve as enablers for a skill course

_7._ to serve as essential prerequisite skill development to support attainment of the chapter terminal objectives

_8._ writing appropriate objectives for each course

_9._
   a. to gain an orientation to the design process
   b. to gain actual design skills
   c. to identify research which is needed
   d. to develop procedures which teachers can use
   e. to identify classroom organization changes
   f. to identify administrative changes

_10._ objectives, instruction, and evaluation of learner performance

Answer Key: Chapter 2 Information Test

_1._
   a. national
   b. state
   c. school or school district
   d. individual "courses," or each year of instruction for each subject area

_2._
   a. an entire curriculum
   b. a single course

_3._
   b. problem; solution

_4._ the gap between the actual situation and the desired situation

_5._ curriculum scope and sequence statement

_6._ performance objectives

_7._
   a. normative need—standard vitamin intake
   b. felt need—something somebody wants (a boat)
   c. comparative need—something another school has (a library)
   d. future need—future need for leisure-time activities
   e. expressed need—demand for an offered item or service (an automobile)

_8._ none

_9._
   a. national study groups
   b. conventions of the past curricula
   c. professional societies
   d. legislation

_10._ job analysis

_11._
   a. identify an appropriate group of people
   b. identify a broad range of possible goals
   c. rank order goals in importance
   d. identify discrepancies between desired and actual pupil performance
   e. set priorities for action

1. scope and sequence statement

2.

    a. to be sure that the chosen delivery system can be developed with existing resources and constraints

    b. to remove constraints, if possible

    c. to choose a delivery system that will meet the objectives and be acceptable to the users

3.

    a. time and money

    b. type of personnel available

    c. existing laws and regulations

    d. institutional practices

    e. attitudes of users

4.

    a. change in preferred delivery system

    b. reassign priorities to goals

    c. modify goal expectations and expected level of pupil achievement

5.

    a. to defend each specific objective in terms of its contribution to achievement of a broader goal or objective

    b. to show a link or "audit trail" among layers of objectives

    c. to eventually identify necessary lesson objectives

6. A delivery system includes all media as well as all other components to make the system operate as planned

7.

    a. group instruction

    b. individualized instruction

    c. work-study programs

    d. small-group instruction

    e. home study

8.

    a. self-pacing

    b. a variety of media for each objective

    c. varying objectives for individual learners

9.

    a. instructional time varies among learners

    b. tests are given on an individual schedule

    c. second attempts on an objective are permitted

_10._

    a. a fixed quarter or semester duration limits the feasibility of self-pacing

    b. "incompletes" are discouraged

    c. some students procrastinate

    d. lack of resources

1. *there are different sets of conditions of learning for each domain; classifying objectives allows one to determine teaching strategy for clusters of objectives into domains, thus making fewer strategies to be designed*

2.
   a. *verbal information*
   b. *motor skills*
   c. *attitudes*
   d. *cognitive strategies*
   e. *intellectual skills*

3.
   a. *decide the domains needed, and write objectives for each*
   b. *write objectives, then classify by domain*
   c. *use the standard capability verbs when writing objectives, thus automatically classifying them (if written correctly)*

4.
   a. *memorized verbatim: names, labels, poems*
   b. *facts (not necessarily verbatim)*
   c. *substance learning*

5.
   a. *discrimination*
   b. *concrete concepts*
   c. *defined concepts*
   d. *rules*
   e. *problem solving*

6.	Type of Outcome	Standard Verb	Action Verb
a.	*discriminations*	*discriminate*	*by matching*
b.	*concrete concepts*	*identify*	*by pointing to*
c.	*defined concepts*	*classify*	*by sorting*
d.	*rule using*	*demonstrate*	*in writing*
e.	*problem solving*	*generate*	*a written solution*
f.	*verbatim memory*	*list, recite*	*orally*
g.	*facts*	*state*	*in writing*
h.	*substance*	*summarize*	*orally*
i.	*attitudes*	*choose*	*by selecting activity*
j.	*motor skills*	*execute*	*by performing*
k.	*cognitive strategies*	*originate*	*a written novel plan*

_7._ *by comparing the capability and performance described in the objective with the kind of behavior required by the test item*

_8._ *adequacy of measurement of the capability being tested; dependability (often related to the length of the test and its freedom from distortion)*

_9._
   a. *situation*
   b. *standard capability verb*
   c. *action verb*
   d. *object*
   e. *tools and constraints*

_10._ *to not mislead students as to how their performance on the objectives will be measured*

_11._
   a. *agreement with objectives*
   b. *congruence with objectives*
   c. *testing what was intended to be tested*

_12._ *measuring what you intended to measure as defined by the objective*

_13._ *measuring well and adequately what you intended to measure*

Answer Key: Chapter 5 Information Test

_1._

    a. *it has a recognizable starting point and finishing point*

    b. *it deals with an organized set of content*

_2._

    a. *course ICM*

    b. *unit ICM*

    c. *lesson ICM*

_3._

    a. *broad to narrow*

    b. *problem solving to rules, concepts, discriminations*

    c. *long-term outcomes to immediate outcomes*

    d. *lengthy curricula to short lessons*

_4._ *to remind us to look for relationships among courses in a curriculum, and to relate the curriculum to lifelong learning*

_5._

    a. *flat*

    b. *vertical (hierarchical)*

    c. *combination of a and b.*

Answer Key: Chapter 6 Information Test

_1._ intellectual skills domain

_2._ one to five: (discriminations, concrete concepts, defined concepts, rules, and problem solving)

_3._
    a. course-level ICM
    b. unit-level ICM
    c. lesson-level ICM

_4._ an ICM shows all relevant domains of outcomes, while a hierarchy shows only intellectual skills; an ICM shows domain interactions

_5._
    a. learning hierarchies
    b. information-processing analysis
    c. procedural analysis
    d. teaching experience (plus domain interactions, recording your own performance, and research data)

_6._ when entry skills are encountered

_7._ to justify each objective in terms of a more complex objective

_8._ there are arguments each way; decide it by considering sequencing of the unit being designed

_9._ by lines and domain symbols

_10._ because they may be recallable by a simple verbal cue to do so

Answer Key: Chapter 7 Information Test

<u>1.</u> the unit ICM.

<u>2.</u>

    a. time available
    b. nature of learners
    c. nature of the objective
    d. avoidance of boredom
    e. avoidance of overwhelming amounts of information

<u>3.</u> subordinate

<u>4.</u> as many as necessary to teach all objectives in the unit ICM, considering time schedules and learner characteristics

<u>5.</u> information-processing theory

<u>6.</u> the principle of transfer, or cumulative learning

<u>7.</u> essential prerequisite skills

<u>8.</u> a prerequisite skill is an actual part of the terminal skill; a supporting objective is not essential to learning, but it facilitates learning

<u>9.</u>

    a. essential sequence relationships
    b. time allotted for lessons

Answer Key: Chapter 9 Information Test

1. the lesson ICM

2.
   a. media characteristics
   b. learner characteristics
   c. task characteristics
   d. the kind of stimuli the media can convey
   e. attitudes of users

3. events of instruction and conditions of learning

4. information presenter to that of manager of instruction, guidance, and remedial learning

5.
   a. more reliable (stable)
   b. more easily subjected to formative evaluation

6. conditions

7. both

8.
   a. media analysis worksheet
   b. time-line sequencing chart for events

9. information-processing theory

10.
   a.—1
   b.—2
   c.—4
   d.—5
   e.—6
   f.—7
   g.—3

11.
   a. scripts
   b. production
   c. tryout (formative evaluation)
   d. summative evaluation

1.

   a. *measure the subordinate components*

   b. *measure a simulated performance*

   c. *sample objectives at random*

2.

   a. *norm-referenced: using a curve system*

   b. *criterion-referenced: setting standards in advance of test administration*

3.

   a. *end-of-course: for grading or predicting success in an advanced course or on a job*

   b. *end-of-unit: to measure a moderately complex performance; to decide to go on to the next unit*

   c. *single objective: to determine mastery and readiness for the next objective*

   d. *subordinate competency: for diagnosis and remedial study*

*4. in productive learning, the student uses concepts and rules to solve a whole **class** of problems; in reproductive learning, the student **repeats** exactly what he or she has been taught*

5. for reproductive learning; for productive learning, the test content must involve different examples from those used for instruction

6.

   a. *grade depends on how other students score*

   b. *accomplishments or competencies not described*

   c. *no reference to objectives*

7. using tests for qualifying for an advanced course or a job

8. subordinate competencies and the terminal objective

9. when generation of an answer rather than recognition of an answer was called for by the objective

*10. what is it **supposed** to measure*

11. objective

*12. **test** with the **objective***

*13. **indirect***

*14. **experts***

15. stable; adequate; consistent; thorough; internally consistent

Answer Key: Chapter 11 Information Test

1. 3	9. 1
2. 2	10. 1
3. 1	11. 1
4. 1	12. 2, 3
5. 2	13. 2, 3
6. 3	14. 2, 3
7. 1	15. 3
8. 1	

R.U. .... 1. The student will be able to write a paragraph using a topic sentence, developmental sentences, and a transition or concluding sentence.

C.C. .... 2. The student will be able to "select the wingnuts" from a bucket of assorted nuts and bolts.

M.S. .... 3. The student will be able to sharpen a pencil.

M.S. .... 4. The student will be able to do a back dive in pike position.

Attitude .... 5. The student will listen to popular music.

V.I. (verbatim) 6. The student will be able to recall verbatim the names of the Presidents of the United States in the order in which they served.

V.I. (facts) 7. The student can tell where to obtain auto license tags.

R.U. .... 8. Before changing lanes, the student glances in the rear mirror to see if the lane is clear.

D.C. .... 9. The student can select articles about segregation from newspapers or magazines.

V.I. (facts) 10. The student can match paintings with the names of their painters.

Attitude .... 11. The student helps other students with their work.

Discr. .... 12. The student can select socks that match the color of his pants.

Discr. .... 13. The student puts different shaped blocks in similar shaped holes.

R.U. .... 14. The student uses electrolysis to convert water to oxygen and hydrogen.

C.S. .... 15. The student designs a traffic plan for Tallahassee.

R.U. .... 16. The student can use a city map when he or she is unfamiliar with the area.

C.S. .... 17. The student develops a way to keep salt water fish alive in fresh water.

P.S. .... 18. The student can detect loopholes in contracts.

R.U. .... 19. The student determines the composition of a chemical compound by collecting appropriate data.

C.S. .... 20. The student develops a new semiconductor material that produces an electric current when touched.

V.I. (verbatim) 21. The student supplies the symbol for chemical elements.

V.I. (substance) 22. The student gives the meaning of the Declaration of Independence.

Answer Key: Exercise No. 2

1. Shown pictures of rattlesnakes and copperheads, the student will be able to *identify* the copperheads by pointing to the pictures; the pictures will be in both black and white and color.

2. On all term papers submitted, the student will be able to *demonstrate* correct APA bibliographic format as indicated by entries in the bibliography for a variety of resource types.

3. Given a sample of cloth, the student will be able to *discriminate* the color of the cloth by comparing it to a color reference chart and selecting an example of the same color. The chart will be a paint sample chart.

4. The student will *choose* to follow the "golden rule," without being told.

5. Given a list of English words, upon request the student will *state* in writing the correct Spanish words, using no references.

6. Given an impromptu speaking exercise, the student will be able to *generate* and deliver the impromptu speech about beanbags.

7. Asked to cut a board to a given length, the student will be able to *execute* the crosscutting of the board using the saw in a safe and appropriate manner.

8. Given a child who cannot read, the student will be able to *originate* a method of teaching reading to the child so that a significant amount of progress can be shown at the end of two months. A significant amount will mean an increase in the reading level of the student equivalent to one-sixth of a grade level from baseline performance.

9. Given a research study, the student will be able to *classify* those variables that are considered to be "independent" or "treatment" variables.

10. Upon request, the student will *summarize* orally in his or her own words the main ideas in Chapter 4, without references.

11. Given a list of dates in history, the student will *state* in writing the events they stand for.

Answer Key: Exercise No. 3

Valid test items:

1. d
2. d
3. a
4. b
5. a
6. d
7. c
8. c
9. d
10. a
11. d
12. d

All other alternatives are invalid.

Answer Key: Exercise No. 4

Note: This key is intended to serve as a model for comparison. There are many other items that could be valid for these objectives.

1. Define in your own words the term "normal distribution."

2. (The teacher sets up a driver education car along the side of a road and softens one tire by letting air out.) Teacher: "Ok, I want you to change this tire. I will be evaluating your performance on how safely you change the tire, as well as your use of the correct procedure." The teacher could have a checksheet for determining if the student followed the correct procedure and safety rules.

3. Pretend that you are the owner of a small clothing store and you need to order parkas for the coming winter. Write how you would determine how many parkas to order and the logic that went into your procedure. Generate an order list for several such items.

4. Using the Smith pressure chamber, bring the pressure of the steam inside to 15 lbs/sq. in.
    (a) Record the temperature of the water in the following space ....
    (b) What is the temperature at 22 lbs/sq. in.? ....
    (c) What is the pressure when the steam is 107 degrees Celsius? ....

5. Using the supplied PLATO computer program, draw a line between statements where the program changes the mode of the computer from regular state to judging state, or from judging state to regular state.

6. In the next three minutes, sort the resistors from the capacitors in this bin into two piles. One pile should contain all the resistors and the other pile should contain all the capacitors.

7. Using the chart on the table, sort the electrical parts in the bin into piles on the chart so that each kind of part is in a pile over its picture.

8. Since this is an unobtrusive measure, an item cannot be directly constructed; however, a method for observing the behavior could be described as follows: In an informal discussion with the student or his or her advisor, the evaluator will elicit statements about the importance of statistics.

9. Develop a method for subtracting that works with any two numbers and does not involve borrowing methods.

10. Recite the poem "Old Ironsides" from memory (the criteria include accuracy and speed; five min.).

11. Our personal rights are protected by the "Bill of Rights"; summarize four of the rights that are protected by this Bill.

Now see the Notes on page 240.

Notes:

(a) The directions are included in the test items, except where the student is not to use outside resources. Notice of this condition can be given at the beginning of the test.

(b) The only motor skill objective is the tire changing (No. 2.). Even though the objective about Boyle's law involves the use of apparatus, the use of the apparatus is not being evaluated except through the attainment of a correct value. The criteria sheet for the tire changing objective might look like this:

		yes	no
a.	sets out trouble markers, flares, or turns on emergency flashers	....	....
b.	takes spare and jack from the trunk	....	....
c.	blocks the wheels so the car won't roll	....	....
d.	removes hubcap and breaks studs loose	....	....
e.	installs the jack in the proper location	....	....
f.	jacks the car safely until the tire can be removed	....	....
g.	removes the flat tire safely	....	....
h.	mounts the good tire and replaces wheel lugs securing wheel	....	....
i.	lowers the car and tightens the lug bolts	....	....
j.	puts the flat and jack into trunk and secures it properly	....	....
k.	student completes the process of picking up markers, turning off flashers, putting on hubcap, etc.	....	....

(c) The criteria for some of the objectives are stated in the objective; e.g., "Old Ironsides" specifies a five-minute time allowance. The degree of correctness is not stated (will the teacher allow one or two errors?). If not stated, one should assume 100%. Sometimes a single item is a whole test, and the criteria for mastery may involve consideration of the parts of the total performance. On other objectives (intellectual skills), items may be needed for both the test terminal task and the essential prerequisites. This is discussed in detail in Chapter 10.

Answer Key: Exercise No. 5

Label the following objectives as either
(a) lifelong objectives
(b) course objectives
(c) unit objectives

I. *Course Title—Aerobics*

b.... 1. The student will be able to execute ten sit-ups in a period of one minute.

a.... 2. The student will choose to participate in a schedule of exercise that will keep him or her fit.

a.... 3. The student will be healthier as a result of proper exercise, weight control, and diet.

b.... 4. The student will be able to generate a program of exercise that corresponds to his or her body weight and caloric intake.

c.... 5. The student will demonstrate the calculation of the number of exercises necessary to burn up 3,000 calories.

II. *Course Title—Television Production*

c.... 1. The student will generate a script for a television program.

b.... 2. The student will write and produce a 20-minute television program designed to meet certain instructional objectives.

c.... 3. The student will demonstrate the operation of a television camera.

c.... 4. The student will direct the production of an instructional program.

Answer Key: Exercise No. 6

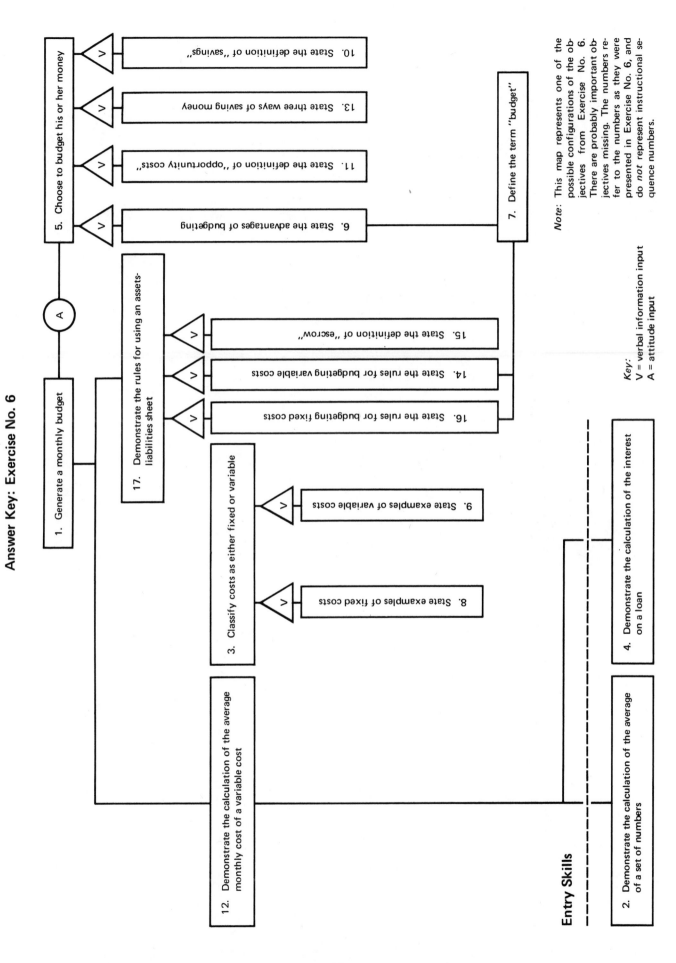

Note: This map represents one of the possible configurations of the objectives from Exercise No. 6. There are probably important objectives missing. The numbers refer to the numbers as they were presented in Exercise No. 6, and do *not* represent instructional sequence numbers.

1. Generate a monthly budget

5. Choose to budget his or her money

10. State the definition of "savings"

13. State three ways of saving money

11. State the definition of "opportunity costs"

6. State the advantages of budgeting

7. Define the term "budget"

17. Demonstrate the rules for using an assets-liabilities sheet

15. State the definition of "escrow"

14. State the rules for budgeting variable costs

16. State the rules for budgeting fixed costs

3. Classify costs as either fixed or variable

9. State examples of variable costs

8. State examples of fixed costs

12. Demonstrate the calculation of the average monthly cost of a variable cost

4. Demonstrate the calculation of the interest on a loan

Entry Skills

2. Demonstrate the calculation of the average of a set of numbers

Key:
V = verbal information input
A = attitude input

243

Answer Key: Alternate Exercise No. 6

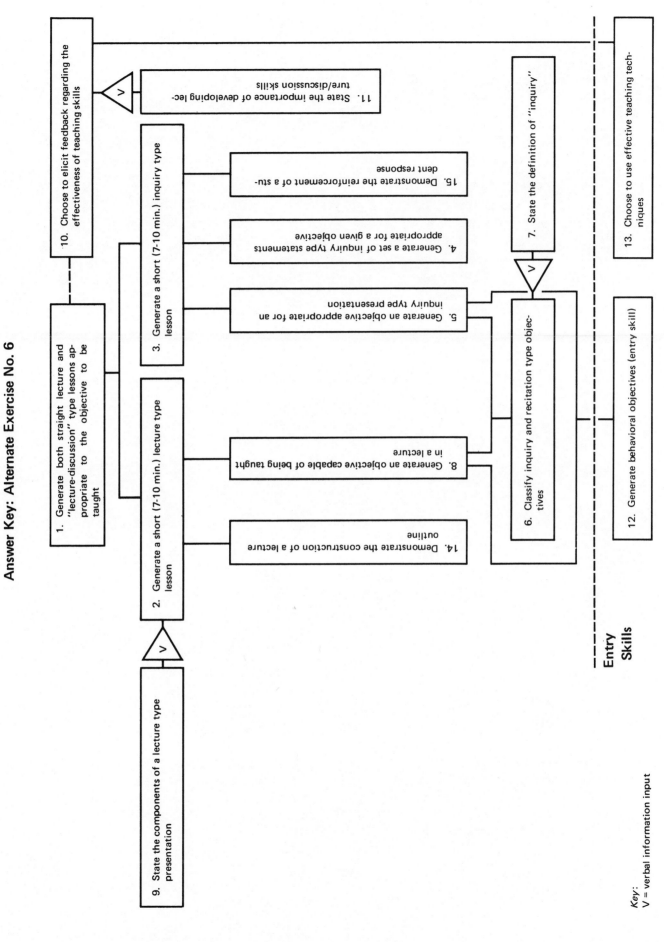

10. Choose to elicit feedback regarding the effectiveness of teaching skills

11. State the importance of developing lecture/discussion skills

1. Generate both straight lecture and "lecture-discussion" type lessons appropriate to the objective to be taught

3. Generate a short (7-10 min.) inquiry type lesson

15. Demonstrate the reinforcement of a student response

4. Generate a set of inquiry type statements appropriate for a given objective

5. Generate an objective appropriate for an inquiry type presentation

7. State the definition of "inquiry"

13. Choose to use effective teaching techniques

2. Generate a short (7-10 min.) lecture type lesson

8. Generate an objective capable of being taught in a lecture

6. Classify inquiry and recitation type objectives

12. Generate behavioral objectives (entry skill)

14. Demonstrate the construction of a lecture outline

9. State the components of a lecture type presentation

Entry
Skills

Key:
V = verbal information input

245

Answer Key: Exercise No. 7

```
┌─────────────────────┐
│ Demonstrate         │
│ calculation of      │
│ the monthly sum of  │
│ fixed and variable  │
│ expenses            │
└─────────────────────┘
```

```
        ┌─ V ─┐ ┌─────────────────────┐
              │ State examples of       │
              │ fixed expenses          │
              └─────────────────────────┘

        ┌─ V ─┐ ┌─────────────────────┐
              │ State examples of       │
              │ variable expenses       │
              └─────────────────────────┘

┌──────────────────┐  ┌─ V ─┐ ┌─────────────────────┐
│ Classify expenses│         │ State examples of       │
│ as either fixed  │         │ seasonal expenses       │
│ or variable      │         └─────────────────────────┘
└──────────────────┘
        ┌─ V ─┐ ┌─────────────────────┐
              │ State attributes of     │
              │ fixed expenses          │
              └─────────────────────────┘

        ┌─ V ─┐ ┌─────────────────────┐
              │ State attributes of     │
              │ variable expenses       │
              └─────────────────────────┘
```

```
┌─────────────────────┐
│ Demonstrate         │
│ calculation of the  │
│ average monthly cost│
│ of a variable       │
│ expense             │
└─────────────────────┘

┌─────────────────────┐
│ Demonstrate         │
│ calculation of the  │
│ annual cost of a    │
│ variable expense    │
└─────────────────────┘

┌─────────────────────┐
│ Demonstrate         │
│ calculation of the  │
│ average of a set of │
│ numbers             │
└─────────────────────┘

┌─────────────────────┐
│ Demonstrate         │
│ calculation of the  │
│ interest on a loan  │
└─────────────────────┘
```

entry skills

```
┌─────────────────────┐
│ Demonstrate         │
│ summation of        │
│ periodic expenses   │
└─────────────────────┘
```

Answer Key: Exercise No. 8

1. a. R
   b. V
   c. - V
   d. - V
   e. - R
   f. - R
   g. R
   h. - V
   i. V
   j. - V

2. a. - E
   b. - P
   c. - P and - E
   d. E
   e. P and E
   f. - E because it
      leaves little time
      for a number of learner
      responses; also - P

Answer Key: Exercise No. 9

1. d   6. b
2. c   7. a
3. d   8. b
4. c   9. b
5. a

Answer Key: Exercise No. 10

1. The purpose of one-on-one formative evaluation is to identify *the primary and most obvious* problems which exist in a rough-draft form of the instructional materials and to make revisions in the materials in accordance with collected data. The purpose of a small-group evaluation is to identify *the more subtle* problems which still exist in the instruction. A small-group evaluation is also used to determine the effectiveness of revisions made at the one-on-one stage and to begin to address the administrative feasibility of using the instruction in its intended environment. The purpose of a field-trial evaluation is to determine the administrative feasibility of using the materials under intended conditions. Also, the effectiveness of revisions from the small-group stage is checked.

2. The inputs into each stage of formative evaluation are as follows:
One-on-one evaluation: a rough-draft copy of the materials to be tested; any graphics which are critical to understanding in reasonably good form; for non-print media, a rough-draft, written script, rough art sketches, or a storyboard; data-collection instruments selected for the one-on-one stage.
Small-group evaluation: revised version of the materials which have been improved in appearance; in the case of non-print media, a rough-cut film or low-fidelity tape recording; data-collection instruments selected for the small-group stage.
Field-trial evaluation: all materials to be used in the instruction, including teacher's manual, tests, and any laboratory equipment; materials must be in polished form; for non-print media, one may use an 8mm film which is later to be reshot in 16mm or 35mm format; data-collection instruments selected for the field-trial stage.

3. The three criteria for selecting formative evaluation participants are:
   a. The students must be members of the target population.
   b. They should represent several segments of the population in terms of their characteristics.
   c. Students should possess the entry skills but not the terminal skills for the lesson being tested.

4. The following numbers of students are required for the three stages of formative evaluation:
   One-on-one evaluation: one to three students
   Small-group evaluation: eight to 24 students
   Field-trial evaluation: approximately 30 students

5. The major role of the subject-matter expert is to ensure that the instructional materials are accurate, authoritative, and up-to-date. Review of the materials by a subject-matter expert is especially recommended during the one-on-one evaluation stage; but such a review may be desirable whenever substantial revisions have been made and the designer perceives a need to verify content accuracy. The subject-matter expert should *not* suggest revisions to the instructional strategy (events of instruction and conditions of learning) incorporated into the materials.

6. When scheduling a time to conduct one-on-one formative evaluations, a useful rule of thumb is to double the estimated time of the lesson itself.

7. The following types of data-collection instruments may be useful during formative evaluation: background information questionnaire, entry skills test, pretest, within-course test items or responses, evaluator's comments to students, students' questions and remarks, length of time required, posttest, attitude questionnaire, debriefing interview, and questionnaire for subject-matter experts.

8. Weaknesses in instruction that can be revealed in formative evaluation data include:
   (a) inadequate analysis of objectives in terms of the proper sequencing of teaching the subordinate competencies or enabling objectives;
   (b) inadequate provisions for needed interaction among categories of objectives and domains of learning;
   (c) failure to incorporate the conditions of learning into the instructional events for the lesson;
   (d) omission of needed instructional events, such as guidance to thinking, student responding and feedback, and generalizing experiences;
   (e) unclear writing style and faulty preparation of pictures, graphs, and other illustrative material; and
   (f) test items which are not valid measures of performance objectives.

9. Responses to this question may vary; however, the critical aspect of any response is that one must *not* use formative evaluation data to immediately revise the instructional materials. The designer will first want to place item analysis data into learning hierarchies and/or instructional maps. This step will allow the designer to study the validity of assumptions about sequencing, subordinate relationships, domain interactions, and implied transfer effects. After this step, the designer should examine the objectives and corresponding test items to ensure that the tests are valid measures of performances. Then, the events of instruction and conditions of learning incorporated in the events should be reviewed for completeness. Only after examining these components of the design process should the designer work with the instructional materials.

10. Formative evaluation of materials is important because instructional design principles are still in an early stage of development. Designing instruction is not an exact science, and it requires many subjective judgments on the part of the designer. Even experienced designers need to use formative evaluation to improve the instructional strategies incorporated into materials and lesson plans.

Answer Key: Exercise No. 11

1. A bi-modal distribution such as the one shown would indicate to the designer that the two groups of people probably had very different experiences when completing the instruction. This might be the result of initial differences in the learners or inadequate instruction. The designer would want to check stated prerequisite skills, that is, both entry skills and essential prerequisites within the instruction. In examining the skills stated as entering competencies, it may be found that some were overlooked and that the skills were possessed by the high-ranking group but not by the low-ranking group. Checking entry test scores for a similar distribution might be helpful. The designer would also want to review the learning hierarchy and/or instructional map. It may be that some essential prerequisite skills were omitted in the analysis. The high-ranking group may have used cognitive strategies to discover these skills, while the lower group did not. An examination of pretest scores may help pinpoint such an occurrence. Finally, the designer should check other relevant characteristics of the participants to ensure that a representative sample has been tested. Perhaps the materials were written at a twelfth-grade level and a subgroup of participants read only at an eighth-grade level.

2. This graph alone would not signal that revisions are required. Such a negatively skewed distribution, with students "piling up" at the high end, is desired and even anticipated with instructional materials that have undergone a rigorous design process. The data shown on the graph are a welcome indicator that the objectives, materials, and tests are all working together. Unless other data sources, such as attitude questionnaires, show otherwise, it would probably be best to leave this instruction as is.

3. The responses to this question may vary, but some recommended answers are presented below. No credit should be given for non-specific or general responses, such as "The hierarchy is not right," or "The sequencing is wrong."

a. The instruction for Boxes 1, 2, and 3 was poor. The instruction for Box 1 was worse than none at all and, given the sequencing, may have caused confusion on Boxes 2 and 3. The instruction for Box 2 was ineffective, since no gain was evidenced from pretest to posttest scores. The instruction for Box 3 was inadequate, although it was better than Boxes 1 and 2 and resulted in a small pre- to posttest gain.

b. Boxes 1, 2, and 3 may be unnecessary given the 100% performance on Box 4. Perhaps Boxes 1, 2, and 3 represent verbal information rather than essential prerequisites. Perhaps Boxes 1, 2, and 3 are not really subordinate to Box 4; or perhaps learners used cognitive strategies to jump the gap between Boxes 1, 2, and 3 and Box 4.

c. Given posttest scores, the instruction for Boxes 4 and 5 was excellent. Examination of pretest and posttest scores indicates that the instruction for Box 4 resulted in larger gains.

d. Although learners performed well on Boxes 4 and 5, achievement for Box 6 was inadequate. This discrepancy would indicate that perhaps a whole series of competencies is missing prior to Box 6.

e. The results shown suggest that the instruction for Box 6 may be inadequate. Poor performance on this objective may also be due to missing competencies prior to Box 6. Learners in general are unable to use cognitive strategies to bridge the gap between Boxes 4 and 5 and Box 6.

4. The responses to this question may vary, but some recommended answers are provided below.

a. The designer should ensure that the same difficulty level exists in practice and posttest items. Perhaps the practice items present simple, straightforward problems, while the posttest items are more complex.

b. The designer should check for cues or prompts that may be present in the practice exercise. Perhaps hints to the learner result in increased practice scores. Eliminating over-prompting is another means to ensure that the difficulty level is the same for practice and posttest items.

c. Perhaps the posttest items are consistently harder. The designer may decide to pool practice items and posttest items and then randomly assign items to practice exercises and the posttest. This is another procedure for balancing the difficulty level of items.

Answer Key: Criteria for Evaluation of Performance Objectives for Chapter 10

Criteria Sheet for Objectives 26 and 27

There can be so much variety in testing situations that it is impossible to list a simple step-by-step procedure for creating a satisfactory test. Instead, we will present a series of considerations that should be made when developing the test.

1. Are all subordinate objectives represented by items? If not, were objectives omitted through a random selection of items?

2. Is (are) the terminal objective(s) represented by a reliable set of items?

3. Are the items in a suitable format to ensure validity with regard to the type of learning?

4. Is the test long enough to have adequately tested the subordinate and terminal behaviors but short enough to be efficient of the students' and evaluator's time?

5. Is the mastery score related to achievement of the terminal objectives?

6. If there are grades, are they related to mastery and/or the successive approximation of mastery?

The test should be thought of as the closest approximation of direct observance of a learned capability as is reasonably practical, and never as a flawless measure of learning. With this in mind, the test becomes one of the designer's tools for materials improvement and the user's tool for assessing his or her progress.

Author Index

Subject Index